THE LOW COUNTRIES: MULTIDISCIPLINARY STUDIES

Publications of the American
Association for Netherlandic Studies • 3

Margriet Bruijn Lacy, Series Editor

THE LOW COUNTRIES: MULTIDISCIPLINARY STUDIES

edited by
Margriet Bruijn Lacy
North Dakota State University

UNIVERSITY
PRESS OF
AMERICA

Lanham • New York • London

Copyright © 1990 by
University Press of America®, Inc.
4720 Boston Way
Lanham, Maryland 20706

3 Henrietta Street
London WC2E 8LU England

All rights reserved
Printed in the United States of America
British Cataloging in Publication Information Available

"Netherlandic Statemaking through Princely Judicature in the
16th Century" copyrighted 1989 by Hugo de Schepper

"The Flemish Movement in Southwestern Ontario, 1927–1931"
originally appeared in THE BELGIANS IN ONTARIO:
A HISTORY (Toronto: Dundurn) copyright 1987 by
Joan Magee. Reprinted by permission.

Co-published by arrangement with
The American Association for Netherlandic Studies

Library of Congress Cataloging-in-Publication Data

The Low countries : multidisciplinary studies /
edited by Margriet Bruijn Lacy.
p.   cm. — (Publications of the American Association
for Netherlandic studies ; v. 3)
1. Netherlands—Civilization.   2. Dutch philology.   3. Arts, Dutch.
I. Lacy, Margriet Bruijn, 1943–   .
DJ71.L69   1989   949.2—dc20   89–24778 CIP

ISBN 0–8191–7587–0 (alk. paper)

The paper used in this publication meets the minimum requirements of American National Standard for Information Sciences—Permanence of Paper for Printed Library Materials, ANSI Z39.48–1984.

TABLE OF CONTENTS

TABLE OF CONTENTS...v

PREFACE..ix

HET MES SNIJDT AAN TWEE KANTEN:
    ON THE SEMANTICS AND PRAGMATICS OF THE DUTCH
    SENTENCE-FINAL PARTICLE *HOOR*..............................1
Robert S. Kirsner and Jeanine Y. Deen,
  University of California, Los Angeles

PRONUNCIATION NORMS IN THE DUTCH LANGUAGE AREA...................13
Uus Knops,
  Katholieke Universiteit, Nijmegen

THE EDUCATION OF LINGUISTIC MINORITIES
    IN THE NETHERLANDS...21
Marisa Garrett Castellano,
  University of California, Berkeley

DUTCH IN TRANSLATION...27
André Lefevere, University of Texas, Austin and
  Ria Vanderauwera, Austin

PRONUNCIATION ERRORS IN DUTCH:
    THEORETICAL AND PRACTICAL ASPECTS..........................35
S. De Vriendt,
  Vrije Universiteit, Brussel

NEDERLANDS TUSSEN ENGELS EN DUITS
    A TYPOLOGICAL COMPARISON...................................45
Thomas F. Shannon,
  University of California, Berkeley

EVALUATING THE INFLUENCE OF *ZUIDNEDERLANDS* ON THE
    LANGUAGE OF HOLLAND IN THE 16TH AND 17TH CENTURIES..........61
Gregory Hanson, Bradley Holtman and Robert Howell
  University of Wisconsin, Madison

MAPPING LIBRARY RESOURCES IN DUTCH STUDIES
    THROUGH THE CONSPECTUS.....................................77
Martha L. Brogan,
  University of Minnesota, Minneapolis

DUTCH, FLEMISH, AND FRISIAN MATERIALS AT BERKELEY:
    COLLECTIONS AND ACCESS.....................................87
James H. Spohrer,
  University of California, Berkeley

ACCESS TO DUTCH STUDIES MATERIAL IN THE ENGLISH LANGUAGE:
    THE CLIO PROJECT...97
Michael Wintle,
  University of Hull, Hull

RECONSTRUCTION OF A DISFIGURED DUTCH HISTORY PAINTING..........105
Mary Ann Scott,
  University of Denver, Denver

BUITENPARTIJEN: GARDENS OF LOVE OR GARDENS OF LUST?...........111
Kahren Jones Arbitman,
  The Frick Art Museum, Pittsburgh

NEW VISTAS ON NETHERLANDIC LANDSCAPE
    AND THE NATURAL WORLD......................................123
Anne W. Lowenthal,
  New York

A FEMALE FAUST: *MARIEKEN VAN NIEUMEGEN*........................131
Johanna C. Prins,
  Columbia University, New York

MAX HAVELAAR: A ROMANTIC NOVEL FOR SOCIAL FLUIDITY............139
Gary L. Baker,
  University of Minnesota, Minneapolis

ASPECTS OF MYTH IN FERDINAND BORDEWIJK'S *KARAKTER*.............147
Augustinus P. Dierick,
  University of Toronto, Toronto

THE OCCUPIED MIND: REMEMBERING AND FORGETTING
    SOME RECENT EXAMPLES IN DUTCH LITERATURE...................157
Jolanda Vanderwal Taylor,
  University of Wisconsin, Madison

CHILDREN, CHURCH, AND SICKBED?
    THE LIVES OF DUTCH IMMIGRANT WOMEN.........................165
Suzanne Sinke,
  University of Minnesota, Minneapolis

THE FLEMISH MOVEMENT IN SOUTHWESTERN ONTARIO, 1927-1931........175
Joan Magee,
  University of Windsor, Windsor

SYSTEM-THREATENING OR SYSTEM-TRANSFORMING?:
    THE SIGNIFICANCE OF *VERZUILING*...........................183
Stanley W. Carlson-Thies,
  Northwestern College, Orange City

MEDIEVAL NETHERLANDS HISTORY
   THE BURGUNDIAN PERSPECTIVE..................................195
Arthur L. Loeb,
   Harvard University, Cambridge

NETHERLANDIC STATEMAKING THROUGH PRINCELY JUDICATURE
   IN THE 16TH CENTURY...211
Hugo de Schepper,
   Katholieke Universiteit, Nijmegen

REPUBLICAN CULTURE IN EARLY MODERN EUROPE:
   THE DUTCH REPUBLIC AND THE SEARCH
   FOR DIPLOMATIC RECOGNITION..................................227
Matthew T. Holland,
   University of North Carolina, Chapel Hill

THE DUTCH REVOLT AND ITS IMPACT ON ENGLAND
   DURING THE FIRST HALF OF THE SEVENTEENTH CENTURY...........237
Hugh Dunthorne,
   University College, Swansea

POPULAR SONG-BOOKS IN THE SIXTEENTH-CENTURY LOWLANDS...........247
Hermina Joldersma,
   University of Calgary, Calgary

PREFACE

A quick look at the table of contents will confirm that the articles in this third volume of the *Publications of the American Association for Netherlandic Studies* represent many disciplines and range, chronologically, from the Middle Ages to the most recent years. It is gratifying to see such diversity; it demonstrates convincingly that the "Low Countries" do indeed provide numerous opportunities for scholarly pursuits. The editor admits, however, that she felt at times rather overwhelmed by this diversity and the concomitant challenge to create some degree of uniformity, at least in the formal presentation of the articles. In order to comply as much as possible with the individual authors' preferences with regard to style, some variety was maintained, but in several instances the editor had to make decisions that may not have pleased everyone.

The articles in this volume are all based on papers presented at the fourth Interdisciplinary Conference on Netherlandic Studies, held at the University of Minnesota (Minneapolis) in June, 1988. The conference was sponsored by the American Association for Netherlandic Studies, with financial assistance from the *Taalunie* and the University of Minnesota.

In addition to thanking the authors for their cooperation and understanding, the editor wishes to express her sincere gratitude to her secretary, Ms. Cheryl Silcox, who spent countless difficult hours trying to make sense of the editor's instructions, notes, and comments, and who was more or less "forced" by this assignment to become interested in the Low Countries. A word of appreciation is also due to Ms. Cathy Heiraas, who provided insightful and prompt administrative assistance.

All who were involved in the preparation of this volume - authors, assistants, and editor - hope that the articles will contribute to stimulating new insights within and across the disciplines represented.

Margriet Bruijn Lacy
Editor

HET MES SNIJDT AAN TWEE KANTEN:
ON THE SEMANTICS AND PRAGMATICS OF THE DUTCH
SENTENCE-FINAL PARTICLE *HOOR*[*]

Robert S. Kirsner and Jeanine Y. Deen
University of California, Los Angeles

1. *Hoor* as a linguistic stepchild. Any foreign linguist or student of Dutch who keeps his ears open will daily encounter numerous utterances containing the sentence-final particle *hoor* (here glossed as 'prt', for 'particle'):

Nou, dag *hoor*.
'Well, goodbye, prt.'

Moeilijk *hoor*. Ik zal erover na moeten denken.
difficult, prt.
'That's difficult. I'll have to think about it.'

And if he or she reads modern literature — whether short stories by Carmiggelt, novels by Hermans, or essays by Renate Rubinstein — he cannot avoid encountering this particle either:

De vraag blijft: wat wil de man. Na levenslange studie van het onderwerp is mijn antwoord: meer.
Ik weet het, omdat iemand bij mij eens in zware dronkenschap op de vloer lag te beuken met zijn vuisten. Ik was totaal gemystificeerd, wrong mijn handen en jammerde: Wat wil je dan toch? Want ze laten je raden *hoor*, de mannen, als ze dronken zijn laten ze je nog langer raden. . . .   (Rubinstein 1978:93)

'The questions remains: what do men want. After a life-long study of the subject, my answer is: more.
I know, because once at my house someone heavily intoxicated lay pounding on the floor with his fists. I was totally mystified, wrung my hands and lamented: What then do you want? For they *really* keep you guessing, men; if they are drunk they keep you guessing even longer. . . .'

All the stranger, then, that — for all practical purposes — the particle *hoor* has been virtually ignored by all those whom one might expect to have something to say about it: grammarians, lexicographers — even teachers of Dutch as a second language; cf. Abraham 1986, Auwera and Vandeweghe 1984, and Foolen 1986. Although some grammarians go so far as to explicitly mention *hoor* and to classify it as an 'interjection', they do not enlighten us as to HOW it is an interjection. Specifically, they do not indicate how *hoor* differs from other interjections it might be compared with, such as *hè* and *zeg*; cf. Geerts et al. (1984: 563,674) and Van den Toorn (1981:249). The purpose of the present paper is to open discussion on this important particle and to sketch several working hypotheses as to [1] the kinds of meaning *hoor* signals and [2] the various pragmatic mechanisms whereby speakers are induced to infer messages from this meaning.

2. The core semantic components of *hoor* in *X hoor*. Perhaps the most profitable way to explain the myriad of uses of the sentence-final particle *hoor* is to assume that it is a sign in the Saussurean sense: the pairing of a concept or cluster of concepts (i.e., a meaning) with some signal. According to this view, Dutch speakers employ the relatively abstract but invariant meaning signaled by *hoor* in *X hoor* to communicate a wide range of messages. These messages — which are potentially infinite in number and sometimes even mutually contradictory — are in turn viewed as pragmatic inferences from the signaling by speakers of the invariant meaning in different (i.e., varying) linguistic and extralinguistic contexts.[1]

In the case at hand, the signal seems easy enough to state: the particle *hoor* in sentence-, clause-, or utterance-final position. First of all, native speakers agree that synchronically the sentence-final particle has quite a different feel to it than the bare verbal stem *hoor*, with which it might be compared on formal grounds. Consider the following:

??Dat is gevaarlijk voor kleine kinderen. *Hoor*, afblijven.
'That is dangerous for small children. Hear, keep away.'

Dat is gevaarlijk voor kleine kinderen. Afblijven, *hoor*.
'That is dangerous for small children. *Be sure to* keep away.'

Separation of the particle from the verbal stem is thus synchronically justified.[2] A second point is that unlike the particle *toch*, which some speakers can use as an independent sentence all by itself, the particle *hoor* must always follow something else: *Nee hoor* 'No prt.', *Ja hoor* 'Yes prt.', etc. Accordingly, the signal must be defined not as simply *Hoor* but as *X hoor*, where X is a cover symbol for linguistic material (ranging from a single word, as in *Nee hoor*, to a full sentence followed by a pause).

The meaning signaled by *hoor* in *X hoor* is more difficult to define, because it is concerned (as we attempt to elucidate below) with social interaction rather than with entities. It is perhaps most easily stated as a cluster of separate facets or semantic components. As a working hypothesis, we postulate four such components:

NONQUESTION: In saying X to the hearer H, the speaker S is explicitly <u>not</u> asking H for information or confirmation.[3]

INVOLVEMENT: In saying X to the hearer H, the speaker S is explicitly <u>involving</u>, <u>engaging</u> H with a view towards some sort of <u>interaction</u> rather than a matter of fact, neutral transfer of information.

DOMINANCE: In saying X to the hearer H, the speaker suggests that s/he is <u>higher</u> <u>on</u> <u>some</u> <u>scale</u> [e.g., authority, class, intelligence] than some other, contextually obvious entity, typically the hearer H, but sometimes some third person(s).

FRIENDLINESS: In saying X to the hearer H, the speaker is signaling a <u>friendly</u> <u>intent</u> to H.[4]

Postulating the first component, NONQUESTION, accounts for the fact that sentences with *hoor* are not questions. Whereas the first sentence below, with *hoor*, is affirmative and used as a softened command, the second, with *hè*, asks for confirmation, while the third — in which *hoor* is used with question intonation — is ungrammatical:

Jij komt morgen ook, *hoor.*
'You're coming tomorrow too, prt.' [Assignment] 'You *be sure to* come tomorrow.'

Jij komt morgen ook, *hè?*
'You're coming tomorrow too, *aren't you?*'

*Jij komt morgen ook, *hoor?*

The second component of INVOLVEMENT, in turn, accounts for the fact that sentences with *hoor* are interpreted as contextualized utterances rather than as abstract, timeless, neutral statements. They are taken as specific chunks of communication aimed by a specific speaker or speakers S at a specific hearer or hearers H in order to involve H in the communication. For example, whereas the sentence *Dit gaat fout* 'This isn't working right' is taken as a neutral report of an unsatisfactory state of affairs, the sentence *Dit gaat fout, hoor* — with *hoor* 'grabbing at' the hearer — is taken as a warning and call to action: 'This isn't working right (so <u>do</u> something!).' Note also the contrast between *Mooi strand, hoor!* 'Pretty beach, prt' and *Wat een mooi strand!* 'What a pretty beach!'. The latter sentence would be said when one stumbles unexpectedly across a beach and is overwhelmed by its beauty. But the former sentence, with *hoor*, is said when the speaker knows ahead of time that the hearer was going to show him a beach and wishes to acknowledge his guide's kindness in having him see it. In the *hoor*-sentence, then, the speaker-hearer interaction outweighs the evaluation of the beach's beauty, which might even not be genuine (see further section 3.5, below).

The third component, DOMINANCE, is postulated to explain the fact that use of *hoor* can communicate that the speaker is somehow 'parenting' the hearer or some other persons to whom s/he is superior in some sense. For example, *Stikstof is een gas, hoor* 'Nitrogen is a gas, prt' suggests that, in imparting the information, the speaker is being kind to a hearer who is more ignorant. On the other hand, in the Rubinstein quote above in section 1., where the reader is encouraged to feel solidarity with the writer's persona, *hoor* suggests superiority not to the hearer but to a third entity: men.

The final semantic component of *hoor* is FRIENDLINESS. For instance, when a mother praises her male child by saying *Knappe jongen, hoor!* 'Smart lad, prt!', use of *hoor* underscores the positive affect in her remark. A second illustration would be the difference between the brusk command *U kunt wel afruimen* 'You may clear the table' (said to one's private servant) and the more 'friendly' *U kunt wel afruimen, hoor* (said to a waiter in a restaurant, where the hierarchical relationship is more diffuse).

We note parenthetically that explicit postulation of FRIENDLINESS explains why *hoor* does not show up in environments where one might expect it to if all it did was to 'intensify' utterances, as it is characterized in the *ANS* (Geerts et al. 1984). If *hoor* really were an 'intensifier,' then it should be used in both of the following:

*Val dood, *hoor*!
'Drop dead, prt!'

*D'ruit, *hoor*![5]
'Get outa here, prt.!'

Clearly, the incoherence here (the versions without *hoor* being impeccable) results from the clash between the unfriendliness of the command itself with the friendliness normally associated with *hoor*. We may also note that *hoor* is similarly inappropriate where the issue of friendliness does not even arise, as in the military. A sergeant calling his troops to attention does not need to be friendly to get them to comply and any hint of friendliness or politeness (suggesting erroneously that the troops have a choice in the matter) is ludicrous:

Geef acht!
'Ten-HUT! = atTENtion!'

??Geef acht, *hoor*![6]
'Be sure to pay ten-HUT!'

Similarly, *hoor* does not occur in formal written language, as in public notices, whose only purpose is to inform:

> *GEEN TOEGANG VOOR ONBEVOEGDEN, *HOOR*.
> 'NO ENTRY FOR UNAUTHORIZED PERSONNEL, prt.'

3. **The pragmatics of *hoor*.** Having postulated core semantic components for *hoor*, we will now informally sketch some provisional inferential mechanisms underlying its use.

   3.1 Urging. The first mechanism is the combination of NONQUESTION with INVOLVEMENT to communicate some sort of 'emphasis', which can be felt as urging. Consider the following example from Carmiggelt (1975: 54), where *hoor* reinforces the 'natural' insistence of the imperative *neem* 'take' and the adverb *gerust* 'calmly, certainly, without question':

> Wel, wel, wel dat doet me genoegen. Wil je thee, jongen? De koekjes staan op het dressoir. Neem er gerust een paar, *hoor*.
>
> 'Well, well, well. That makes me glad. Do you want tea, my boy? The cookies are on the sideboard. *Go ahead* and have some.' [Literally: take of them certainly a couple, prt.]

In the Netherlands, where one expects to get only one cookie with tea, such extra urging is culturally necessary.

   A second example of 'urging' is provided by the difference between *Zegt u het maar*. 'What'll it be?,' said by an employee to a customer in a sandwich shop, and the version with *hoor*: *Zegt u het maar, hoor*. The first sentence is the normal request, used when the hearer has been waiting attentively for his turn; the second is used only if the customer had been staring off into space and had not realized that s/he could now place an order.

   3.2 **Countering contrary expectations.** A second, related pragmatic mechanism involves the use of the 'simple emphasis' achieved with NONQUESTION and INVOLVEMENT to override what might be called 'contrary expectations.' Consider:

> Maar heus *hoor*, die schoorstenen *roken*.
> but really prt., those smokestacks smoke. (Evenhuis 1979:26)

> But you can see the smoke from the chimneys. (Evenhuis 1978:37)

   Here one can also observe a *de facto* overlap with the particle *wel*. But whereas *wel* is often used to contradict explicit denial, as in *Ik heb je wel gezien* 'I did see you' opposing *Ik heb je niet gezien* 'I did not see you', *hoor* usually counters a more subtle, implied negation: *Ik heb je gezien, hoor* 'I saw you.' However, since *hoor* – like *wel* – suggests the possibility of a contrary state of affairs, it can be employed to underscore the impact of *wel*. The particles can thus be doubled up:[7]

> Ik heb je *wel* gezien *hoor*, met je nichie   (Evenhuis 1979:53)
> I have you indeed seen prt., with your cousin-diminutive
>
> I saw you, with your little cousin.   (Evenhuis 1978:81)

3.3 FRIENDLINESS countering the assumption of unfriendliness.
We now turn to the remaining semantic components listed in section 2. One reason a speaker can have for explicitly signaling FRIENDLINESS (along with the other components of *hoor*) is to indicate that he is being conciliatory, that the hearer should not take offense at what the speaker has just said. In an interview published in a Flemish journal, the author Willem Frederik Hermans remarks as follows:

> Ik heb vrij veel met Walen verkeerd. Ik verbaas me er wel eens over dat ondanks alle taalstrijd veel Vlamingen niet beseffen hoe zeer ze door de Walen worden geminacht -- ik wil niet stoken, *hoor*.   (Janssen 1979:322)
>
> 'I've had a lot of contact with Walloons. I am often surprised that, inspite of all the language conflict, many Flemings do not realize how much the Walloons despise them – I don't want to make mischief, prt.' = 'I don't want to make mischief; *don't understand me wrong*.'

3.4   FRIENDLINESS for mitigation.
A second reason for signaling FRIENDLINESS is to 'soften the blow' to the hearer of the announcement of unexpected negative events. Consider the following dialogue between Koot and his wife as they calculate the costs of hiring a cleaning service to clean their house:

> 'Jemig', zei mijn vrouw verbijsterd, 'wat een percentages allemaal!'
> 'Tja, dat krijg je als je het helemaal legaal en volgens de regels doet', wist ik. 'Maar we zijn er nog niet *hoor*.'   (Van Kooten 1984:97)
>
> "Wow,' my wife said astonishedly, 'what a lot of percentages!'
> 'Yeah, that's what you get if you do it legally and according to the rules', I replied. 'But we still aren't through yet, prt.'

What is particularly interesting here is the co-occurrence of *hoor* with the adversative conjunction *maar* 'but'. *Maar* warns the hearer that something unexpected is coming up, but the sentence-final *hoor* dampens, as it were, the negative connotations.

3.5 FRIENDLINESS and the mechanism of 'cognitive weakening'.
Given that there is always a choice between saying simply X and saying X *hoor*, with an added component of FRIENDLINESS, one conclusion that can be drawn from the explicit *hoor* in the latter is that the X is being said only to be friendly. But this can suggest that the X in X *hoor* need not be taken as literally true. Accordingly the FRIENDLINESS component of *hoor* may well 'weaken' the cognitive context of X.[8]

We may see this in 'display questions' (cf. Weijdema et al. 1982:79): A mother asks her child: 'How many marbles am I holding, Jantje?' The child responds 'Three!' And then the mother says: *Knappe jongen, hoor!* 'Smart boy, prt.!' Although the child is being praised, the compliment is not as strong as it would be without *hoor*. Compare the unmitigated *Jantje is een wonderkind!* 'Johnny is a child prodigy/genius!' with *Jantje is een wonderkind, hoor!*, where the speaker is being friendly and leaves it open whether s/he is sincere: 'Johnny is a genius (and/but I am being friendly in saying so).'

From here it is not far to the use of *hoor* to tell 'white lies,' when the context of X is in fact untrue. In the following dialogue, Koot tells his wife that the bird which they had rescued and fed is still alive, even though both he and the reader know it has been eaten by the family cat:

'Thijs nog gezien?' vraagt mijn vrouw, zodra ze weer thuis is. 'Nee *hoor*', glimlieg ik, 'die zien we hier niet meer. Die heeft lekker de vrijheid verkozen.'
(Van Kooten 1984:71)

'Have you seen Thijs [the bird]?,' my wife asks as soon as she has come back.
'No, prt,' I smlie [smile-lie]. 'We won't see him anymore. He has chosen for freedom.'

Note that the playful neologism *glimlieg*, blending *glimlachen* 'smile' and *liegen* 'lie' complements the FRIENDLINESS signaled with *hoor*.

3.6 Cutting both ways: 'Inappropriate' signaling of DOMINANCE and/or FRIENDLINESS. Sarcasm can be achieved when what one says is the opposite of what one intends, provided that the clash is obvious from context. Simple utterances, such as *That was a really GREAT weekend* or *You're a REAL FRIEND* can all be sarcastic when it is clear that the speaker could not really mean what he is saying.

With *hoor* there are two main ways in which sarcasm is effected. The first is when the component of DOMINANCE which *hoor* signals is inappropriate. It may be friendly for a teacher to say to a pupil *Stikstof is een gas, hoor* 'Nitrogen is a gas, son,' but when a fellow-student says it, who does not have the teacher's genuine authority, it can be a putdown: You are really stupid for not knowing that nitrogen is a gas.

The second way to effect sarcasm is to signal FRIENDLINESS in a context where friendliness is being deliberately withheld. Consider the following, from Carmiggelt (1967:40):

'Ga je dat lezen?' vroeg mijn vrouw 's avonds.
'Ja, wat dacht je dan, gewichtheffen of zoiets?' zei ik geprikkeld, want ik haat dat sceptische toontje, waarmee zij mijn serieuze ondernemingen altijd ondergraaft. Goed, goed, lees maar,' riep ze, 'kennis is macht, *hoor*.

'Are you going to read that?' my wife asked in the evening.
'Yes, did you think that I was going to lift weights with it instead?,' I said, irritated, for I hate that sceptical little tone with which she always undermines my serious projects. 'Fine, fine, go ahead and read,' she called out. 'Knowledge is power, prt.'

It is the signaling of FRIENDLINESS with *hoor*, when you know that the wife doesn't mean it, which delivers the crushing blow here.

4. Summary and conclusions. We may summarize the above informal discussion with a diagram showing the pragmatic effects achieved with the various semantic components:[9]

```
NONQUESTION   --> a. response expected, not information
INVOLVEMENT   --> b. emphasis --> countering adversative
                     expectation
DOMINANCE     --> c. 'parenting' versus putdown
FRIENDLINESS  --> d. counters assumption of unfriendli-
                     ness; cf. b.
              --> e. cushions bad news
              --> f. cognitive weakening --> white lies
              + unfriendly context --> g. irony.
```

We conclude by noting some implications of our article.

First, under theoretical implications, we would suggest that particles are knowable and analyzable; cf. Wierzbicka 1976. Furthermore, a Saussurean approach to the particles, treating them as signs (unified signals of unified meanings) has much to offer: cf. Cook 1987 on Japanese *no*. And finally, the Saussurean notion of a 'system of oppositions' (cf. Garcia 1975, Kirsner 1979) may well prove useful in elucidating further properties of particles.

It seems clear, for example, that *hoor* is indeed opposed to *hè* in signaling something like NONQUESTION versus QUESTION. Compare *Leuk hoor* 'Nice!' versus *Leuk hè* 'Nice, isn't it?'

Second, there are the practical implications. If *hoor* is analyzable, it is also teachable in an explicit, precise way. One can (and therefore should) devise lessons to get students to use particles. They are an essential ingredient of the Dutch language.

Finally, there are the descriptive implications. With utterances of the form *X hoor*, the social interaction achieved by speaker and hearer becomes almost more important than the propositional content of *X*. This influences both [i] the kinds of elements which turn up within *hoor*-sentences as opposed to 'plain' sentences and [ii] the environments in which *hoor*-sentences are used. To discuss such matters in any depth, however, we would need to consider quantitative data going beyond the space limitations of the present study.[10]

NOTES

*The research reported on here was supported by Grant 2964 from the Academic Senate of the University of California, Los Angeles. We wish to thank P. Broeder, J. Heemskerk, R. de Jonge, and J. Pacilly for helpful comments.

[1] For extensive discussion and exemplification of the concepts of meaning, message, and inference, see Garcia 1975 and Kirsner 1979. Because the contribution of a meaning to a message may be indirect as well as direct, our concept of message encompasses Searle's notion of perlocutionary effect.

[2] It is of course justified on historical grounds since, according to the *WNT*, the particle *hoor* derives from the interpolated phrase *hoort ge* 'you hear.'

[3] The contrasting particle *hè*, which does ask for confirmation, will be dealt with briefly below.

[4] But, as we discuss below, depending on both the linguistic and extralinguistic context, the message ultimately inferred by the hearer from the explicit signaling of FRIENDLINESS may be either genuinely friendly or bitingly sarcastic.

[5] There are contexts in which this utterance is indeed appropriate, as for example when one is wrapping Christmas presents (which are supposed to be a surprise) and is interrupted by someone coming into the room. But the friendly interpretation imposed upon, say, *D'ruit, hoor! Ik ben even bezig.* 'Get out, Okay? I'll be busy for a few more minutes.' merely confirms our analysis.

[6] Compare the equally absurd ??*Geef eens acht!* 'Ten-HUT, please', which is relatively incoherent for the same reason. For the sake of completeness, we note that Bob de Jonge has pointed out to us that one could use a sentence like *Geef eens acht!* or *Geef 's acht!* to ask an off-duty soldier attending a party to 'please show what the 'attention' posture looks like.' But in a strictly military context, friendliness and politeness are irrelevant.

[7] One theoretical issue raised by this particular example (which is not interpreted as a friendly utterance) is whether the core component FRIENDLINESS has been stated too specifically and should be replaced by the more neutral term AFFECTIVITY. The incoherent examples discussed in section 2, however, could not be explained if this were done. There would be no 'clash' between FRIENDLINESS and an unfriendly or 'antifriendly' context.

[8] In other words, given that one could always have said simply X, the content of X in X *hoor* may be interpreted in a way which <u>maximizes the contribution of *hoor* to the total message</u>. Compare Grice's Maxim of Quantity discussed in Sperber and Wilson (1986:33).

[9] It will be obvious that we have not discussed in this article how the core components might be related to one another (e.g., in a hierarchy) or whether pragmatic effects which we have attributed to one component (e.g., FRIENDLINESS) might not better be attributed to the simultaneous signaling of <u>all</u> components.

[10] An expanded version of the present article is in preparation.

SELECTED REFERENCES

Abraham, Werner, ed. 1986. Partikels. TTT: Interdisciplinair Tijdschrift voor Taal- & Tekstwetenschap 6, 83-210.

Auwera, J. van der, en W. Vandeweghe, eds. 1984. Studies over Nederlandse Partikels. Antwerp Papers in Linguistics 35. Antwerp: Universitaire Instelling Antwerpen.

Cook, Haruko Minegishi. 1987. Social meanings of the Japanese sentence-final particle *no*. Papers in Pragmatics 1, 123-168.

Foolen, A. P. 1986. 'Typical Dutch noises with no particular meaning': Modale partikels als leerprobleem in het onderwijs Nederlands als vreemde taal. In A. van Seggelen, ed. Verslag van het Negende Colloquium van Docenten in de Neerlandistiek aan Buitenlandse Universiteiten. 's-Gravenhage: Internationale Vereniging voor Neerlandistiek, 39-57.

García, Erica C. 1975. The Role of Theory in Linguistic Analysis: The Spanish Pronoun System. Amsterdam: North Holland.

Geerts, G., W. Haeseryn, J. de Rooij and M. C. van den Toorn. 1984. Algemene Nederlandse Spraakkunst. Groningen: Wolters-Noordhoff.

Kirsner, Robert S. 1979. The Problem of Presentative Sentences in Modern Dutch. Amsterdam: North Holland.

Searle, John R. 1970. Speech Acts: An Essay in the Philosophy of Language. Cambridge: Cambridge University Press.

Sperber, Dan and Deirdre Wilson. 1986. Relevance: Communication and Cognition. Cambridge, Massachusetts: Harvard University Press.

Toorn, M. C. van den. 1981. Nederlandse Grammatica. Groningen: Wolters-Noordhoff.

Weijdema, Willy, Simon Dik, Margo Oehlen, Clara Dubber and Akke De Blauw. 1982. Strukturen in Verbale Interaktie. Muiderberg: Coutinho.

Wierzbicka, Anna. 1976. Particles and linguistic relativity. International Review of Slavic Linguistics 1, 327-367.

DATA SOURCES

Carmiggelt, S. 1967. Vliegen Vangen. Amsterdam: ABC-Boeken.

Carmiggelt, S. 1975. Slenteren. Amsterdam: De Arbeiderspers.

Evenhuis, Gertie. 1979. En Waarom Ik Niet. Amsterdam: Van Goor Jeugdboeken.

Evenhuis, Gertie. 1978. What About Me? Transl. Lance Salway. Harmondsworth: Puffin Books.

Janssen, Frans A. 1979 ed. Scheppend Nihilisme. Interviews met Willem Frederik Hermans. Amsterdam: Loeb & Van der Velden.

Kooten, Kees van. 1985. Modermismen. Amsterdam: De Bezige Bij.

Rubinstein, Renate. 1978. Niets te Verliezen en Toch Bang. Amsterdam: Meulenhoff.

PRONUNCIATION NORMS IN THE DUTCH LANGUAGE AREA[*]

Uus Knops
Katholieke Universiteit, Nijmegen

1. Introduction

It is generally known that there is a rather great discrepancy between normative and empirical views on Dutch standard pronunciation. From a normative point of view Dutch standard pronunciation is envisioned as a point, i.e., as a variety with no variation between forms. It is identified by linguists and recorded in pronunciation dictionaries (e.g., De Coninck 1976, Paardekooper 1978), but it is more a construct or something postulated than something real. Yet in the Dutch speech community there are some people who are considered to be pretty close to it. From an empirical point of view Dutch standard pronunciation is a range. It is the set of pronunciation features, including a lot of variation, that is recognized and accepted as standard by the Dutch-speaking population (cf. Bartsch 1985).

The discrepancy between these two points of view — though not at all typical of or exclusive to the Dutch language area — can be the cause of many practical problems. Dutch language teachers, on the one hand, will have to rely upon the normative description of the standard pronunciation and teach it to their students. However, their own pronunciation may differ considerably from what they are supposed to teach. Students of the Dutch language, on the other hand, may be perplexed with the variation in standard pronunciation upon their first contact with the average Dutch standard speaker. Deviations from what they have learned as the correct pronunciation may be so numerous that intelligibility problems frequently arise.

It appears to me that many of these and related problems could be lessened or even solved, if language teachers disposed of descriptions of the whole range of pronunciation features that is recognized and accepted as standard by the Dutch-speaking population. Of course, some of this diversity is described in introductions to pronunciation dictionaries and in Dutch pronunciation manuals (e.g., Blancquaert 1969, Hermkens 1967). However, these descriptions tend to be incomplete, obsolete or based upon few or defective empirical data.

The investigation I want to present here is a first and modest attempt to gain some more insight into the empirical base of Dutch standard pronunciation and its relation to the normative standard pronunciation model. In setting up this investigation an attempt was made to reconcile two research traditions, both of which are concerned with the examination of the nature of listeners' reactions to speech.

The first research paradigm is that of language attitude studies in the matched- and verbal-guise tradition (e.g., Giles and Powesland 1975, Ryan and Giles 1982). In these studies stimulus materials usually consist of running speech fragments produced by mono- or bilingual speakers using different languages or language varieties. Listener-judges are asked to evaluate the speakers of those varieties on a number of personality traits and these evaluations are then taken to be language attitudes. Although these studies provide insight about the attitudes towards different groups of speakers marked by their language, one does not get insight with regard to the evaluation of the linguistic stimuli themselves, nor can anything be said about direct links between particular pronunciation features on the one hand and evaluative reactions towards speakers on the other hand.

The second paradigm is that of language attitude studies in a more sociolinguistic tradition. These studies have concentrated more on the evaluation of short-term segmental features i.e., pronunciation features. For instance, in the subjective reaction tests of Labov (1966) and Trudgill (1972) stimuli consisting of isolated words and differing in the realization of only one phonological variable at a time are presented to listeners with the request to indicate the variants they consider correct or that correspond to their own use. These studies - contrary to those conducted within the matched- and verbal-guise tradition - give detailed information about the evaluation of segmental phonological and phonetic features. However, neither the presentation of words in isolated forms, nor the kinds of reactions elicited in connection with these forms permits one to generalize to more realistic communicative situations where attitudes towards speakers are usually formed on the basis of larger fragments of running speech.

Therefore both paradigms were combined into one, leading to a design where both normal fragments of running speech and isolated words originating from these fragments constitute the stimulus materials. The evaluative reactions elicited in connection with these stimuli pertain to characteristics of the speech as well as the speakers. It must then be possible to get insight into the particular pronunciation features that play a determining role in the formation of language attitudes. And it may be hypothesized that these features will differ according to listeners' national and regional background. Further consequences of the design are that the relation between the evaluation of decontextualized words and larger fragments of running speech can be examined, as well as the relation between the evaluation of speech and personality traits. In short, the goals of this study were the examination of

1. the relation between the evaluation of speech and personality traits;
2. the relation between the evaluation of isolated, i.e., decontextualized, words and larger fragments of running speech;
3. the influence of particular pronunciation features upon the evaluation of running speech;
4. the influence of listeners' national and regional background upon the evaluation of different standard varieties of Dutch.

2. Method

A 30 second fragment of neutral prose was read on tape by seven speakers, two of which could be characterized as standard speakers (one speaker being a Dutchman, the other a Fleming). The remaining five speakers all had a regional accent, typical of various regions in the Netherlands and in Flanders. Two speakers came from what is regarded as the socio-economic center of the Netherlands and of Flanders respectively (the Dutchman had a North-Holland accent, the Fleming a Brabant accent). Two other speakers had a regional accent typical of the southern periphery of the Netherlands (a North-Brabant and a Limburg accent), and the last speaker had a West-Flemish accent, characteristic of the western periphery of Flanders. In all, there were four Dutch and three Flemish speakers. All of them were male, they had the same professions and were 30 to 35 years old.

From each of the seven fragments 15 words were isolated with the help of a porting system. These 15 words were the same for each speaker and represented approximately 25% of the reading fragments. In the case of the accented speakers, the words contained various phonological and phonetic deviations from the normative Dutch standard pronunciation model.

Both the decontextualized words and the fragments of running speech were presented to different audiences of judges. These consisted of five groups of about 50 students, originating from the same areas as the accented speakers used in this study: thus, they were natives of North-Holland, North-Brabant and Limburg in the Netherlands and of Brabant and West-Flanders in Belgium.

The 250 students all had to evaluate the stimuli in the same way. Therefore an evaluation instrument was constructed, containing semantic differential scales with five scale positions and two antonymic adjectives at the end of each scale. Two kinds of adjectives were used: adjectives designed for the evaluation of a speaker's speech (the so-called speech scales) and adjectives designed for the evaluation of the speaker as a person (the so-called personality scales).

The speech scales were: the pronunciation is clear - unclear; pure - not pure; beautiful - ugly; cultivated - uncultivated; pleasant - unpleasant; careful - sloppy; and natural - affected. The personality scales were: the speaker is intelligent - unintelligent; congenial - uncongenial; modest - arrogant; confident - unsure; friendly - unfriendly; reliable - unreliable; and respectful - disrespectful.

3. Relation between speech and personality judgements

First, the relation between the speech and personality scales was examined. Pearson product-moment correlation coefficients were computed for the different types of scales and the different types of stimuli, i.e., the standard prose passages as well as the decontextualized words. The coefficients were mostly highly significant suggesting a strong relation between the two different types of scales. However, two personality scales form an exception in that they show rather weak correlations with the speech scales. These are the scales "modest - arrogant" and "respectful - disrespectful." It was decided to eliminate these scales from further consideration.

On the remaining scales a factor analysis for each type of stimulus was performed which generally resulted in a two-factor solution. The personality scales loading on the first factor refer to the social and intellectual status of speakers (confident - unsure; intelligent - unintelligent), whereas those of the second factor display raters' concern for speakers' social attractiveness (congenial - uncongenial; friendly - unfriendly; reliable - unreliable). These dimensions can easily be interpreted in terms of competence (Lambert 1967), status (Ryan 1979) or superiority (Zahn and Hopper 1985) on the one hand, and social attractiveness (Lambert 1967) or solidarity (Ryan 1979) on the other hand. Speech scales that load on the first dimension turn out to refer to traditional prescriptive norms for good or correct articulation (clear - unclear; cultivated - uncultivated; careful - sloppy; pure - not pure), whereas those that load on the second dimension refer to the naturalness and aesthetic qualities of speech (beautiful - ugly; natural - affected). The model found shows remarkable resemblance with the one Zahn and Hopper (1985) extracted with their speech evaluation instrument, except that the latter found a third factor, termed dynamism. New is the fact that the two-factor model pertains to both reading fragments and isolated words. The latter stimuli were not included in the stimulus materials of Zahn and Hopper.

4. Relation between the evaluation of isolated words and larger fragments of running speech

Second, the relation between the evaluations of isolated words and their corresponding reading fragments was examined by calculating Pearson product-moment correlations between the evaluation of each reading fragment and the sum of evaluations of the 15 words isolated from this fragment. Since half of the different speech and personality scales showed high and consistent correlations with a status dimension, reflecting the normative views of Dutch and Flemish judges on standard speech, the correlations on this dimension only were examined. Though in most cases the correlation coefficients were highly significant, the highest coefficient to be found was still no more than .67. This means that even in the best case only 44% of the variation in the evaluation of running speech can be predicted from the variation in the evaluation of single words produced by the same speaker under the same circumstances.

The results of the second part of the investigation therefore hold an important warning to language attitude studies in a sociolinguistic tradition. Since the stimulus materials of these studies usually consist of isolated words differing in the realization of only one phonological variable at a time, precise information concerning the evaluation of particular pronunciation features can be revealed. Researchers in this tradition have to face the fact, however, that the external validity of their results in terms of the generalizability to running speech is rather limited. A relatively low predictability will all the more pertain to studies where the stimulus materials consist of words that are produced in isolation. After all, it is reasonable to expect that the use of decontextualized instead of isolated words gives a more favorable view on the relation existing between the evaluation of words spoken in isolation and running speech (cf. Koopmans-Van Beinum 1980).

5. Pronunciation features as determinants of language attitudes

In a next step of the analysis I looked at the pronunciation features that served as cues in the evaluation process, i.e., the determinants of language attitudes. These were defined as the pronunciation features, occurring in decontextualized words, the evaluations of which correlated significantly with the evaluations of the corresponding reading fragments. More specifically, it was examined whether certain pronunciation features have more perceptual relevance than others.

A distinction was made between phonological and phonetic deviations from standard pronunciation. Phonological deviations are those that pertain to a different phonemic sound system or to varieties that allow types of phonemic sequences different from the standard pronunciation model (cf. Laver and Trudgill 1979).

Examples from my own materials are the use of voiceless fricatives instead of voiced ones (typical of Northwestern speakers in the Dutch language area) and the omission of /h/ in prevocalic positions (typical of many Brabant dialects). Phonetic deviations from standard pronunciation on the other hand concern the way particular phonemes are actually pronounced. For instance, /w/ can be pronounced as a bilabial or a labiodental semivowel in Dutch; /o./ and /e./ can be pronounced as monophthongs or as diphthongs. These are purely realizational differences between speakers of various regions in the Dutch language area; they do not concern deviations in phonological resources.

It was hypothesized that phonological deviations from standard pronunciation are perceptually more salient and evaluated less positively than purely phonetic deviations. The reason is that deviations of the first kind produce a larger dissimilarity, i.e., a larger linguistic distance regarding the standard system than deviations of the second type. On the whole, the first part of this hypothesis proved to be true. Phonological deviations from standard pronunciation do have more perceptual salience as determinants of attitudes than purely phonetic deviations. The former are evaluated more reliably, i.e., they show greater consistency with the evaluations of the corresponding language varieties than variants of a phonetic kind.

The second part of the hypothesis relates to the question whether phonological deviations from standard pronunciation are evaluated less positively than purely phonetic deviations. Comparison of the mean evaluations of both kinds of deviations revealed, however, that this hypothesis is only partly true. In most cases phonological deviations were indeed evaluated less positively than purely phonetic deviations. In some cases, however, the phonological deviations were evaluated more positively than the phonetic deviations and even more positively than the standard features themselves. In other words, the factor "prestige" plays an important role in determining the direction of evaluation. When devoid of positive prestige, phonological deviations from standard pronunciation are evaluated less positively than purely phonetic deviations. But when these phonological features are endowed with positive prestige, their evaluations turn out to be more positive than for likewise positively evaluated phonetic deviations. Therefore, it has to be concluded that phonological deviations are evaluated more "extremely," in either a positive or negative way, than purely phonetic deviations. The more "extreme" evaluation of phonological versus phonetic deviations is moreover in accord with their larger perceptual relevance as segmental features typically associated with a particular variety.

6. Influence of judges' national and regional background upon the evaluation of different varieties of Dutch

Since the factor "prestige" plays a determining role in the acceptance of deviations from the Dutch standard pronunciation model, differences in evaluations among the various groups of listener-judges are to be expected. This is all the more so since the accented varieties presented to the listener-judges are located in different countries, each of which has its own area that functions as a socio-economic center. One might hypothesize that submodel varieties that are located in the economic and political center of an area will be accepted more as standard than submodel varieties that are located in the periphery. The most salient differences in evaluations are indeed those between the Dutch and Flemish judges. The Flemish judges systematically upgrade the Flemish accents in comparison with the Dutch judges. On the other hand, they downgrade the Dutch standard speaker as well as the North-Holland speaker. The latter has much prestige for the Dutch judges, whereas the Belgian Brabant speaker has more prestige for the Flemish judges. This means that the prestige of a standard language variety is not only or necessarily due to the similarity of that variety to a standard pronunciation model, which would have been the case if phonological deviations from the standard model were systematically downgraded in comparison to phonetic deviations. Rather, it is an extralinguistic factor, namely the prestige of the group that is located in the area which is regarded as the socio-economic center of a particular speech community, that determines the prestige of the language variety associated with that group. In other words, we have to make a clear distinction between linguistic features that seem to be important as factors playing a role in the more cognitive task of identifying speakers, and extralinguistic factors that seem to determine the evaluation process. This result would not have been found if the search for a way of combining different approaches in the study of language attitudes had not been undertaken. It can therefore be concluded that the reconciliation of both designs has proved useful in learning something about the intricate interplay of linguistic and extralinguistic factors in language evaluation.

* This research was made possible through a grant of the Netherlands Organization for Scientific Research (N.W.O.).

BIBLIOGRAPHY

Bartsch, R., *Sprachnormen. Theorie und Praxis*. Tübingen: Niemeyer, 1985.

Blancquaert, E., *Praktische uitspraakleer van het Nederlands*. Antwerpen: De Sikkel, 1969.

Coninck, R.H.B. de., *Groot uitspraakwoordenboek van de Nederlandse taal*. Antwerpen: De Sikkel, 1976.

Giles, H. and P.F. Powesland, *Speech Style and Social Evaluation*. London: Academic Press, 1975.

Hermkens, H.M., *Fonetiek en fonologie*. 's-Hertogenbosch: Malmberg, 1967.

Koopmans-van Beinum, F.J., *Vowel Contrast Reduction. An Acoustic and Perceptual Study of Dutch Vowels in Various Speech Conditions*. Amsterdam: Academic Press, 1980.

Labov, W., *The Social Stratification of English in New York City*. Washington D.C.: Centre for Applied Linguistics, 1966.

Lambert, W.E., "A Social Psychology of Bilingualism." In *Journal of Social Issues* 23 (1967), 91-109.

Laver, J. and P. Trudgill, "Phonetic and Linguistic Markers in Speech." In K.R. Scherer and H. Giles (eds.), *Social Markers in Speech*, 1-32. Cambridge: Cambridge University Press, 1979.

Paardekooper, P.C., *ABN-uitspraakgids*. Hasselt: Heideland-Orbis, 1978.

Ryan, E.B., "Why Do Low-Prestige Language Varieties Persist?" In H. Giles and R.N. St. Clair (eds.), *Language and Social Psychology*, 145-157. Oxford: Blackwell, 1979.

Ryan, E.B. and H. Giles, eds., *Attitudes Towards Language Variation: Social and Applied Contexts*. London: Edward Arnold, 1982.

Trudgill, P., "Sex, Covert Prestige and Linguistic Change in the Urban British English of Norwich." In *Language in Society* 1 (1972), 179-195.

Zahn, C.J. and R. Hopper, "Measuring Language Attitudes: The Speech Evaluation Instrument." In *Journal of Language and Social Psychology* 4 (1985), 113-123.

THE EDUCATION OF LINGUISTIC MINORITIES IN THE NETHERLANDS

Marisa Garrett Castellano
University of California, Berkeley

INTRODUCTION

Since World War II, immigration to the Netherlands has increased greatly. Immigrant children face the problem of receiving an education in a language they may not understand or speak. This paper attempts to describe the programs and policies designed for these children, and then to provide some evaluative comments about the goals and outcomes of the programs.

The foreign population of the Netherlands is estimated at about 5% of the total population. However, the foreign population under the age of 25 is much higher. In Utrecht it is 24%, and in Amsterdam it is 35%.

THE EDUCATION OF LINGUISTIC MINORITIES IN THE NETHERLANDS

To understand the initial actions taken by the Dutch government, we must look at the situation within the broader framework of the European Economic Community. At first, the EEC did not interfere with the educational systems of the member states, mostly because that issue had not been addressed in the Treaty of Rome, which created the Community. Educational policies were national matters and the sole responsibility of the country concerned. But since 1974 the EEC has issued annual reports and directives on the situation of the education of immigrant workers' children, and has also implemented various pilot programs, including reception methods, mother tongue teaching, in-service teacher training, and vocational guidance for young immigrants.

By far the major limitation of any Commission directives is their limited scope: they only refer to workers who immigrate to member states from other member states; that is, they are only concerned with other European children (Neave, 1984). Of course, each individual country has the freedom to apply or not apply the directives to any population within its borders.

The Netherlands was involved in two of the EEC's 1977 pilot projects investigating various "reception" techniques. Newly-arrived children were taught in their native language by someone of their own nationality. Dutch was gradually introduced until, after two years, the children joined a Dutch-speaking class of their own age group in a neighborhood school. These pilot projects became the model for current Dutch reception programs.

Subsequent research in the second language acquisition of immigrant children, however, has revealed that two years is not enough time to learn a language well enough to be able to succeed in an academic setting exclusively in that language (Cummins, 1982). Maybe after two years, children seem to have a working knowledge of Dutch, and maybe they can communicate fairly well with teachers and peers, but this is not enough to accomplish cognitively demanding classwork and activities. If such children are mainstreamed into regular all-Dutch instruction too early, they will continue to fall behind their peers.

By 1978, the Netherlands had also begun a program of education in mother tongue and culture (OETC), directed towards recently arrived students who do not speak Dutch. While the situation varies greatly among Dutch schools, all OETC teachers must be qualified teachers in the mother countries of the pupils.

If a student arrived in the Netherlands at <u>secondary</u> school age, and there were at least eight students of the same nationality in the school, a separate class would be formed, called an *Internationale Schakelklas* (ISK). These transition classes are meant to link (*schakelen*) the students' previous education in their homeland with the Dutch system, and to prepare them to enter a Dutch secondary school in one or two years. OETC does not exist for these classes, although some have interpreters.

The short duration of the ISK together with a lack of any formal evaluation method almost guarantees its failure and the failure of its students. Many do not even finish the program, and the majority of adolescent immigrants end up with a job much like that of their parents: in the lower echelons of the working class. Not surprisingly, they are underrepresented in higher education.

In 1981, the *Beleidsplan Culturele Minderheden in het Onderwijs* (Policy Plan for Cultural Minorities in the Netherlands) was released, in which two goals were stated: first, to aid linguistic minority children prepare for social and economic participation in Dutch society from the vantage point of their cultural background; and second, through intercultural education, to foster the acceptance and valuing of these minorities into Dutch society. So now the government's concerns became the fostering of a positive self-concept in these students so that they can function in society, and, of great importance, the education of Dutch children about their non-Dutch peers. However, nowhere in this statement does the Dutch Minister consider the maintenance of the mother tongue as an explicit goal of the OETC program.

Since 1984, immigration to the Netherlands has decreased (Sociaal en Cultureel Planbureau, 1986). Thus the need for "reception" classes per se will also decrease, but the need for genuine intercultural education for both the Dutch-born minorities and Dutch majority children will not.

In 1986, the European Ministers of Education published an article describing the current state of the problem of migrant children's education. In it, they consider "cultural identity" to be a major factor for educational and integration difficulties, and suggest that intercultural education is a possible solution. Since migrants tend to come from underdeveloped rural areas, it is sometimes difficult for them to understand urban life or adapt to an industrialized society. But the children of these migrants often learn to speak the language of the host country better than their parents, and better than their mother tongue. If parents are determined to preserve cultural or religious traditions that seem to have no place in the mainstream society, conflicts between them and their children can result. So an important task of the host country is to "legitimize" as much of the home culture as possible through the schools. The Ministers go on to admit that intercultural education will be a challenge to the ethnocentricity of Europe, and that many aspects of education will have to be reanalyzed. The aim should be to take advantage of the other cultures present in a given society, in order to critically review the ways in which the dominant culture is constructed.

EVALUATION OF THE DUTCH PROGRAMS

In evaluating the programs mentioned above, the framework adopted here is that of Tove Skutnabb-Kangas, an advocate of minority language education as a means of social change, the type of change envisioned by both the EEC and the Netherlands concerning intercultural education and the future shape of European society. Skutnabb-Kangas creates four classifications for educational programs for children, distinguished by the linguistic organization of the program (mono- or bilingual), and the goal of the program (mono- or bilingualism).

1. Monolingual education leading to monolingualism: This is standard education, where students are taught in the dominant language. They might take foreign languages as subjects, but seldom to the point of fluent bilingualism.

For minority children taught in Dutch, in what is known as the "submersion" model, the goal is to assimilate children into the mainstream and to socialize them into accepting majority norms; little value is placed on maintaining the mother tongue. If they hold on to their cultural background, they sense frustration at not being able to partake of the prosperity they see in the host country. But if they have assimilated, they may find themselves discriminated against by the members of the dominant society. Minorities educated in this way do not feel completely a part of either the majority or minority community. These types of submersion programs educate future assembly line workers or the future unemployed, such as the ISK students mentioned above.

The other goal in this model is monolingualism in the minority language, where children do not learn the power language of that society and are thus cut off from receiving their share of the economic prosperity of the host country. Fortunately, this model does not exist in the Netherlands.

2. Bilingual education leading to monolingualism: The reception or transitional bilingual education programs belong to this second model. Because they are transitional in nature, the goal is monolingualism in Dutch. The message to the minority child is to assimilate. But once children are transferred to all-Dutch instruction, many fall further and further behind, because they do not have the academic abilities in Dutch that their Dutch-speaking peers do.

3. Monolingual education leading to bilingualism: If bilingualism for majority children is the goal, it is called an immersion program, where majority children begin their schooling in a minority language. They do not receive instruction in their own language, but it is the dominant societal one, so they are in no danger of losing it. This model is used in Canada and Spain, but does not exist in the Netherlands.

If bilingualism for minority children is the goal, it is called a language maintenance program. These are not implemented in the Dutch school system either. However, some minority groups have their own programs which offer children a chance to use the mother tongue in an academic setting, reinforcing it, and helping the children realize that their language is just as proper a vehicle for learning as Dutch.

4. Bilingual education leading to bilingualism: The goals for this last model are high levels of competence in both the majority and minority languages, for both majority and minority students. Whichever language would be otherwise less likely to develop (usually the minority language) receives most of the resources and time inside the school. This is not presently realized anywhere on a large scale, but Skutnabb-Kangas recommends this as the model of choice for Europe, given its present demographic make-up and the consequences that could follow if significant changes do not take place.

CONCLUSION

The stated goals of the Dutch educational policy are intercultural education and social and economic participation for all. Skutnabb-Kangas' framework is thus insightful and appropriate to use as a yardstick for the Dutch system, since recent policy statements have rejected assimilation as a goal. But despite what is on the books, the Dutch system is not working towards realizing its goals. Lip service is paid to intercultural education but no one knows exactly how to proceed with it. There are no minority language maintenance programs run by the government. The failure of the ISK programs has not yet been rectified. Finally, the bilingual programs (reception and OETC) are purely transitional in nature, and have been subjected to much criticism.

If intercultural education is indeed the goal, the first step would be to look at such programs in different areas of the world. Intercultural education means providing complete and sufficient materials in the minority languages in order to promote functional and recreational reading in any of the languages spoken in the Netherlands. It means having school assemblies in minority languages – in short, it means putting the minority languages on an equal footing with Dutch within the school system.

In addition, intercultural education should become a means of eliminating racism and stereotypes. For this to take place, it has to become a part of the entire Dutch school system, not only in those schools with a large minority population.

The third step is to discover means of evaluating current programs. There must be criteria for successful programs and a way to correct those that do not meet these criteria. Minority groups should be consulted in order to discover what they would like education to accomplish. At the present time, they are far too seldom consulted concerning these issues.

These are some of the directions in which the Netherlands must now go. It has been claimed that Dutch society has become the most varied multicultural society in Western Europe. If this is so, intercultural education is all the more necessary so as to break down ethnocentricity and give minority children the personal stability needed to cope with and take part in the society in which they live.

SELECTED BIBLIOGRAPHY

1. Altena, Nelleke and Dorian de Haan. "Taalpolitiek en etnieskulturele migrantengroepen in Nederland." *Interdisciplinair Tijdschrift voor Taal- en Tekstwetenschap.* Vol. 4 (no. 4), Dec. 1984. 295-316.

2. Appel, Rene. "Minority Languages in the Netherlands: Relations Between Sociopolitical Conflicts and Bilingual Education." *The Sociogenesis of Language and Human Conduct.* Ed. Bruce Bain. New York: Plenum, 1983. 517-26.

3. Council of Europe. "Principales initiatives tendant à développer l'éducation des enfants migrants aux Pays-Bas." *Migrants Formation*. Vol. 46. Paris, 1981. 32-40.

4. Cummins, James. "The Role of Primary Language Development in Promoting Educational Success for Language Minority Students." *Schooling and Language Minority Students: A Theoretical Framework*. Sacramento: California State Department of Education, 1982. 3-47.

5. Van Esch, W. "Dutch Concepts for the Education of Migrant Workers' Children." *The Education of Migrant Workers' Children*. (Council of Europe). Lisse: Swets & Zeitlinger, 1981. 162-66.

6. European Ministers of Education. "The Education of Migrant Children: Problems and Prospects." *Western European Education*. Vol. 18 (no. 2), 1986. 8-49.

7. Extra, Guus. "Taalminderheden en onderwijs in vergelijkend perspektief." *Levende Talen*. Vol. 368. Coevorden, the Netherlands, 1982. 2-11.

8. Neave, Guy. *The European Economic Community and Education*. Great Britain: Trentham Books, 1984.

9. Skutnabb-Kangas, Tove. "Children of Guest Workers and Immigrants: Linguistic and Educational Issues." *Linguistic Minorities: Policies and Pluralism*. Ed. John Edwards. New York: Academic Press, 1984. 17-48.

10. Sociaal en Cultureel Planbureau. *Sociaal en Cultureel Rapport 1986*. 's Gravenhage: Staatsuitgeverij, 1986.

11. Vermeulen, Hans and Trees Pels. "Ethnic Identity and Young Migrants in the Netherlands." *Prospects: A Quarterly Review of Education*. Vol. 14 (no. 2), 1984. 277-82.

DUTCH IN TRANSLATION

André Lefevere
University of Texas, Austin
and
Ria Vanderauwera
Austin

We shall briefly deal with three aspects of Dutch in translation, try to show to what extent they are related, and give some do-it-yourself hints.[1]

The first aspect is that of pedagogical translation. We think it should, again, be part and parcel of the teaching of Dutch as a foreign language. It seems to be the best way to actually illustrate the differences between English and Dutch. This can be done on the morphosyntactic level (*ik zat in mijn bad en was zingen weg* is not the same as "I sat in my bath and was singing away"), on the semantic level (*drie slechte achterwerken* is not "three bad bums") and, especially, on the level of style and register, pun and "cultural" connotation (i.e., the connotation that requires the introduction of cultural background before it can be made clear to the student). *Een stuk koek* is not "a piece of cake" and *klaar is Kees* is not "Kees is ready now." There is also an ulterior motive for the introduction of pedagogical translation into the classroom: it is a fascinating challenge for some of the brighter students, who will then go on to translate Dutch into English outside of the classroom. Since it is an open secret that we need translators who can translate Dutch into American (or, if need be, "Transatlantic") and not British English, there is a lot to be said for "catching them young."

The second aspect is that of the translation of literature. It is important to distinguish, right at the outset, between "translation of literature" and "literary translation." A "translation of literature" is usually written for a scholarly audience. It tries to make the original available for further study, usually of a comparative nature within a wider European context. One thinks of Egbert Krispijn's projected anthology of the literature of the Golden Age in this respect, or of the facing translation of the collected works of Ruusbroec, which is definitely intended for theologians, medievists, and students of mysticism. The "translation of literature" does not claim any literary merit of its own. It comes close to a kind of "glossary" designed to make the original text available.

A "literary translation," on the other hand, tries to compete with the literary production in the target literature (American literature, in our case) on a footing of equality or, to put it more cautiously, on its own merits. Needless to say, neither type of translation is easily found in its "pure" form. They often overlap to some extent, and there are all kinds of gradations between the two.

Prospective translators of Dutch literature would be well-advised to take into account a series of factors, which will be dealt with in the next few pages: patronage, audience, author, text-type, poetics, and universe of discourse.

Patronage is the umbrella term that covers questions like: "Who is going to publish what?." If there is a Dutch book you would like to translate, you should familiarize yourself with the American publishing world and find out which publishers might be interested in a book of this kind. It is also advisable to check with the Foundation for the Promotion of the Translation of Dutch Literary Works in Amsterdam to find out if anybody else is already translating the book, and what the copyright situation is like. Before you start translating, you should also ask yourself what kind of market there is or might be for the book: does it stand a chance on the general market, or should it be translated for more specialized markets? A further problem is that of the "image" of Dutch literature in America. One finds that it is still mostly defined by the events of World War II and the holocaust. "Dutch literature" tends to evoke Anne Frank, Miep Gies, Hetty Hillesum and *De aanslag*. If your potential translation fits in with this image you will have less trouble getting it published than if it does not. But if it does not and you do get it published, you will have achieved more for the image of Dutch literature in America than if it did.

Audience is a convenient shorthand for questions like: "Is this book for a general audience?" If not, what target audience can you, as a translator, imagine for the book? This question should also be dealt with at the outset, because you, as the translator, will have to be able to convince the potential publisher that there is a potential audience for your translation - out there. That audience is very often a specialized sub-audience, i.e., an audience which consists either of scholars reading "translations of literature," or of the reader in the street who is somewhat of a mystery buff. In that case he may well be a potential audience for the Van de Wetering or Van Gulik mysteries. If the man in the street is somewhat of a poetry buff, he may be interested in an anthology of Dutch poetry.

If your **author** does not have "name recognition" in America, your task will be made that much more difficult. Publishers don't really want to publish people they have never heard of. And they have never heard of most Dutch authors. A sensible strategy to counteract this lack of name recognition is to either point out the similarities between the author you are translating and famous authors in the target literature. (This should not be overdone, of course, because it runs the risk of becoming counterproductive very easily: "If this author of yours is so much like our author X, then why translate him at all? Why publish Adriaan Roland Holst in a translation that has to compete with Yeats on his home ground?") The alternative strategy is to portray your author as belonging to a "general European movement" of which he is the "local" representative. The particular "Low Countries" variation on the common theme might, therefore, be of interest.

If your author has name recognition, your problems are minor, except if a particular work by that author does not fit in too well with the pre-existing image. Multatuli evokes *Max Havelaar*, of course, but has *Woutertje Pieterse* really been written by the same man? You may face yet another problem if your author is perceived as "marginal" in his or her own culture, if he or she is Flemish, to draw attention to a mild case, or if he or she hails from Surinam or the Dutch Caribbean (e.g., Astrid Roemer, Bea Vianen, Tip Marugg, Boeli van Leeuwen, Frank Martinus Arion).

Dealing with the authors you want to translate may not always be particularly easy either. Contrary to common belief, not all authors want to be translated. Alternatively, writers who are "world famous in Holland" may not want to be published in America if the publisher happens to be a small press, or if the publisher is not willing to fork out large advances. Authors who are somewhat proficient in some variety (temporal – what they were taught when they were in high school, or spatial – British) of English will not always be satisfied with a translation into American English, not out of prejudice, but out of ignorance. Again, the Translation Foundation in Amsterdam has done a very good job in bringing egoes together in the past, and will no doubt continue to do so. It is hard to know when it is best to approach an author directly, or when it is best to go through the Foundation. Fate plays a part here, too.

Certain **text-types** travel (a lot) better than others. Publishers love to see novels, because novels sell best. Essays are not terribly in demand, and neither are collections of poetry or short stories. On the other hand, magazines (little or not so little) are usually willing to print translations of Dutch poetry or of Dutch short stories. Publishers might be more favorably disposed towards anthologies of Dutch poetry, giving a survey of the production of a certain period, than in the work of just one poet. It is almost impossible to get drama published for a general audience. If the play has not been performed in America, it will not be published in America – and often it will not be published even if it has been performed.

The **poetics** of Dutch and American literature are not necessarily the same, even though both literatures are part of a bigger entity called "Western." In other words: what is considered literature in Holland is not necessarily considered literature in America, and vice versa. The Dutch reaction to Janwillem van de Wetering's success in the US is a case in point. Van de Wetering is probably the best selling Dutch author abroad, but in Holland he is looked down on as a "mere" purveyor of "detective" fiction. The Dutch novel is much more introspective in nature than its American counterpart, which is much more action oriented, and faster paced. The American novel is also much longer than its Dutch counterpart, which is why US publishers will occasionally publish two short Dutch novels by the same author (e.g., Geeraerts) in one volume and pass them off as "one" novel.

Finally, the **universe of discourse** of Dutch literature does not always travel well. Objects do not exist in the target culture, concepts are difficult to carry across without extensive footnoting or explanation in the text. (Think of so thoroughly Dutch a concept as *verzuiling* in this respect.) This is probably even more the case in novels written in Dutch but set in Indonesia, Surinam, or the Caribbean, which will contain many objects and concepts which are hard to understand for the Dutch reader who is not familiar with the former Dutch colonial possessions. On a somewhat smaller scale, the same holds true with regard to the work of older generations of Flemish writers. Alternatively, the sheer exotic flavor of things and concepts may well give the novels which contain them a kind of "lure" which is lacking in "Dutch-Dutch" novels. It is clear that language and universe of discourse do by no means overlap: are the novels written by Caribbean writers who use Dutch as a literary medium novels which belong to "Dutch literature", or are they "really" Latin American literature which happens, through some fluke of history, to have been written in Dutch?

The point of it all is, of course, to make Dutch literary works enter the canon of world literature. For the time being that canon exists, for better or worse, in both English and Russian. Literature which is not translated into either of those languages (or preferably both), does not exist on a global scale. For Dutch literature, the situation is not as dismal as it was even five years ago: Multatuli, Mulisch, Couperus, Nooteboom, Emants, and soon Claus and Streuvels are available in editions campus bookstores can actually find and order. It will soon be possible to teach "Dutch Literature in Translation" courses without having to resort to extensive xeroxing.

Yet there is more to be done. The translator who wants to get his or her translation into the canon of world literature has to deal with the factors enumerated above. Most of these factors can be dealt with by means of methods not beyond the bounds of human reason. Yet there is one factor over which the translator has no control: Dutch literature has a certain image (or, sometimes, in some places, no image at all), and that is the given the translator has to live with. He or she can try to exploit it, or change it, to refer to both ends of the scale of possible strategies, but whatever a translator does, he or she does not start out from virgin territory. The image problem can never be "solved," but there seem to be two contradictory ways to deal with it. One way would be to stress what is "really original" in Dutch literature, i.e., what does not exist in other Western literatures, or not to anywhere near the same extent. This strategy is bound to take us back in time, mostly to the Middle Ages: the *abele spelen*, Arthurian literature, the animal fables, mysticism. This strategy will, most likely, produce translations mainly for more or less specialized sub-audiences. The other strategy would be to unabashedly hitch the Dutch wagon to a European (or even "Western") star. Whatever is "in" at the moment in the target culture and can be shown to exist in Dutch also is a good bet for translation. This strategy allows us to range through genres and periods, form the medieval *boerden* (there is widespread interest in the *fabliaux*, these days) to the metaphysical wit of the Golden Age and the feminist novel of our own time.

If we want to link pedagogical with literary translation, we might consider opening some of the pages of *PAANS* to facing translations of short pieces of literature, mainly poems and short stories, chosen for their literary merit, their potential use in the classroom, and their historical relevance. That way we might be able to both sensitize students to translation and offer them an outlet for their first translations. We might also make it possible to offer more literature classes, or simply "reading on an advanced level" classes if we could deal with texts that would be available together with facing translations. We could still make grammatical, stylistic and register points, but the actual translation work would have been done, comprehension would be facilitated, and there would be more time left for discussion in the classroom.

The differences between technical and literary translation are not as great as they are often made out to be. If, for example, you want to translate Stijn Streuvels' *De Vlaschaard*, you had better make sure that you know a lot about flax and the way flax was grown and processed at the end of the nineteenth century. In addition, you will also have to know about idiolect, sociolect, and register – the selfsame features which occur in many non-literary texts which need to be translated.

The main difference between literary and non-literary translation is definitely an extrinsic one: money. You make more money as a non-literary translator. Depending on the amount of work you get, you might even make a living as a non-literary translator. It is very unlikely that you will ever make a living as a literary translator from the Dutch, which is why literary translations are mostly made by scholars, or people who can afford to make them for fun and/or out of genuine interest for an author or a text.

Since non-literary translation is better paid, the constraints under which the non-literary translator has to work also tend to be more rigorous. Deadlines are there to be met, not as vague guidelines which can nearly always be extended or revised. And the client is omnipotent: if he or she does not like the translation, the translator has very little recourse, other than going back to the word processor. There is no independent court of appeal, such as transcendental beauty or the wisdom of the ages that can bail out non-literary translators.

The ideal technical translator should have a number of degrees, of course. First of all, a language degree in a foreign language, or a degree in linguistics combined with near-native knowledge of a foreign language. He or she should also have a technical degree in, say, engineering, business, computer science, or chemistry. If the translator is equipped in this manner, he or she can afford to specialize within a certain area — but not if Dutch is that translator's main language. Specialization appears possible only for translators working into or out of the "bigger" languages or, at the outer limit, for translators working with Dutch in Holland and for either Philips or Buitenlandse Zaken. Specialization and Dutch seem to be mutually exclusive in America.

The ideal technical translator, whose profile has been sketched above, tends not to exist in too great numbers. Technical translators often turn out to be people gifted with knowledge of languages, genuine interest and — maybe above all — common sense. More often than not, technical translators have liberal arts degrees, and do not suffer from that fact, or feel inferior or unadapted to their tasks on account of it.

The ideal technical translator also has the courage to refuse assignments. Nobody can know everything, and both clients and agencies appreciate honesty. If you do not succeed in making (common) sense of a text after repeated readings, chances are that you had better say no to any invitation to translate it. If you know you will be unable to meet the client's or the agency's deadline, say so. It will not scare them away.

Next to common sense, the ideal technical translator also needs bibliographical sense. Technical translators need to know, or be able to find out, which dictionaries will be of help, and how to acquire access to those dictionaries. Bilingual dictionaries usually prove to be of limited value. They need to be supplemented by technical dictionaries. Yet for the interested layman/woman, pictorial dictionaries tend to be at least as useful on the initial level. Dictionaries are often supplemented by other forms of information, and by the many words and equivalences the translator jots down while reading and enters into the glossary of his or her word processor.

Translations from English into Dutch are better paid than translations from Dutch into English, but there is more work in the Dutch-English field than in its opposite. Translators also need to be aware of the uneasy relationship between Dutch and Flemish. Since Flemish is often used to refer to the Dutch spoken in Belgium, and since it is often still perceived as a separate language, different from Dutch, it is advisable to make it known that you translate out of both Dutch and Flemish, and into Dutch. The use of the word "Netherlandic" is anathema in this context: it confuses the issue, the client, and the agency. Even though the word has been created to defuse Flemish susceptibilities, it has never really "made" it in the "real" world (i.e., outside of academe) and should not be used there.

Translating out of Flemish can be a problem for those speakers of Dutch who are not Flemings themselves. Most Dutch-English dictionaries are based on Holland Dutch and British English. The translator into Dutch who has lived in America for a while has little difficulty in silently eliminating Britishisms and replacing them with American usage. If the translator is not a Fleming, however, he or she will rarely know what the Flemish word, often not listed in bilingual dictionaries, could possibly mean. If the translator has recourse to Van Dale (the Dutch-Dutch Van Dale), the problem can usually be solved. If not, non-Flemish translators will go on translating the *laf* in *laf weer* as "cowardly," rather than "humid." The worst pitfall for the translator is the problem of official language. The official Dutch used in Belgium differs significantly from the official Dutch used in Holland, simply because, when the Belgian state became bilingual in fact as well as in theory, many French terms were simply – often very literally – translated. *Zaakvoerder* (meaning "executive"), for example, is probably unintelligible to most non-Flemish readers of Dutch. If those readers know French, they can think of *chargé d'affaires*, and that will make things clearer. If they do not know French, the problem persists.

In comparison to the above, translating into Dutch represents fewer problems. Common sense dictates the use of Holland Dutch. If the translated text is to be used in Holland, the client will expect no less. If the text is to be used in Belgium, the reader will be able to make the necessary adjustments. If a Fleming reads *repareren*, he or she will be able to privately translate that word into *herstellen*, if he or she so desires. If a Dutch reader reads *herstellen*, he or she will immediately recognize (stigmatize?) the word as Flemish. If texts are translated into Holland Dutch, they can be used in both main parts of the Dutch linguistic area. If they are translated into Flemish, they will have to be adapted once again for use in the Netherlands.

Translation from English into Dutch tends to create more problems than the other way around. English vocabulary develops faster. There is more to keep up with. The time-lag between the evolution of English and Dutch vocabulary can, paradoxically, also work to the translator's advantage: many specialized terms are simply taken over by Dutch in their English, or "still recognizably English" form. In specialized areas, such as computer science, it would be pointless to invest time and energy into inventing *ad hoc* Dutch equivalents. Syntactically the translator's main cross to bear is the English "ing" construction, which spawns all kinds of subordinate clauses in Dutch. Semantically the problem is mainly one of register. In English texts colloquial and formal language co-exist to a much greater extent than they do in Dutch texts.

Finally: how to find work? The ATA (American Translators Association) lists its members with their languages. Translators should also contact the translation agencies in their area. The agencies usually have a network of clients, and they can significantly shorten the time it takes for an individual translator to become "established" as competent for a language and in several fields. Most agencies require test translations. Reputable agencies will ask you to translate only a few passages from a text. Never translate a whole text: there is no easier way for the agency to have that text translated free. Chances are you will never hear from them again.

It takes a certain type of person to translate, whether he or she translates literature or not. That type of person enjoys the work he or she is doing. That type of enjoyment often shows in the way the person speaks about his or her work. It is often catching.

NOTES

[1] This article was prepared with the assistance of Joost de Wit of the Foundation for the Promotion of the Translation of Dutch Literary Works in Amsterdam.

PRONUNCIATION ERRORS IN DUTCH:
THEORETICAL AND PRACTICAL ASPECTS

S. De Vriendt
Vrije Universiteit, Brussel

> Ick sprack een' Duytscher van de Pest.
> Die noemden hij mij staegh die Best:
> Die Beest! docht ik; de booste plaghen,
> Zijn dat de beste van ons' dagen?
> Mich dunckt der Herr redet zu motest.
> (C. Huygens)

1. Unless one has students interested in developing only one particular skill, e.g., reading, each aspect of the language being taught and learned can be considered important. This does not mean, however, that all teachers will agree on what has to be taught systematically (in an explicit way or not).

According to some courses and teachers, a systematic presentation of the grammar of a language is unnecessary; to others, one does not need to bother about how many and what words one is to teach, whether they are frequent or useful; more teachers think teaching good pronunciation is little more than wasting one's time, since according to them, most pupils will succeed in producing the foreign language in a satisfactory manner anyhow.

I think it is important for our students to have a good, not a perfect, pronunciation as soon as possible, for the following reasons:

a) If there is something like an affective filter (see S. Krashen's writings on this subject), we have no reason to believe that their feeling inhibited when producing utterances in a foreign language should only be caused by their fear for grammatical or lexical errors; some students feel uneasy about their production because they are conscious of their awkward way of pronouncing individual sounds or sound strings.

b) We think that perception is important as a basis for good production (see part 2 of this article), and vice versa, i.e., the fact that a student masters the phonological system of the foreign language and most common realizations of the various phonemes will no doubt facilitate his perception and comprehension of native speaker utterances.

c) After a certain amount of initial lessons (after a few weeks or months), the language being used in class becomes more complex; clusters and successions of difficult sounds are then unavoidable, e.g., in *ze heeft grote kinderen* or *ze heeft geen huis gehuurd*. This last sentence is hopelessly difficult for students who have not learned to produce and distinguish [h] and [x] correctly.

    d) If, as we do, we first teach our students to listen to the foreign language and to produce spoken utterances, delaying for some time the contact with the written form of the language, a good pronunciation, especially the ability to keep phonemes apart, prevents the learner from making quite a lot of errors when starting to write; this is certainly the case when the foreign language has a highly phonological spelling, like Dutch.

2. Within the so-called SGAV framework [the structuro-global audio-visual method, Renard-Van Vlasselaer (1976), was written more than twelve years ago; for a better understanding of recent developments, see the English, German, or Dutch courses by Dickinson et al. (1975), Chaumond et al. (1979), De Vriendt et al. (1987)] we use the so-called verbo-tonal method of phonetic correction (Renard-Vlasselaer, 1976, pp. 42-44, 65-67).

    a) This method stresses the importance of perception. Pronunciation errors are not due to an inability to produce the sounds of the foreign language, but primarily to the wrong perception and identification of perceived sounds.

    b) As sounds do not occur separately in the language as it is spoken by native speakers, the student must learn to identify and to produce them within sound strings; consequently, phonetic correction will never be the correction of sounds in isolation.

    c) Moreover, not being isolated, sounds may be influenced by neighbouring sounds and by prosodic features of the whole string, e.g., they may vary according to where they occur in the intonation pattern of an utterance, to their being part of a stressed or an unstressed syllable, to the relative speed with which the utterance or part of it is pronounced.

    d) Accordingly, the method uses these very characteristics of the sounds-in-context to facilitate, improve, and correct the learner's perception of the sounds:

        – intonation, e.g., emphasizing the high-pitched feature of a vowel by placing it at the summit of the intonation curve;

- <u>rhythm</u>, e.g., slowing down when producing a syllable containing a diphthong or accelerating the production (by the teacher) of a word like *jongen* to emphasize the unicity of the central consonant [ŋ] and to avoid or correct the appearance of a parasitical [g] in the learner's production ([jɔŋgə]);

- <u>combination</u> with other sounds: it has been observed frequently that pronunciation errors occur in some contexts and not in others. A very useful correction strategy consists in presenting a sound in a context favouring its correct perception, and hence production. Another strategy, which can, but need not be combined with the use of favourable neighbouring sounds is the <u>modulated pronunciation</u> by the teacher of the part of a string in which an error was made. Both strategies are illustrated in the following example and at the end of part 4.

It is a well-known fact that anglophones are very bad at pronouncing [y], whether in French (*la rue*), German (*die Tür*) or Dutch. As a matter of fact, we will not say that they are unable to pronounce [my·r]; we think it all has something to do with Trubetskoy's sieve. When Dutch (French, German) people hear [my·r], they perceive correctly that the vowel has the features [+ high] [+ round] and [+ front], whether in their mother tongue or in any one of the other languages possessing the same vowel. Consequently they produce the vowel correctly.

The anglophone, whose ear is not different from the Dutchman's, so that it catches exactly the same vibrations, correctly analyzes the first and the second feature [+ high, + round] but fails to recognize the other feature and consequently interprets the received sound as the only [+ high] [+ round] unit in his system, which is /u·/, the corresponding features of which are [+ high] [+ round] [+ back]. The very fact that he perceives something different from [u] (as in *poor*) appears from his production: [mju̯·r], with a [j̯], a semi-vowel with a "higher" characteristic than [u].

Starting from this analysis and applying the strategies as outlined above, we would propose the following correction:

a. Choose a short sentence (if possible not too different from the sentence in which the learner made the error) containing one or two instances of [y], in which this [y] follows a labial, labio-dental or dental consonant, e.g.,

die muur is wit
vraag het aan je buurman
kiwi's zijn duur

    Note that we avoid the vicinity of velar consonants, as in *kuur* or *guur*, because these have the [+ back] feature which was incorrectly perceived in the [y] -vowel.

b. Pronounce this sentence with a modulated pronunciation of the [y], i.e., a sound between [y] and [i]. We do this to emphasize the [+ front] feature in the vowel.

c. If the learner, when asked to repeat the sentence, pronounces a [y] that can be considered satisfactory, the teacher will first tell him that it is all right, then will produce the same sentence with the same modulated pronunciation once or twice and have the learner repeat it. If the result is good, the teacher will make his pronunciation more like [y], i.e., less like [i], and again ask the learner to repeat it. This strategy, which yields good results, will not prevent errors from appearing again afterwards. The same kind of correction will then be repeated, till the learner hearing a Dutch [y] pronounces [y] and not [ʝu]. How much time this will take depends on the relative difficulty — whatever this may mean — of the sound and the personal qualities of the learner.

    A final remark concerns the fact that Russians, Poles, and Yugoslavs (maybe all speakers of slavonic languages) typically analyze the same [y] differently: they do perceive the frontness of this vowel, but not its being rounded: consequently they produce an [i] -vowel, saying [mi·r], [di·r], [bi·rman], etc. In this case the optimal sentences for phonetic correction will have to contain [y] after a labial consonant (p, b, m) emphasizing the [+ round] feature; if possible the word containing [y] should be placed in the descending part of the intonation curve and the teacher's pronunciation can be modulated in this case towards [u].

3. When, twenty years ago, we prepared an audio-visual Dutch course for francophone secondary school pupils and adults we analyzed the errors made by these categories of learners, tested correction strategies based on the same principles as discussed above and integrated phonetic correction into our course (De Vriendt et al., 1966; the same in De Vriendt et al., 1967, pp. 49-76; presented differently in De Vriendt et al., 1981, *livre du maître*, pp. 21-31).

I cannot offer anything like this about errors made by anglophones learning Dutch, for two reasons: one is that very few anglophones attend Dutch classes in Belgium so that my collection of data is not yet rich enough to propose carefully elaborated strategies (which should first be tested anyway); the other that there may be differences between errors made by British and American learners and even between errors made by Americans coming from different parts of the United States.

As a consequence, I will merely list some errors that seem to be rather frequent among the various kinds of learners I was able to observe:

Vowels: mainly [y] (see above)
[e] and [o] are sometimes clearly diphthongized, more like [eⁱ] and [oᵘ], but as this pronunciation is not unusual in the Netherlands, it should certainly not be corrected.

[e] is sometimes pronounced as [i], as in *geel, kasteel*; as the little girl who made this error had never seen the words written, any influence of the written form was excluded.

Diphthongs: [œy] seems to be very difficult (is mostly "replaced" by something like [ø]; on the whole the pronunciation of [ɔu] and [ɛi] is good, but occasionally I noted a confusion between [ɛi] and [aʃ]: *draaien* is then pronounced [drejə].

Consonants and glides: [r], "replaced" by an English [r].
[l] is a bit too thick and so is bilabial [w] (this can be avoided by teaching a labio-dental w);
Initial [p, t, k] are often slightly aspirated, which is not allowed in Dutch.
Some clusters appear to be difficult, for instance [sχ]; obviously the [ʃ] I heard in *schouders* may be due to influence of the English word "shoulders."

4. In this part I will discuss an interesting error that is made very frequently by Belgian francophones learning Dutch. In such sentences as

Hij doet dat oo<u>k</u>
Dat wist i<u>k</u>
Ik roo<u>k</u>

the final consonant is often not the voiceless velar stop [k], but the voiceless velar fricative [χ]. At first sight, this is very strange, because the francophone learner replaces [k], which he knows from French, a language in which this consonant can appear in final position, as in *Pâques, critique, duc, roc*, by a sound that does not exist in his mother tongue. No production-based theory of phonetic correction can provide an explanation; all it could do, starting from the observation that the student has learned that there is a [χ] consonant in Dutch, is to conclude that he sometimes "overgeneralizes" its use. I will try to show that "overgeneralization" is too vague a term and that it is possible to come closer to an explanation of what causes this frequently observed error.

It should first be noted that when we listen carefully to Dutch and Flemish native speakers and to francophone learners, we can hear a variety of realizations that reminds us of . . . Grimm's law. As Eggers (1963, p. 65) put it,

Man kann sich vorstellen daß z.B. germ.*p* in einem langwierigen Prozeß über *ph* (behauchtes *p*, wie es heute in Norddeutschland gesprochen wird) allmählich zu *pf* und erst im Endergebnis zu *ff* geworden ist. Unter dieser Sicht darf man die Verschiebung, die nur bis zur Affrikata führt, als eine unvollständige ansehen. Sie wäre also auf halbem Wege stehengeblieben."

The switch might have been as follows for the three voiceless stops:

$$p \longrightarrow p^h \longrightarrow pf \longrightarrow f$$
$$t \longrightarrow t^h \longrightarrow ts \longrightarrow s$$
$$k \longrightarrow k^h \longrightarrow k\chi \longrightarrow \chi$$

And indeed, when we listen carefully we can hear the four realizations, in <u>final position</u>, i.e., before a phonological pause:

k : by native speakers (seldom) and by francophone learners
k^h : by native speakers (very often)
$k\chi$: by native speakers (sometimes)
χ : by our learners, never by native speakers

I do not suggest that Dutch has started a shifting similar to the *zweite, hochdeutsche, Lautverschiebung*, but I do believe that at least one of the reasons why some francophone learners make this error is the fact that they perceive the aspiration or the slight affricate, anyway something which is not like "their" [k] and which consequently they interpret as different.

And what about [p] and [t]? These too are often pronounced with some aspiration when in final position, the strength of the so-called aspiration varying, as is the case with [k] according to speaker, register, rhythm, affectivity, etc.

It is interesting to note that Dutch speakers are not conscious of the fact that they produce this aspiration. Phoneticians either do not mention it (e.g., Van den Berg, 1960^2) or, if they do, seem to have heard it accompanying only [t] (Cohen, 1961, p. 40: "het woord /zut/, zoet, gevolgd door een al of niet hoorbare zucht") or [p] (Blancquaert, 1962: "Als slotklank vóór een rust volgt op de ontploffing van de *p* een lichte zucht, die bij ontroerd spreken versterkt en afzonderlijk hoorbaar wordt; ik waarschuw echter tegen overdrijving" [sic]). How shall we interpret Blancquaert's comments? Is it possible that he did not hear the aspiration after the other two voiceless stops, [t] and [k]? It should be noted that he repeatedly mentions the aspiration of <u>initial</u> p, t, k by Germans and Englishmen speaking Dutch ("dit is geen Nederlands," p. 99). Or did he fail to make the generalization for final stops that he made for initial stops? Or is the aspiration of final [t] and [k] a more recent phenomenon than the aspiration of [p]?

We cannot try to answer these questions here. What does interest us is why our francophone students make the error described above, whereas they never produce [f] instead of [p] or [s] instead of [t]. I never heard *dat is wit* pronounced as [datiswis] or *eet het op* as [etətɔf], and this observation was confirmed by all teachers of Dutch that I know.

Possible explanations for the fact that errors are restricted to final [k] are:

a. the fact that the aspiration may be more frequent or stronger after [k] than after [p] or [t]; this is no more than a hypothesis and I cannot prove that this is actually so;

b. the fact that francophones know the oppositions p/f and t/s, not the opposition k/χ; so they are used to distinguishing between p and f, and also between t and s, even when the conditions in which communication takes place are not ideal;

c. the complexity of the system of back consonants in Dutch, even more so if, as is the case for most francophone learners, the Dutch they hear is produced by Flemish speakers or by francophone teachers who have learned Dutch in Belgium; whereas French has only two velar consonants, both stops, voiced /g/ and voiceless /k/, Dutch has four:

- the voiceless stop /k/, which is realized as [g] when followed by /d/ and /b/, but we will ignore this for further discussion;
- the voiceless fricative /χ/
- the voiced fricative /ɣ/
- the voiceless pharingeal /h/

So the only opposition of French, the opposition of voice for stops, does not exist in Dutch, in which language one must distinguish between stop (k) and fricative (χ), different places of articulation (χ versus h) and, in Belgium, the voice opposition for fricatives (ɣ versus χ). Some teachers insist on these phonemes being so difficult and probably increase their students' trouble.

The facts discussed under c. seem most important to me and their relevance is confirmed by the fact that students making the said error also replace final [χ] by [k]: *nog* then becomes [nɔk] and . . . *die ik zag* [dɪɪksɑk].

d. to this, one reason could be added why [t] is identified and produced correctly, namely the fact that final [t] is taught very early as the third person singular morpheme added to the stem of nearly all Dutch verbs, whereas [s] is one of the two frequent plural morphemes for nouns; this may protect not only these morphemes, but all final [t] and [s] consonants from confusion.

How do we avoid and correct the [k-χ] error?

Clearly the optimal position for [k] is the initial (for francophones, who do not aspirate initial [k]) or the intervocalic position. Final position after a liquid or a nasal is safe too: our learners produce *kerk, melk* and *bank* correctly, which may be due to the fact that, in this position, k is aspirated less or less frequently. So, the order of presentation has to be:

1. sentences without final [k], a conscious avoidance strategy;
2. sentences with final [k] after liquid or nasal (e.g., *hij drinkt melk, hij zit op een bank, dat is een kerk*);
3. sentences with final [k] after a vowel.

Errors are likely to appear in phase 3. Then, if the error occurs, one can use the following strategies:

- Pronounce final [k] slightly voiced, a little bit like [g]; after all, even if, imitating his teacher too perfectly, the learner pronounces [ɪkog] (*ik ook*), this does not sound so bad as [ɪkoχ] or [ɪχoχ], does it? At least, for some time. . . .

- Add a short word beginning with a vowel or a nasal (not a fricative!):

> *hij doet dat ook (<u>al</u>)*
> *ik rook (<u>niet</u>)*;

After one or two repetitions, in which [k] should normally be pronounced correctly – it is no longer in final position – it is possible to drop progressively part of and finally the whole of the added word. If necessary, both strategies can be combined.

5. Conclusions:

First, I wanted to show that phonetic correction can be fascinating and even fun, for the successful teacher and . . . learner.

Second, I stressed the importance of perception, of distributional and prosodic features, of (comparing) phonological systems.

Third, I showed that we can learn something about our mother tongue from learners' errors.

Fourth, I indicated that even the knowledge of diachrony can feed meditations on such every day matters as errors made by learners of a spoken language.

Finally, and in accordance with the theory I tried to illustrate in this article, errors made by native speakers of another language than French should be evaluated and corrected differently. For instance, if, as seems to be the case, American students learning Dutch sometimes make the [k/χ] mistake discussed above, the reasons why they do so may be completely different. For one thing, the phonological system of English is not the same as the French system since it has an /h/.
Moreover, [k], like [p] and [t], is aspirated in initial position. This may induce anglophone students to aspirate initial [k] in Dutch – as Blancquaert said, "dit is geen Nederlands" – but it could also help them to recognize [k^h] as a variant of /k/. On the other hand, as was pointed out to me, if they all have learned German before starting learning Dutch, they may simply be making the said error because German has [χ] in words like *Buch, mache, auch*. Again, keen observation of exactly when and where errors occur is necessary: do they also say [makə] for *maken* (German *machen*)? Do they say [buχ] for *boek* and also [buχə]? Or [buχ] and [bukə]?

43

In the first case, German influence is probably the right explanation; not so, if [k] "becomes" [χ] in final position but not in intervocalic position. Another question would be: if they say [ɪχ] for *ik* (German *ich*), how do they pronounce *dik* (German *dick*) and *kaak* or any other word that does not exist in German?

A precise analysis of all errors and non-errors is a necessary base for developing correction strategies.

REFERENCES

Berg, B. van de, *Foniek van het Nederlands*. Den Haag: 1960[2]

Blancquaert, E., *Praktische Uitspraakleer van de Nederlandse Taal*. Antwerpen: 1962.[6]

Chaumond-Klier, A., R. Herrmann, J. Klein, H.G. Lenzen, A. Schneider, H. Stephan, *In Bonn*. Paris: 1979.

Cohen, A., C.L. Ebeling, K. Fokkema, A.G.F. Van Holk, *Fonologie van het Nederlands en het Fries*. 's Gravenhage: 1961.[2]

De Vriendt-De Man, M.J., S. De Vriendt, J. Eggermont, M. Wambach, C. Wuilmart, K. Schutte, *Méthode audio-visuelle de néerlandais*. Bruxelles: 1967.

De Vriendt-De Man, M.J., S. De Vriendt, H. Bijleveld, J. Eggermont, M. Vandermaelen, A.M. Van Eynde, L. Verheyden, M. Vincent, *Steek van wal I*. Bruxelles: 1981.

De Vriendt, S., M.J. Vriendt, M. Wambach, "Correction phonétique des francophones belges qui apprennent le néerlandais," in *Revue de phonétique appliquée*, 3 (1966), pp. 17-40.

Dickinson, Leveque, Sagot, *All's well* . . . . Paris: 1975.

Eggers, K., *Deutsche Sprachgeschichte I*. Reinbek: 1963.

Renard, R., *Introduction to the Verbo-Tonal Methodology*, 1975.

Renard, R. and J.J. van Vlasselaer, *Foreign Language Teaching with an Integrated Methodology: The SGAV Methodology*. Paris: 1976.

NEDERLANDS TUSSEN ENGELS EN DUITS:
A TYPOLOGICAL COMPARISON

Thomas F. Shannon
University of California, Berkeley

0. **Introduction.** It has often been observed that in some sense Dutch occupies a middle position linguistically between its closely related neighbors German and English. This point has been made perhaps most clearly and forcefully in C. B. van Haeringen's brief but illuminating work entitled *Nederlands tussen Duits en Engels*, which in slightly altered form has provided part of the title for this article. Unfortunately, Van Haeringen's pioneering work has largely remained unknown in linguistic circles outside of the Netherlands and was only a beginning in defining the position of Dutch vis-à-vis its close relatives English and German.[1] Other scholars have even attempted to rank the modern Germanic languages along a continuum of relatedness. Thus Hutterer (1975: 454) orders them as follows: 1) Icelandic, Faroese, German; 2) Dutch (and Low German), Frisian, Yiddish; 3) Norwegian, Swedish, Danish; 4) English; 5) Afrikaaans (and Creoles). On the basis of somewhat different criteria, Lass (1987: 318) too comes to a very similar scale: 1) Icelandic, Faroese, German; 2) Frisian; 3) Dutch; 4) Norwegian, Danish, Swedish, Yiddish; 5) English, Afrikaans. Despite a few rather small differences such as the place of Yiddish or Frisian, by and large Hutterer and Lass agree on their relative rankings, in particular in positioning Dutch intermediately between German and English.

However, while such "simple-minded but indicative rankings [offer a rough indication] of overall innovativeness, in terms of typological distance from the archaic Germanic model" (Lass 1988: 318), they are at the same time too coarse-grained and run roughshod over certain important similarities and differences. For example, Afrikaans is always put at the end of the scale, yet in some respects, e.g., in terms of word order, it is much closer to German and Dutch than English. Moreover, criteria for such rankings are seldom explicitly stated and defended. For this reason the precise sense in which Dutch occupies a middle position between English and German is not made clear, i.e., in what important ways it is more like English, more like German, or truly "in between" the two. Finally, such scales offer no general, unifying framework from which to view these contrasts.

For these reasons I would like to consider now in somewhat more detail, albeit still all too briefly, some contrasts among these three languages, using proposals made recently by John Hawkins in his book, *A Comparative Typology of English and German* (1985), as a unifying background for our discussion and extending them to cover Dutch as well, as recommended in Shannon (1988b).

In this work Hawkins argues that the contrasts between English and German are: 1) often in a (proper) subset relation, English having reduced or expanded the set of inherited possibilities which German has retained; 2) sweeping, covering many areas of the grammar; 3) related by general typological principles involving the relation between surface form and meaning, which underlie the direction of contrast. Hawkins' main claim is that where the morphological and syntactic rules of English and German contrast, English shows less correspondence – and hence more "distance" – between meaning and surface form. The result is greater ambiguity, a greater collapsing of semantic distinctions in English surface forms. Here Hawkins sees an inherent tension between rules generating linguistic forms and the rules mapping them onto their meaning: simplicity in one area entails complexity in the other. This forms a typological continuum here along which languages can differ synchronically and move diachronically. In this article I will argue that Dutch fits into an intermediate position along Hawkins' cline, sometimes closely resembling English, sometimes German, and at other times holding the middle between the two. In this way we will begin to give a more precise sense to the claim that Dutch is *tussen Engels en Duits*.

To explain the uniform direction in which English has moved and thus the observed contrasts, Hawkins adopts Sapir's (1921) drift hypothesis, according to which the historically observable trend toward the invariable word has had other important consequences. Phonetic attrition brought about a loss of case marking; all further contrasts are due to the resultant changes in English along the continuum mentioned above. To distinguish clearly between subject and object, English word order became largely fixed on S(ubject)V(erb)O(bject). This has supposedly led in turn to more semantic diversity of basic G(rammatical) R(elation)s and the looser selectional restrictions imposed by English verbs. Moreover, the lack of preposition stranding and the presence of VP Pied Piping in German are also due to case marking, which forces NPs to remain within their governing category. With respect to verb position, the more fixed order in English results in greater ambiguity of surface forms, since verb position largely cannot be put to the same pragmatic and semantic uses as in German (or Dutch). SOV, which signals nonroot clauses in German (and Dutch, of course), is not found in English; moreover, as opposed to German (and Dutch) English consequently cannot use preverbal position as much for pragmatic purposes, and where V-2 structures are still found in English they are only the severely limited remnants of the strict V-2 constraint found in all other Germanic languages.

Let us consider now how Dutch fits into this picture; in so doing we will also from time to time take a side glance at Afrikaans in a very non-systematic way. I must warn the reader that my remarks will be all too brief and cursory and would ask for his indulgence; unfortunately, space does not permit the full investigation which these questions deserve, but a much larger version of this work is in preparation which will treat these matters in much more detail. Nevertheless I feel that certain conclusions can already at this time be drawn concerning the position of Dutch vis-à-vis English and German with respect to Hawkins' typology. To facilitate the discussion, I have provided a table of comparison as an appendix at the end of this article.

1. **Morphological comparison.** To begin with contrasting morphology (cf. app., I), specifically inflectional morphology first (cf. app., I A), note that with respect to the very important nominal case distinctions Dutch and English are of course very similar, both having largely abandoned morphological case markings except in some personal pronouns. This has the consequence that grammatical relations like subject and object are usually not distinguished by different forms. But with respect to gender and plural markers Dutch (2 genders, 2 plural markers) is between German (3 genders, 5 plural markers) and English (no grammatical gender, basically only 1 plural morpheme).[2] However, from the point of view of Hawkins' framework, the former merger is much more significant because of grammatical marking and the purported link to further changes in GRs. When we then look at the verbal morphology on the other hand, the picture is quite different. Both German and Dutch preserve person and number marking on the verb much better than English, which only marks third singular in the present tense; hence German and Dutch both give better indication of subject through agreement marking, even though Dutch has largely lost the ability to mark subject vs. object by case. Moreover, German and Dutch both still have an infinitive marker, BE as a perfect auxiliary, and BECOME as the passive auxiliary. The loss of BE as a perfect auxiliary in English could arguably be considered due at least in part to the loss of the case system and certainly seems to have reduced certain semantic distinctions in English which German and Dutch obligatorily keep apart. In other, less crucial regards Dutch is closer to English, however, in having largely given up the distinction between indicative and subjunctive and using SHALL as the future auxiliary. Note, incidentally, that Afrikaans has gone the farthest in terms of "deflection," having abandoned case, gender, and verbal agreement, as well as the past tense and the distinction between strong and weak verbs.

In derivational morphology, on the other hand, Dutch is much more closely allied with German than with English. As opposed to German and Dutch, English has continued the drift toward the invariant word in giving up diminutive formation – which the other West Germanic languages have preserved so well – and to a large extent also verbal prefixation. Perhaps because there is no characteristic ending for verbs, English has much more conversion, where a noun stem for instance is used as a verb (as in the recent neologism to *Federal Express it*). Here English appears to be blurring semantic distinctions which German and Dutch usually maintain, e.g., the counterparts often express the semantic relations involved much more specifically by the use of a prepositional phrase.

2. **Syntactic comparison.** If we turn now to syntax (cf. app., II), we can note further interesting contrasts, particularly of the type Hawkins envisages. Let us first consider grammatical relations (app., II A). Recall that Hawkins claims that due to case merger English allows many more semantic roles to be coded as subject and object, thus obliterating surface distinctions kept by German through case marking. To a certain extent Dutch follows English in this direction, but surprisingly not as far as one might expect. The loss of case marking has led in any number of instances to prepositions taking over the marking, as with certain verbs (cf. E *to accuse someone of something* = D *iemand van iets beschuldigen*, but G *jemanden einer Sache beschuldigen*) and especially the indirect object, which in both English and Dutch can be alternatively signalled by a preposition expressing direction toward (cf. D *Hij geeft het kind een bal / de bal aan het kind*, E *He gives the child a ball / a ball to the child*, vs. G *Er gibt dem Kind einen Ball / *den Ball an das Kind*.). However, Dutch is more like German in preserving a number of instances (former genitive or dative objects) with no prepositional marking, and it appears that the Dutch examples are a (proper) subset of those in German. For example, just like in German, certain adjectives in Dutch can still govern an object not marked by a preposition, e.g., *dankbaar, vreemd, gunstig, moe(de), zat, vol, kwijt, bijster, gedachtig, indachtig, machtig, waard*. In such cases English must use prepositional marking. Another difference is that the object is frequently found before the adjective in Dutch (*Hij is haar niet waard*) and G (*Er ist ihrer nicht würdig*), but always after it in English (*He isn't worthy of her*), except for those cases – usually involving measurement – where English also allows a non-marked NP object (*ten meters wide, forty years old*). Also, with partitives English uses the preposition *of*, whereas Dutch and German do not use any marking whatsoever; cf. E *a glass of beer* = D *een glas bier* = G *ein Glas Bier*.

Moreover, since they no longer have case distinctions, neither Dutch nor English can now distinguish, as German still does, between sole dative vs. accusative objects of verbs (G *jmem folgen* vs. *jmen verfolgen*).[3] This also may have consequences for the choice of perfect auxiliary in Dutch (but not in English of course, since the latter no longer has a choice of perfect auxiliary): cf. D *Hij is/heeft haar gevolgd* vs. *Hij heeft haar vervolgd*; G *Er ist ihr (dat.) gefolgt* vs. *Er hat sie (acc.) verfolgt*; but E *He has followed/pursued her*). Subsequent possible confusion as to the transitivity of certain verbs (which formerly took non-accusative objects) may have been (in part) responsible for the spread of BE to apparently transitive verbs, as in well-known schoolbook cases like *vergeten* and *verliezen*: *Ik ben je naam vergeten/mijn paraplu verloren*. [For more on this, cf. Shannon (1989b)].

Since the semantic differences signalled by dative vs. accusative are no longer directly marked by the morphology in Dutch and English, the semantic roles of direct objects in these two languages are now commensurately more varied than in German. This in turn has certain consequences for rules which create new subjects like passive.[4] While in German only accusative direct objects — largely only affected entities — can become passive subjects, the other two languages are somewhat more lenient in allowing other semantic roles to become passive subjects, with Dutch preserving somewhat better the semantic "sense" of dative objects. Thus in both English and Dutch what are dative objects in German can become passive subjects, whereas in German this is not possible: cf. D *De kinderen werden niet geholpen*, E *The children weren't helped* vs. G *Den Kindern/*Die Kinder wurde(*n) nicht geholfen*. Furthermore, as Langendonck (1968) observed and despite the continuing criticism of prescriptive grammarians, there is a certain tendency in Dutch to make even indirect objects passive subjects, which is quite common in English but impossible in German. Compare the following examples: *Ze werden/Hun/Aan de heren werd verzocht de zaal so spoedig mogelijk te verlaten* (ANS: 1052); *Op ons bellen werden we/werd (voor) ons opengedaan* (ANS: 1052); *Hij werd daar nogal op zijn tenen getreden* (Langendonck: 105); *Zij mogen geen voedsel geweigerd worden* (Langendonck: 107). However, neither Dutch nor German goes as far as English in allowing even objects of prepositions (e.g., locatives) to become passive subjects, as in E *This bed has been slept in by all the kings of France* (cf. D. **Dit bed is (er) in geslapen door alle koningen van Frankrijk* and G **Dieses Bett ist von allen Königen von Frankreich (dar-)in geschlafen worden*). The consequence of all this is that the semantic roles of passive subjects in English are the most diverse, followed by Dutch, and finally by German, where the semantic roles of passive subjects are the most highly restricted. Therefore, the subject possibilities for the passive in each of these languages appear to be in a (proper) subset relation to each other, in line with Hawkins' observations for English and German.

Similar observations can be made for other constructions in these languages involving non-prototypical subjects.[5] Take for instance so-called reflexive constructions in German. All three languages have referential reflexive constructions, where the subject literally acts upon itself, as in D *Hij wast zich* – G *Er wäscht sich* – E *He washes himself*. However, as far as I can tell, only German and Dutch allow inherent reflexives like *zich schamen/*

sich schämen; English regularly does not use the reflexive here.[6] Cf. D. *Hij schaamt zich* – G *Er schämt sich* – E **He shames himself*. One could arguably claim that the reflexive signals the affected nature of the subject here, and this is not coded in this manner in English, again in keeping with Hawkins' observation that English does not code such semantic roles as explicitly as German (and, we can add, Dutch). Interestingly enough, however, with respect to what Fagan (1984) calls "middles," German always uses a reflexive pronoun, whereas Dutch and English never do; cf. D *Dit boek leest gemakkelijk* – E *This book reads easily* – G *Dieses Buch liest sich leicht*. Once again, German has a more explicit coding of the semantic relations here, since the reflexive arguably indicates the affectedness of the less than prototypical subject, which is not coded in English, or Dutch for that matter. This leads to potentially ambiguous sentences (cf. Jordens and Rohdenburg 1972) such as *Dit type speler verkoopt tegenwoordig heel wat beter* and E *This kind of player sells much better nowadays*, where the subject in English or Dutch could be interpreted as either agent ("seller") or patient ("sold"). In German, however, there is no such ambiguity, since these two senses are coded differently: G *Dieser Spielertyp verkauft sich heutzutage viel besser* vs. *Dieser Spielertyp verkauft heutzutage viel besser*. Both English and Dutch allow the patient to be simply coded as the subject here, but German requires the additional reflexive to indicate the affected nature of the less than prototypical subject. In addition, both Dutch and German allow what Fagan (1984) calls "impersonal middles," as in D *In deze rivier wast het best* – G *In diesem Fluß wäscht es sich gut*, whereas English (**In this river (it) washes the best*) does not, in keeping with its strong tendency to avoid non-referential ("impersonal") subjects altogether and to prefer any referential subject, regardless of semantic role. Here too German uses a reflexive, indicating a non-agentlike subject, but Dutch does not. With regard to these reflexive phenomena then, we find Dutch between the two extremes again, coding like German the non-agentlike subject via the reflexive in one of the cases and leaving it uncoded like English in the other.

While we are on the topic of impersonals here, let us make a few brief relevant observations.[7] As noted already, English is particularly averse to so-called "impersonal" constructions and has gotten rid of many of them in the course of its history, as have its cousin languages Dutch and German, though to a much lesser extent. All three languages agree in having at least some impersonal "weather verbs," but those of English appear to be a (small?) proper subset of Dutch and German: *sneeuwen/schneien/to snow; donderen/donnern/to thunder; hagelen/hageln/to hail; onweren/stürmen/??to storm; bliksemen/blitzen/*to lightning; tochten/ziehen/*to draw*, etc. With few exceptions as far as I know, these tend to be about the only true "impersonal verbs" in English, and they are clearly outnumbered by those in German and Dutch. Moreover,

German has numerous impersonal verbs which express spontaneous sounds (*Es rauscht/poltert/klappert/klopft*), but as far as I have been able to find out, Dutch does not - or at least not as many; English does not seem to have any impersonal verbs of this type. Moreover, both German and Dutch also have a few (sometimes archaic) impersonal verbs expressing physical and emotional experiences like D *Hem duizelt/Hem hongert*; G *Ihm schwindelt/Ihn hungert*. These take or took oblique experiencers in Dutch and German, but in English these former objects have been long since reanalyzed as subjects, in keeping with the tendency of English to code different semantic roles as subject, while German and Dutch remain to a certain extent conservative here.[8] However, in both these languages there are normally also alternative constructions in which the oblique experiencer is the subject (D *Hij hongert*, G *Er hungert*). Finally, there are in Dutch and German a number of verbs which take a personal experiencer as object and the thing experienced as subject, where in English the GRs are reversed: D *Het mankeert hem aan geld/Het kan me niet schelen/Het bevalt me niet*; G *Es fehlt ihm an Geld/Das ist mir egal/Das gefällt mir nicht*; E *He needs money/I don't care/I don't like it*.

Viewed against the background of these impersonal constructions, it is not very surprising that while Dutch and German allow impersonal passives, English does not; cf. D *Er werd gelachen, gegeten en gedronken/Aan tafel mag niet gerookt worden*; G *Es wurde gelacht, gegessen und getrunken/Am Tisch darf nicht geraucht werden*; E **There was laughed, eaten, and drunk/*At the table there may not be smoked*. Moreover, as was mentioned earlier, Dutch and German allow impersonal middles, but English does not. Given the fact that English is a very strict Subject-Verb-Object language, this avoidance of subjectless sentences is quite understandable: by and large all (full) sentences in English must have a subject, and usually in fact it must be referential, regardless of its semantic role. In Dutch and German, not all sentences must have a subject, though of course most in fact do. These languages are also, as we have seen, more choosy about the semantic role of the subject - it must normally be fairly agentlike, and if it is not, this fact is often coded, e.g., by a reflexive pronoun.

As we have seen here, the subject possibilities of Dutch appear to be in between those of English (less restricted in terms of semantic roles) and German (more restricted); in fact, the possibilities seem to be in a (proper) subset relation. However, there is at least one instance where Dutch is more permissive than English (and certainly German) in its subject possibilities. Of these three languages, as far as I know only Dutch allows middles in which the subject has some sort of oblique semantic role, such as locative or instrument. As Jordens and Rohdenburg (1972) point out, Dutch allows sentences of this kind, which are impossible in German (and English): D *Deze muziek danst fijn/Zulke schoenen* lopen lastig; G *Diese Musik tanzt schön/*Solche Schuhe laufen mühsam; E *This music dances nicely/*Such shoes run terrible. However, apparently the alternative impersonal construction is always possible in Dutch (and German), though of course not in English: D *Op deze muziek danst het fijn/In/Met zulke schoenen loopt het lastig*; G *Nach dieser Musik tanzt es sich schön/In/Mit solchen Schuhen läuft es sich mühsam*; but E **It dances nicely to this music/*In such shoes it runs terrible*. Thus, at least to this extent, the subject possibilities of Dutch are not a proper subset of English, but rather go beyond even this very tolerant language.

However, at this point Dutch apparently halts and does not go as far as English in allowing non-prototypical subjects, especially apparently transitive counterparts of intransitive sentences, which as Hawkins observes occur in English but not in German: E *A few years ago a dollar would buy a glas of gin* – D **Een paar jaar geleden kocht een gulden een glaasje jenever* – G **Vor ein paar Jahren kaufte eine Mark ein Gläschen Schnaps*; E *This tent sleeps four* – D **Deze tent slaapt vier* – G **Dieses Zelt schläft vier*. While English allows non-prototypical non-agent subjects of these kinds (e.g., instrumentals and locatives), Dutch and German agree in requiring a different construction in which the noun in question is not the subject but rather some sort of oblique, usually coded in a prepositional phrase, and the subject is the true agentlike entity: D *Een paar jaar geleden kon je nog voor een gulden een glaasje jenever kopen/In deze tent kunnen vier personen slapen* – G *Vor ein paar Jahren konnte man noch für eine Mark ein Gläschen Schnaps kaufen/In diesem Zelt können vier Leute schlafen*. Both languages agree in coding the instrument and locative by a preposition and do not make it subject as in English. Apparently the subject possibilities of Dutch are much different here, as is the case for German as well: thus Dutch and German are more explicit in coding the semantic roles of these arguments and do not allow the semantic diversity of subject roles that English tolerates.

There seems to be a great difference between English and Dutch here: whereas both have by necessity collapsed certain semantic distinctions in objects due to the loss of case distinctions, only English seems to have greatly expanded the semantic variety of subjects, which is not a necessary consequence of case syncretism. Hawkins offers some interesting speculation on why English and German should differ here, and it turns out to be potentially applicable to Dutch as well. English subjects have increased beyond what would be predicted by case merger alone because, due to the fixed word order of English, the only way to get certain NPs in the at times pragmatically preferred initial position is to make them subject. Given the freer word order of Dutch and German, this motivation is lacking and hence neither language has followed the drift of English this far. If correct, this analysis offers a nice explanation for the observed differences here.

In addition to the points covered so far, there are any number of other areas of syntax which could be explored and discussed in this context; Hawkins himself covers a wide range of phenomena in his work. Especially interesting are the word order differences - and similarities - between these languages (cf. app., II C). For instance, despite the loss of case marking in Dutch, the language has remained surprisingly close to German in its basic word order regularities: it has maintained the so-called "sentence frame" construction, finite verb second order in main clauses, finite verb final word order in subordinate clauses.[9] Interestingly enough, Afrikaans, which has gone the farthest in giving up case marking, still maintains word order regularities which are practically identical with those of Dutch. This would appear to be rather problematic for Hawkins' proposals, as he links case merger in English with the rise of strict SVO word order and hence the abandoning of V-2 and split SVO-SVO order. Since Afrikaans has lost case marking even more than English, it is inexplicable on Hawkins' account why Afrikaans has not also gone over to English-style word order. Unfortunately, space does not allow us to pursue these matters further in the present article; this will have to be postponed for a later study.

3. **A brief look at lexical comparison.** For our final comparison let us consider briefly lexical fields. Here Hawkins adopts some ideas of Plank: it is claimed that as opposed to English, German verbs regularly impose more strict selectional restrictions on their arguments - the English verbs are broader in meaning, they cover a wider slice of the relevant semantic field than their German counterparts. Hence English is once again collapsing diverse semantic distinctions onto common forms. According to Plank, languages whose basic grammatical relations (subject, direct object, indirect object) are semantically well differentiated typically have much more specific selectional restrictions associated with their verbs, as seems to be the case in German: the tighter the selectional restrictions in a language, the narrower the range of semantic interpretations for its basic grammatical relations, and vice versa, quantitatively speaking. Since Hawkins does not give too many examples and Plank's work is to my knowledge still unpublished, it is difficult to judge these claims accurately and especially to see how Dutch fits in this scheme, but let us make the following few tentative remarks at least.

Generally speaking, we would expect Dutch to fit in between English and German, and by and large it does seem to. For instance, both Dutch and German have different verbs of knowing (D *kennen -- weten*, G *kennen -- wissen -- können*) - each with more specific meanings and selectional restrictions - whereas English makes do with the single word *to know*. Furthermore, in Dutch and German a more specific verb of location or placing is preferentially used: D *liggen -- staan -- zitten, leggen -- stellen -- zetten;* G *liegen -- stehen -- sitzen, legen -- stellen -- setzen*, while in English the general verbs *to be* and *to put* are commonly employed. Similarly, we may note here, English prefers to use the all-purpose verb of motion *to go*, whereas Dutch and German prefer much more specific verbs which indicate the manner of locomotion: D *gaan* vs. *rijden* and *varen*, and G *gehen* vs. *fahren*. Hawkins also cites differences in verb choice in German but not English based on the difference between affected and effected object, and Dutch often resembles German here, though not always; cf. EFFECTED: E *to dig a grave/hole/tunnel* - *ein Grab/Loch/(-en) Tunnel graben* - *een graf/gat/tunnel graven*; AFFECTED: E *to dig the ground* -- G *den Boden umgraben* - D *de aarde omspitten*; EFFECTED: E *to burn a hole* - G *ein Loch brennen* - D *een gat branden*; AFFECTED: E *to burn the meat* - G *das Fleisch ver-/anbrennen* - D *het vlees verbranden*. Similar observations could be made about verbs of putting on clothing, where Dutch and German often prefer a more specific verb denoting the exact action involved but English makes do with just *to put on*. Finally, Dutch shares with German, though apparently to a much lesser extent, a lexical sensitivity to the difference between human and non-human: E *to die* - D *doodgaan* (*/sterven*) vs. G *verenden/verrecken* (for animals), *eingehen* (for plants); E *to drown* vs. G *ersäufen, ertrinken* - D *verzuipen(?)*, *verdrinken*.

Based on this admittedly very scant evidence, Dutch does seem to range between English and German in this respect as well. However, extreme caution should be exercised in such a comparison, since the vocabularies of various languages - even closely related ones like these - are often not isomorphic anyway. Moreover, one can easily cite other examples which go fully counter to the claims which Hawkins makes. For example, both Dutch and German agree in having basically only a single verb for the English pairs *bear* vs. *carry* and *bite* vs. *sting* (of insects): D *dragen, steken* and G *tragen, stechen*. Similarly, German only has *schwimmen*, where English insists on differentiating between *swim* vs. *float* and Dutch has *zwemmen* vs. *drijven*. As such examples clearly demonstrate, sweeping generalizations concerning the comparability of the vocabularies of these languages should not be made too hastily. Any final conclusions concerning these claims - based as they are on Plank's as yet regrettably unpublished work - must therefore await further, more detailed scrutiny.

4. **Conclusion.** In this brief article I have tried to look somewhat more closely at the well-known claim that Dutch in some sense stands between English and German. Specifically, Hawkins' (1985) typological framework and observations about English and German have been used as a background for comparing and contrasting Dutch with these two closely related languages. On

the whole we have found that Dutch does indeed range between English and German with respect to specific points in Hawkins' proposed typology, that most of the (proper) subset relations Hawkins found for English and German hold true for Dutch as well, and that most of Hawkins' claims held up when considered in the light of the further data adduced from Dutch.

Presumably, for anyone who knows all three languages many of the empirical observations made here will have been rather obvious. However, I hope to have made at least some remarks which have been novel, gathered together as much diverse data as was possible in our brief space, and put things in a different and hopefully interesting light by adopting Hawkins' principled typological proposals as a unifying framework for our study. In this way I have attempted on the one hand to subject Hawkins' claims to further empirical testing via data from a closely related language which he did not consider in his study and on the other hand to characterize more clearly in what precise ways Dutch truly is *tussen Duits en Engels*.

APPENDIX

TYPOLOGICAL COMPARISON OF G, D, E

	GERMAN	DUTCH	ENGLISH
I. MORPHOLOGY:			
A. INFLECTIONAL			
1) substantival:			
case:			
article	4(3)	1	1
pronoun plural	3	2	2
pronoun singular	4	2	2
noun singular	2(3)	2(1)	2(1)
noun plural	2	1	1
relative pronoun	4	1(3)	1(3)
adjective declension:	+	+	−

	GERMAN	DUTCH	ENGLISH
case: singular	3	–	–
plural	3	–	–
gender	3	2	1
plural:			
# basic markers	5	2	1
Ø-plural	+	–	–
2) verbal:			
pers/# endings present	6/5	5/3	1/1
past	4/3	4/3	0/0
infinitive ending	+	+	–
BE as perfect auxiliary	+	+	–
passive auxiliary	BECOME	BECOME(BE)	BE
separable vs insep prefixes	+	+	–
modals = separate class	–	–	+
ind vs subj (synthetic)	+	–	–
future auxiliary	BECOME	SHALL	SHALL/WILL
obligatory progressive	–	–	+
strong vs weak	+	+	+
past tense (synthetic)	+	+	+

B. DERIVATIONAL

diminutives	+	+	–
verbal prefixation	much	much	little
conversion (N --> V)	little	little	more

	GERMAN	DUTCH	ENGLISH

II. SYNTAX

A. GRAMMATICAL

obliques:

	GERMAN	DUTCH	ENGLISH
prepositionally marked indirect objects	−	±	±
non-prepositionally marked objects of certain adjectives	+	+	−
partitive phrases	−	−	+

subjects:

	GERMAN	DUTCH	ENGLISH
"dative" obj=passive subject	−	±	+
indirect object= passive subject	−	±	+

impersonal constructions:

	GERMAN	DUTCH	ENGLISH
weather verbs	many	many	few
sounds	+	few (?)	−
w/ oblique experiencer (*mich hungert*)	+	fewer	−
impersonal passive	+	+	−
impersonal middles	+	+	−

reflexive constructions:

	GERMAN	DUTCH	ENGLISH
thematic (= "true")	+	+	+
non-thematic:			
inherent reflexives	+	+	−
reflexive ergatives	+	+	−
middles:	+	+	+
reflexive	+	−	−

	GERMAN	DUTCH	ENGLISH
impersonal middles:	+	+	−
reflexive	+	−	

B. WORD ORDER

	GERMAN	DUTCH	ENGLISH
word order freedom:	most	more	least
sentence frame (SVOV)	+	+	−
main clause = V-2	+	+	−[10]
split: SVO-SOV	+	+	−

III. LEXICON

A. LEXICAL FIELDS

	GERMAN	DUTCH	ENGLISH
"know"	3	2	1
locational verbs (vs "be")	+	+	−
locational verbs (vs "put")	+	+	−
different verbs for [± human]	+	few	no

B. GENERAL VOCABULARY

	GERMAN	DUTCH	ENGLISH
Germanic words	most	least	more
French words	least	most	more

NOTES

[1] To forestall any protests at this point: in proclaiming that Dutch in some sense holds an intermediate position between its "bigger brothers" English and German I of course do not mean to question the independent status of the Dutch language or to intimate in any way that it is derivative of one or both of the other two languages.

[2] For discussion of the plural markers in these languages from the perspective of linguistic naturalness theory, cf. Shannon (1989a, to appear a).

[3] This often signals the difference between a less affected vs. more affected entity and thus affects the transitivity of the

verb; for discussion of this, cf. Shannon (1987, 1989b, to appear b).

[4] For further discussion of passive in Dutch and German, cf. Shannon (1987).

[5] For an enlightening discussion of protypical subjects, cf. Van Oosten (1984).

[6] The same can be said for what Fagan (1984) calls "reflexive ergatives," but space does not allow us to go into this here.

[7] For a discussion of so-called "dummy subjects" in Dutch, cf. Shannon (1988a).

[8] As my Berkeley colleague Johan P. Snapper has reminded me, there are of course one or two highly archaic verbs of a similar type in English like *Methinks*. However, that such a verb is really only a frozen relic form is shown by the fact that it can only occur in this form: **Him/Us/Themthinks, Methought*.

[9] Apparently English alone is unusual among the modern Germanic languages in having abandoned the so-called "V-2" constraint; all of its other modern relatives in fact have it. The same, however, cannot be said for SOV word order in subordinate clauses.

[10] Except for rare (archaic) instances.

REFERENCES

ANS = Geerts, G., et al. 1984. *Algemene Nederlandse spraakkunst*. Groningen: Wolters-Noordhoff.

Fagan, Sarah M. B. 1985. "The Syntax and Function of Non-Thematic Reflexives in German and Dutch." Unpublished Cornell University dissertation.

Haeringen, C. B. van. n.d. *Nederlands tussen Duits en Engels*. The Hague.

Hawkins, John A. 1986. *A Comparative Typology of English and German. Unifying the Contrasts*. Austin: University of Texas Press.

Hutterer, Claus Jürgen. 1975/1987^2. *Die germanischen Sprachen. Ihre Geschichte in Grundzügen*. Wiesbaden: Drei Lilien.

Jordens, Peter and Günter Rohdenburg. 1972. "Sekundäre Subjektivierungen des Niederländischen und Deutschen in Aktivsätzen." In Gerhard Nickel (ed.), *Reader zur kontrastiven Linguistik*, 106-121. Frankfurt: Athenäum Fischer.

Langendonck, W. van. 1968. "Het meewerkvoorwerp van de aktieve zin als onderwerp van de passieve zin." In *LB* 57: 101-118.

Lass, Roger. 1987. *The Shape of English*. London: Dent.

Sapir, Eduard. 1921. Language: *An Introduction to the Study of Speech*. New York: Harcourt Brace.

Shannon, Thomas F. 1987. "On Some Recent Claims of Relational Grammar." In *BLS* 13: 247-262.

_____. 1988a. "Relational Grammar, Passives, and Dummies in Dutch." In Ton J. Broos (ed.), *Publications of the American Association for Netherlandic Studies. Papers from the Third Interdisciplinary Conference on Netherlandic Studies*, 237-268. Lanham/London: University Press of America.

_____. To appear a. "The naturalness of noun plurals in German, Dutch, and English." To appear in Irmengard Rauch and Gerald Carr (eds.), *The Semiotic Bridge: Trends from California*. Berlin: Mouton/de Gruyter.

_____. 1988b. Review of *A Comparitive Typology of English and German* (1985), by John A. Hawkins. In *Language* 64/4: 820-821.

_____. 1989a. "On Different Types of Naturalness in Morphological Change." In *Zeitschrift für Phonetik, Sprachwissenschaft und Kommunikationsforschung* 42/1: 20-33.

_____. 1989b. "Perfect Auxiliary Variation as a Function of Transitivity and *Aktionsart*." In Joseph Emonds et al. (eds.), *Proceedings from the Western Conference on Linguistics. WECOL 88*. Vol. 1: 254-266. Department of Linguistics: California State University, Fresno.

_____. To appear b. "The Unaccusative Hypothesis and the History of the Perfect Auxiliary in Germanic and Romance." To appear in Henning Andersen (ed.), *Proceedings of the VIIIth International Conference on Historical Linguistics*. Amsterdam: Benjamins.

Van Oosten, Jeanne H. 1984. *On the Nature of Subjects, Topics and Agents: A Cognitive Explanation*. UC Berkeley dissertation, distributed by Indiana University Linguistics Club.

EVALUATING THE INFLUENCE OF *ZUIDNEDERLANDS* ON THE LANGUAGE OF HOLLAND IN THE 16TH AND 17TH CENTURIES

Gregory Hanson, Bradley Holtman and Robert Howell
University of Wisconsin, Madison

Standard accounts of the historical development of the Dutch language place heavy emphasis on the importance of the successive waves of immigration from the southern provinces of the Netherlands to the cities and villages of Holland in the period roughly between 1560 and 1630. The attention paid to a demographic shift of such great magnitude seems entirely justified. The northward flight from the restrictive and economically ruinous Spanish occupation resulted in an infusion of highly skilled, well-educated and generally cosmopolitan Flemings and Brabanders whose arrival brought about fundamental changes in the society and economy of the northern provinces.[1] Given the great number of southern immigrants (Briels [1978.19] places their eventual number in the North at approximately 150,000) and the key positions these new arrivals came to occupy in the economic and cultural life of Holland, it would hardly be surprising to find that southern linguistic norms enjoyed a period of influence on the written and spoken language of the northern provinces. Evaluating the degree to which the southern immigration left an enduring imprint on the language of Holland remains, however, a matter of considerable controversy – particularly when we turn to the question of the direct influence of spoken Flemish and *Brabants* on the spoken language of Holland. Kloeke's (1927) *expansietheorie*, which attributes the spread in the North of the diphthongization of Middle Dutch $\hat{\imath}$ and $\hat{u}$ to [ɛi] and [øy] (*mîn, hûs > mijn, huis*) to the influence of prestigious diphthongizing Brabanders in Holland has gained wide acceptance. Nonetheless, clear indications that direct contact with the speech patterns of the southern immigrants left any lasting impression on the spoken language of Holland prove exceedingly difficult to isolate. And yet linguistic historians who accept Kloeke's theory in any form find little difficulty reconciling the massive influx of well-educated and culturally advanced southerners, a seductive language-external development, with the paucity of linguistic evidence which might demonstrate that immigration was of any direct decisive importance to the spoken language of Holland. This "evidence gap" is conveniently bridged with sentences relying on assumptions rather than evidence. De Vooys (1952.65) states, for example, "Maar vooral waar ze [de Brabanders en Vlamingen] optraden als geestelijke leiders en opvoeders **moet** de invloed van hun taal groot **zijn** geweest." But **was** this influence as great as is commonly supposed?

When considering the linguistic effect of the southern immigration it is important to maintain a rather careful distinction between the southern influence on the development of the eventual written standard language in the North and the influence of the southern dialects on the spoken language of Hollanders resulting from direct, face-to-face contact. The mechanisms involved in the incorporation of regional features into a written standard prove in most instances to be quite different from those resulting in the imitation of features of a prestige dialect (e.g., *Brabants*) by speakers of a local dialect (e.g., *Hollands*). The paths of potential south to north influence can be schematized as in figure 1:

Fig. 1

Northern spoken varieties ⟵ - - - - - Northern written varieties
↑   ⟵ _ _   ↑
| _ _ _ |
Southern spoken varieties _ _ _ _ ⟶ Southern written varieties

We will concern ourselves primarily with the evaluation of the influence indicated by the solid arrow in figure 1, the influence exerted by southern spoken varieties of Dutch on the speech of Holland during and after the period of northward migration.

Theoretical studies of language contact situations based on extensive empirical data have shown that the linguistic domains most commonly affected by borrowing are the lexicon, or word stock, and to a lesser extent the derivational morphology. Far more resistant to borrowing is a language's grammatical structure – its syntax, inflectional morphology and phonology. This basic scale of more common versus less common types of borrowing, aptly labeled by Van Coetsem (1988) as the **stability gradient**, would lead us to expect at the very least a large number of lexical borrowings from Flemish and *Brabants* in the spoken language of Holland resulting directly from the extensive linguistic contact between native Hollanders and the southern immigrants. Demonstration that a significant number of southern lexical items were incorporated into the spoken language of Holland would seem especially important if we are to accept Kloeke's hypothesis that the presence of Brabanders in the cities of Holland resulted in a fundamental change in the phonological structure of spoken *Hollands*, the diphthongization of ↑ and *û*. Adoption of foreign phonetic characteristics is far less common than exchange of lexical material.

Before embarking on a discussion of the immigration proper it is important to note that Hollanders were no strangers to southern linguistic forms even prior to the migrations. From the 13th century onward the political and economic superiority of Flanders and, subsequently, Brabant assured that early written Dutch carried a strong southern imprint. Written texts originating in Holland prior to the 16th century, although replete with Hollandisms, generally conform to the contemporary scribal practices of the southern provinces. By the 16th century the linguistic importance of Brabant is easily demonstrated in the development of the *rederijkerstaal*. Even in plays originating from the West Flemish *kamer* of Ieper clear preference is shown for the linguistic forms of Brabant, examples of which are given in figure 2:

Fig. 2

Brabants *cleyn, eysch, vleysch* for Flemish *cleen, eesch, vleesch*
Brabants *gras* for Flemish *gers*
Brabants *duer* for Flemish *dore* (De Vooys 1952.63)

Plays emanating from the *rederijkerskamers* of Brabant also found their way into the repertoire of the *kamer, Trouw moet Blijcken* in Haarlem and *Eglantier* in Amsterdam, although in some cases not before undergoing linguistic adjustment to the audiences of Holland. De Vooys (1952.63) cites an interesting example of the replacement of words in the southern *Bekeringe Pauli* with words more acceptable to the public of Holland:

Fig. 3 Brabants original =====> Hollands replacement
. . . dies sij *succumbeerden* =====> *verneerden*
Ghij hebste al gestraft, die u *refuseerden* =====> *onteerden*
Tweick hier te lang waer om te *narreren*, =====> *vertellen*
Al sijn se geplaegt, die u wet *corrumperen* =====> *verteerden*
Als een rechtveirdig godt in al u *useren*. =====> *stellen*
U rechtveirdigheyt en was noyt om *gronderen*, =====> *rebellen*

Of course the originally southern verse would also take on a definite northern accent in the mouth of a northern *rederijker*, but exposure to the lexicon, syntax and morphology of *Brabants* through such texts was considerable.

In short, the written language of Holland prior to the flood of southern immigration, whether it is reflected in municipal records or the works of the *rederijkers*, bore a distinctly southern flavor, reflecting the long-standing economic and cultural superiority of the provinces of Flanders and Brabant. Since a primary concern of the *rederijkers* was to develop and eventually to purify the literary language, it seems probable that forms present in the written language made significant contributions to emerging elevated registers of the spoken language of the cities of Holland in the 15th and 16th centuries long before the flood of immigrants arrived from the South. It also seems likely that the Hollanders could rather easily reinterpret differing features between the arising *cultuurtaal* and the regional vernacular of Holland no longer as a juxtaposition of *Brabants* versus *Hollands* but rather as a juxtaposition of elevated language versus *plat*. As Heeroma (1941.125) states, "De algemene beschaafde uitspraak van het Renaissance-Nederlands heeft zich ongetwijfeld gevormd op de grondslag van de 16de-eeuwse Amsterdamse volkstaal, maar dan een volkstaal die al tal van elementen uit de conventionele literatuurtaal in zich had opgenomen."

The theory that the southern immigration exerted decisive influence on the development of the language of Holland finds its greatest support merely from the extent of the demographic shift and the composition of the immigrant population. By the year 1622 the population of a number of pivotal northern cities was comprised of a substantial minority of immigrants from Flanders and Brabant. In a few cases the southerners had even come to outnumber the original northern inhabitants:

Fig. 4

city	population	number of immigrants	immigrants as % of population
Alkmaar	12,417	1,800	14.5%
Amsterdam	104,932	35,000	33.4%
Delft	22,769	4,000	17.6%
Dordrecht	18,270	6,000	32.8%
Gouda	14,627	5,500	37.6%
Haarlem	39,455	20,000	51.0%
Leiden	44,745	30,000	67.0%
Middelburg	40,000(?)	25,000	62.5%
Rotterdam	19,780	8,000	40.1%
Total	316,995	135,300	42.4% (vs. 10% for the Republic as a whole)

(from Briels 1978.21)

Although many of the immigrants were simple laborers and artisans, they could also count among themselves numerous prominent merchants, statesmen, military leaders, printers, clergymen and men of letters. Linguistic histories (cf. De Vooys 1952.65f.; Donaldson 1983.103) cite above all the influence on the northern language potentially exerted by the large number of southerners occupying positions as professors, school teachers and clergymen. In addition, the establishment of Flemish and *Brabants* chambers of rhetoric such as *De Oranje Lelijkens* in Leiden (Flemish), *De Witte Angieren* in Haarlem (Flemish), *De Geele Fiolette* in Gouda (Flemish) and *Twit Lavendel* in Amsterdam (*Brabants*) assured an ongoing southern contribution to literary endeavors in Holland. The imitation of southern manner, dress and indeed also language in Holland by the youth of certain upperclass circles becomes the subject of some contemporary comment by, among others, Roemer Visscher:

Fig. 5 De meyskens van de courtosye,
stellen op Brabants haer fantasie:
Op Brabants setten sy het cap:
Op Brabants is huyfken met den oorlap:

> Op Brabants zijn haer lubbekens gheset:
> Op Brabants is haer fluwelen klet:
> Op Brabants knoopen sy haer mouwen:
> Op Brabants fronsen sy haer bouwen:
> Op Brabants segghense jae voorwaer:
> Op Brabants spreken sy alle gaer:
> Op Brabants singhense haren sangh:
> Op Brabants makense haren gangh:
> Op Brabants
> Op Brabants
> Amsterdamse dochters doet mijn bescheyt,
> Schaemt ghy u van de Hollantsche botticheyt?
>
> (*Quicken*, VII, 41)

The southerner's propensity in the late 16th and early 17th centuries for referring to the Hollander as *bot* or *botkop* certainly underscores his feeling of cultural superiority. Visscher's poetry clearly indicates that certain segments of the population of Holland were all too ready to admit their cultural inferiority by mimicking southern customs.[2] Nonetheless he praises in the same work *een Leydse tong* and a *Goutsche stem*.

Although the social and economic importance of the Flemings and Brabanders to the development of the provinces of Holland in the 16th and 17th centuries must not be underestimated, a number of factors seem to work against the permanent incorporation of southern linguistic forms into the spoken language of Holland as a direct result of exposure to the spoken language of immigrants. One of the most important of these factors must be that the language of the immigrants was itself by no means uniform. Thus if we take a single feature central to Kloeke's theory of *Brabantse expansie*, the diphthongization of $\hat{i}$ to [ɛi], we see that immigrants from Flanders generally retained the undipthongized form [i:] in *mijn*, *zijn*, etc., while Brabanders would have already diphthongized the [i:] to [ɛi]. This fact renders suspect the rather impressive percentages of southern immigrants in northern cities in terms of a specifically *Brabantse expansie*. Marriage figures for Arnemuyden in Zeeland, for example, show that fully 46.5% of the 426 people married between 1590-95 were southern immigrants. Of these, however, the majority appear to have come from Flanders, a non-diphthongizing area (Meertens 1937.44). A similar distribution of Flemings and Brabanders seems to hold true for the oft-cited presence of southern school teachers and professors in the North. Thus while Van Schelven (1921.81) shows that 18 of 22 registered school teachers in Middelburg in 1591 were southerners, approximately half of these came from Flanders, not from Brabant. Briels' (1978.51) list of the most well-known professors on the faculty of the university at Leiden shows a similar heavy contingent from Flanders.

The influence of southern clergymen preaching in the North is for similar reasons difficult to evaluate. In addition to

Flemings and Brabanders there seem to have been a considerable number of preachers from Germany and Frisia (De Vooys 1952.61) and it seems highly likely that each of these churchmen would have addressed his audience essentially in his own language or dialect. It is equally likely that a preacher, whatever his origin, might have made linguistic concessions to his audience for the sake of greater intelligibility and general social acceptance. Southern teachers may well have done the same. In any event, the varied linguistic backgrounds of the immigrants arriving in Holland in the 16th century, not only from the South but also from the North and East, indicate that the northern cities represented linguistic melting pots. Inhabitants were not faced with a simple binary juxtaposition of *Hollands* versus *Brabants*.

Although the cultural superiority of the southern immigrants was undoubtedly most acutely evident in the early years of the northward migration, the linguistic influence exerted by Flemings and Brabanders was not necessarily enhanced by the relative cohesiveness of the immigrant populations in their new northern environment. To a certain extent the slow assimilation of the southerners must be directly attributable to their clear intention to return to Brabant and Flanders should the political and economic climate permit. There are obvious indications that northerners and immigrants alike were convinced of the temporary nature of the southerners' residence in the North. Nothing provides more convincing proof of this desire to return to the South than the numerous clauses in contracts between northern cities and southern preachers, teachers, weavers and merchants stipulating that southerners entering into contractual agreements would be free to return to the South should a pacification with Flanders be achieved or restrictions on practice of the reformed faith be eased (Briels 1978.39).

As the years pass after the fall of Antwerp in 1585 contemporary commentators begin to provide palpable evidence of a growing dislike of the haughty southerners in the North. This reaction to the southerners seems to arise from a mixture of envy, resentment, and even aversion. Although there do seem to be indications that the language of the Brabander enjoyed a certain prestige relative to other regional variants of Dutch, its superiority, as attested by available documents, seems to be supported primarily by Brabanders. It is therefore hardly surprising to hear from the Brabander Van de Noot the following:

>**Fig. 6** Alzoo wordt in Brabant met d'allersuetste voys Gesproken en ghebruyct het alder beste duyts.
>(De Vooys 1952.70)

Far less impressed with southern language and custom were northern commentators such as Visscher, who makes his feelings about the immigrants' supposed superiority clear in two versions of a poem "aen de Flaminghen" written in 1599 and revised in 1614:

Fig. 7   1599 version
Den Visscher vangt de Bodt in zee,
De landtman maeckt de botter vant groove vee:
En ghy O alderbotste indien hoochsten graet
    ghestelt,
Waer om geeft ghy noch voor Bot en botter U gelt?

1614 version
De botte Hollander haelt de Bot uyt de zee,
De vette botter melckt hy van het grove vee:
Dan ghy alderbotst, die voor bot den Hollander
    schelt,
Waerom gheeft ghy hem voor bot en botter cooren en
    ghelt?

The poet Jan van der Veen (from Deventer) makes specific reference to the "bastardized" language of Antwerp and mercilessly ridicules the overuse of French loanwords by southerners in a short poem written in 1628 on the occasion of a wedding in Amersterdam.[3]

Fig. 8   Kost ick nu met hoofsche streken,
Als den Vlaemschen Lieven spreeken
. . . .
Ik kome hier met reverentie,
Om u te groeten met eloquentie,
Om na mijn ingenieuse scientie,
Ende begaafde inventie,
Van dese gehuw'de te maken mentie,
By soo verre ik mach hebben credentie,
Dus geef my goede audientie,
Soo sal ick sonder violentie,
Ofte eenige insolentie,
Met alle vroome prudentie,
Na mijn uyterste diligentie,
Verstaet wel mijn intentie. . . .(Briels 1978.63)

The extensive use of Brabants by certain characters in works by Bredero (*Spaanse Brabander*, 1619), Hooft (*Warenaar*, 1617) and Coster (*Rijckeman*) for the clear purpose of amusing an audience of Hollanders also does not seem to support the hypothesis that southern speech patterns gained wide acceptance in the northern Netherlands. On the contrary it would seem that southern speech was adopted, perhaps temporarily, by very limited segments of the native population of Holland such as the affected young women, reminiscent of the French *précieuses*, chastised by Visscher (Fig. 5 above).

The overt mockery of southern speech by the early 17th century clearly indicates that the economic and political growth of the northern Netherlands was accompanied by a parallel growth in cultural and linguistic self-confidence. This growing sense of

pride in the spoken language of Holland versus that of the South
is nowhere more eloquently stated than in the description of a
Brabants immigrant woman's speech in *Claas Kloet* (1619):

Fig. 9 Sy spreekt oock alries so plat Amsterdams,
dat je se iens ginck hooren,
Je sout seggen, s'isser ewonnen en eboren.
(Geerts 1975.86)

Given the nature of contemporary comment on the negative reception
of *Brabants* in northern cities such as Amsterdam, it would seem
prudent not to overestimate the importance of this particular contact situation to the development of northern varieties of spoken
Dutch. As Van Coetsem (1988.13f.) states: "A speaker using
borrowed words may be motivated to do so by prestige, while such a
usage is rejected as pretentious by another." The clear victory
of northern Dutch over competing southern forms is signaled by the
southerner Vondel's adoption of northern forms such as the replacement of [e:] with [a:] before the consonant cluster -rd: *sweerd*
'sword'> *zwaard* (Polomé 1986.75).

If we turn to purely linguistic evidence, the case for heavy
direct influence of spoken southern Dutch on spoken northern Dutch
appears to find little support. The idea that diphthongization of
$\hat{\imath}$ and $\hat{u}$ resulted from attempts to imitate the pronunciation of
Brabanders arriving in urban centers such as Amsterdam does not
seem to square with the facts. First of all, linguists have
demonstrated that diphthongization of [i:] seems to have occurred
in at least some parts of Holland by the late 15th century, e.g.,
graphemic *schreynmaker* in municipal records for MDu. *schr$\hat{\imath}$nmaker*
(cf. Salverda de Grave 1928.79). In the face of this kind of evidence, most modern histories of Dutch have simply watered down
Kloeke's theory of *Brabantse expansie* by stating that the immigration probably **contributed** to the expansion of a diphthongization
process which had already begun in Holland (cf. Van Bree
1977.168f.). Of course the scope of the Brabanders' influence on
the diphthongization process represents the central issue, but
this question is rarely addressed with relevant specific linguistic
arguments. An Amsterdammer impressed with a Brabander's dissimilated diphthong *mayn, tayd* etc. (= *mijn, tijd*) could easily have
imitated the southerner's pronunciation by substituting the [ai]
present in his native dialect (<WGmc. */ai/) for his native reflex
of MDu. $\hat{\imath}$ but seems to have retained well into the 17th century a
distinct difference between reflexes of MDu. *ei* as in *leiden* 'to
lead' and MDu. $\hat{\imath}$ as in *lijden* 'to suffer'. In fact, as late as
1723, Lambert ten Kate (p. 155) can still comment on the retention
of this distinction, uncharacteristic of *Brabants*, saying that
older Amsterdammers clearly remembered "dat ze in haer jonge tijd
bij den **deftigen grijzen Ouderdom** van Amsterdam dit Onderscheid . . .
nog in gebruik vonden." Bredero's clear parody of *Brabants* speech
in his *Spaanschen Brabander Jerolimo* (1617) makes extensive use of

the distinction between the haughty Brabander Jerolimo's highly dissimilated diphthong, indicated with graphemic <ay> in figure 10, and the good-hearted Amsterdammer servant Robbeknol's less dissimilated diphthong (or retained monophthong!!), indicated with graphemic <ij>:

Fig. 10   Jerolimo
           Bay woor sayde gay, dagge me niet en kuyst
           Mayn Mantel en wambays? sach say zaijn so
              bepluist.
490   Kom hier en sieget eens, gay moetme voorts wat
              keeren.
           En hedy geen borstel?

           Robbeknol
           En hebdy gien swijns veeren?
           Daar isser gien in huys.

Given this rather obvious parody of the Brabander's exaggerated diphthongization of ↑ some thirty-two years after the fall of Antwerp, it would be difficult to maintain that this pronunciation had gained general acceptance or lasting prestige value in Amsterdam.

It is interesting to note that debate on the hypothesis of the *Brabantse expansie* focuses so heavily on the questions of diphthongization. If the southern influence on the spoken language of the North had been a major factor, we would expect the contact situation to have left an imprint on linguistic domains which have been shown to be more unstable than the phonological system, namely the lexicon. Surprisingly enough, however, the large number of high-frequency lexical items contributed to *ABN* by the southern Netherlands generally remains confined to the *schrijftaal* in the North, a fact which no doubt reflects the entry of these items into *ABN* through the written language. If *Brabants* had enjoyed great prestige and extensive imitation, these southern lexical items could logically be expected to have gained wide acceptance in the spoken language of the North. Even if some of these forms had been absorbed, but eventually lost ground to northern equivalents, one would expect some trace of these southern items in the modern *spreektaal* or dialectally in relic areas. Goossens (1980), however, provides isoglosses for a number of high-frequency southern words which imply that these words never penetrated the northern *spreektaal* to any great extent:

Fig. 11 | southern word | northern equivalent |
           |---|---|
           | zenden | sturen |
           | gaarne | graag |
           | geheel | heel, gans |
           | gij | jij, jullie |
           | gehuwd | getrouwd |

lommer	schaduw
nu	nou
opheffen	(op)tillen
peinzen	denken
reeds	al
smart	pijn, zeer
zieden	koken
rieken	ruiken
werpen	gooien

In closing, we should make clear that we have in this article made no attempt to deny the contribution of southern Dutch to the development of the eventual written standard, *ABN*, nor do we wish to assert that the southern immigration to the North after the fall of Antwerp in 1585 had no effect on the development of the spoken language in the northern cities. We would, however, like to suggest that the primary source of influence exerted by the South came from its long-standing importance to the development of the written language rather than from any far-reaching effect of direct contact with the spoken language of the southern immigrants. In light of the evidence introduced above, the scheme in figure 1 above might then be modified, as in figure 12, with the solid lines indicating the most important paths of southern influence, the dotted line indicating secondary path of influence:

Fig. 12

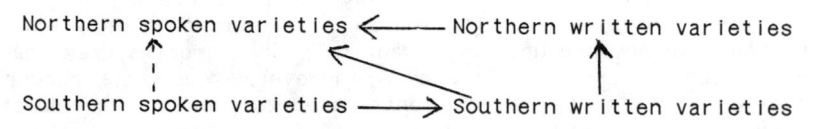

Northern spoken varieties ⟵——— Northern written varieties

Southern spoken varieties ———⟶ Southern written varieties

The resettlement of a large segment of the southern intelligentsia in the North during the years so crucial to the formation of the standard language no doubt assured the future of a number of southern forms in *ABN*. Above all, we believe that a thorough study of all linguistic and language-external evidence will prove crucial to a more accurate evaluation of the impact of the immigration on the language of the North, and that such a study has yet to be undertaken.

NOTES

[1] It is worth providing some concrete manifestations of the oft-cited cultural superiority of the southern provinces. Briels (1978.59) notes, for example, that marriage records for the city of Amsterdam indicate that far more southerners than northerners could write. Briels also cites Giucciardini's (1612.27) commentary on the general literacy in the southern provinces even among peasants and rural populations.

Furthermore many southerners seemed to have knowledge of foreign languages.

[2] Expressions indicating clear disdain for Hollanders are relatively easy to find. Briels (1978.59) cites the southern playwright Sinne's negative characterization of a woman's gait: "Gy loopt alsof gij een Hollantse meid waart."

[3] Robbeknol's wry answer to Jerolimo's assessment of *Brabants* shows a similar disdain for the overuse of non-Dutch loanwords:

Jerolimo
175 Een dingen jammert may, dat is dagge so bot Hollants spreckt.
O de Brabantsche taal die is heerlyck, modest en vol perfeccy,
Soo vriendelayck, so galjart, so minjert, en so vol correccy
Datment niet gheseggen kan. . . .

Robbeknol
185 Ja 't is een moye mengelmoes, ghy meuchter wel van spreken,
Ghy luy hebt de Fransche, de Spanjersen d'Italianen vry wat of ekeken.
De Brabanders slachten d'Engelsche of de spreeuwen, sy kennen van elcks wat.

REFERENCES

Berg, Berend van den. 1938. *Oude tegenstellingen op Nederlands taalgebied. Een dialektgeographisch onderzoek.* Leiden: Dubbeldman.

----. 1943. Boers en beschaafd in het begin der 17de eeuw. *Nieuwe Taalgids* 37.242-246.

----. 1971. *Inleiding tot de Middelnederlandse syntaxis.* Groningen: Wolters-Noordhoff.

Bree, Cor van. 1977. *Leerboek voor de historische grammatica van het Nederlands.* Groningen: Wolters-Noordhoff.

Briels, J.G.C.A. 1976. De emigratie uit de Zuidelijke Nederlanden omstreeks 1540-1621/30. *Opstand en Pacificatie in de Lage Landen. Bijdrage tot de studie van de Pacificatie van Gent*, 184-220.

----. 1978. *De Zuidnederlandse immigratie 1572-1630.* Bussum: Knieboek.

Caron, Willem Johannes Hubertus. 1972. *Klank en teken. Verzamelde taalkundige studies.* Groningen: Wolters.

Coetsem, F.C., van. 1988. *Loan Phonology and the Two Transfer Types in Language Contact.* Dordrecht: Foris.

Daan, Jo and Klaas Heeroma. 1965. *Zuidhollands.* (Bijdragen en mededelingen der Dialectkommissie van de Koninklijke Nederlandse Akademie van Wetenschappen te Amsterdam [BMDC].) Amsterdam: North-Holland.

Daan, Jo and P.J. Meertens. 1963. *Toelichting bij de taalatlas van Noord- en Zuidnederland I.* Amsterdam: Noord-Hollandsche Uitgeversmaatschappij.

Franck, Johannes. 1910. *Mittelniederländische Grammatik mit Lesestücken und Glossar.* 2nd ed. Leipzig: Tauchnitz. (Reprinted 1967. Arnhem: Gysbers and Van Loon).

Geerts, Guido. 1979. *Voorlopers en varianten van het Nederlands. Een gedokumenteerd dia- en synchroon overzicht.* Leuven: Acco.

Goossens, Jan. 1977. *Inleiding tot de Nederlandse dialectologie.* Groningen: Wolters-Noordhoff.

————. 1980. De Zuidelijke oorsprong van Nederlandse schrijftaalwoorden. *Liber Amicorum Weijnen,* ed. by J. Kruijsen, 101-108. Assen: Van Gorcum.

Heeroma, Klaas Hanzen. 1935. *Hollandse dialectstudies. Bijdrage tot de ontwikkelingsgeschiedenis van het algemeen beschaafd Nederlands.* Groningen: Wolters.

————. 1938. De herkomst van de Hollandse diftongering. *Tijdschrift voor Nederlandse Taal- en Letterkunde* 57.276f.

————. 1939. Opmerkingen over de methode der expansiologie. *Nieuwe Taalgids* 33.60.

————. 1941. De waardering van de volkstaal. *Nieuwe Taalgids* 35.117-127, 145-160.

————. 1964. Ingwäonisch in niederländischer Sicht. *Niederdeutsches Jahrbuch* 87.7-23.

————. 1965. De herkomst van het Nederlandse vocalisme. *Taal en Tongval* 17.162-180.

————. 1970. Structuurgeschiedenis van het Hollands. *Taal en Tongval* 22.106-117.

Hellinga, W. 1938. *De opbouw van de algemeen beschaafde uitspraak van het Nederlands.* Amsterdam: Ph.D. Diss. (Reprinted 1968, Arnhem: Gysbers and Van Loon.)

Helten, Willem Lodewijk van. 1973. *Middelnederlandsche spraakkunst.* [Reprint of 1887 ed.] Groningen: Wolters.

Hol, Adriana Roelandina. 1937. *Een tegenstelling Noord: Zuid in de praeterita en participia van de sterke werkwoorden. Een dialectgeografisch-historisch onderzoek.* (Noord- en Zuid-Nederlandsche dialectbibliotheek, 6.) The Hague: Nijhoff.

————. 1939. Het prefix in het verleden deelwoord. *Tijdschrift voor Nederlandse Taal- en Letterkunde* 60.249-293.

Kate, Lambert ten (ed.). 1723. *Aenleiding tot de kennisse van het verhevene deel der Nederduitsche sprake.* Amsterdam: Wetstein.

Kloeke, Gesinus Gerhardus. 1927. *De Hollandsche expansie in de 16de en 17de eeuw en haar weerspiegeling in de hedendaagse Nederlandsch dialecten.* The Hague: Nijhoff.

————. 1939-1958. *Taalatlas van Noord- en Zuid-Nederland.* (Nieuwe Noord- en Zuid-Nederlandse dialectbibliotheek, 1.) Leiden: Brill.

————. 1952. *Verzamelde opstellen.* (Taalkundige Bijdragen van Noord en Zuid, 3.) Assen: Van Gorcum.

Loey, Adolphe van. 1937. *Bijdrage tot de kennis van het Zuidwestbrabantsch in de XIIIe en XIVe eeuw.* (Nomina Geographica Flanderica Studien, 4.) Brussels-Tongeren: Michiels-Broeders.

————. 1970. *Schönfeld's Historische grammatica van het Nederlands.* 8th printing. Zutphen: W.J. Thieme.

————. 1975. *Inleiding tot de historische klankleer van het Nederlands.* Zutphen: W.J. Thieme.

————. 1976. *Middelnederlandse spraakkunst. 1. Vormleer.* 7th ed. Groningen: H.D. Tjeenk Willink.

————. 1976a. *Middelnederlandse spraakkunst. 2. Klankleer.* 7th ed. Groningen: H.D. Tjeenk Willink.

Labach, Adolf Edzard. 1891. *Over de verbuiging van het werkwoord in het Nederlandsch der 16de eeuw.* Groningen: Wolters.

Meertens, P.J. 1937. Het Vlaams karakter der Zeeuwse dialecten. *Onze Taaltuin* 6.39-45.

Obreen, H. and A. van Loey. 1934. *De oudste Middelnederlandsche Oorkonden voor onderwijs en eigen studie verzameld en naar het oorspronkelijk uitgegeven*. Vlaamse Academie voor Taal- en Letterkunde 1934.329-471.

Overdiep, G.S. 1940. *De volkstaal van Katwijk aan Zee*. Antwerp: Standaard-Boekhandel.

Pauwels, A. 1953. *De plaats van hulpwerkwoord, verleden deelwoord en infinitief in de Nederlandse bijzin. 1-2*. (Werken uitgegeven door de Koninklijke Commissie voor Toponymie en Dialectologie, 7.) Louvain: Symons.

Pée, Willem. 1958. *Dialektatlas van Antwerpen. 1. Teksten*. Antwerp: De Sikkel.

Salverda de Grave, J.J. 1928. Over de diftongering van $\underline{i}$ en $\underline{u}$. Nieuwe Taalgids 22, 65-79.

Schelven. A. A. van. 1921. Zuid-Nederlandsche schoolmeesters en schoolvrouwen in Noord-Nederland. *Tijdschrift voor geschiedenis*. afl. 1-2.80-83.

Sterkenburg, P.E.J. van. 1977. *Een Glossarium van zeventiende-eeuws Nederlands*. Groningen: Wolters-Noordhoff.

Stoett, Frederik August. 1923. *Middelnederlandsche spraakkunst: syntaxis*. 3rd edn. The Hague: Nijhoff.

Toorn, M.C. van den. 1977. Kloekes expansietheorie na vijftig jaar. *Nieuwe Taalgids* 70.1-14.

Vangassen, Hendrik Frans. 1954-1964. *Bouwstoffen tot de historische taalgeographie van het Nederlands. 1. Hertogdom Brabant. 2. Noordhollandse Charters*. (Bouwstoffen en studien voor de geschiedenis en de lexicografie van het Nederlands, 3, 8.) Tongeren: Michiels.

Verdam, Jacob. 1923. *Uit de geschiedenis der Nederlandsche taal*. 4th ed. ed. by F.A. Stoett. Zutphen: W.J. Thieme.

Vooys, C.G.N. de. 1952. *Geschiedenis van de Nederlandse taal*. Groningen: Wolters.

Weijnen, Antonius Angelus. 1941. *De Nederlandse dialecten*. Groningen: Noordhoff.

----. 1952. *De dialecten van Noordbrabant*. Antwerpen: De Sikkel.

----. 1965. *Zeventiende-eeuwse taal*. Zutphen: W.J. Thieme.

----. 1966. *Nederlandse dialectkunde.* 2nd ed. (Studia theodosica, 10.) Assen: Van Gorcum.

----. 1971. *Schets van de geschiedenis van de Nederlandse syntaxis.* Assen: Van Gorcum.

----. 1974. *Het algemeen beschaafd Nederlands historisch beschouwd.* Assen: Van Gorcum.

Wijk, L.E. van. 1950. De ontwikkeling van oudgermaans u in het Nederlands en Zeeuws. *Tijdschrift voor Nederlandse Taal- en Letterkunde* 67.161-208.

Willemyns, Roland. 1979. *Het niet-literaire Middelnederlands. Een Leerboek met Bloemlezing.* Assen: Van Gorcum.

Winkel, Jan te. 1899-1901. *De noordnederlandsche tongvallen. Atlas van taalkaarten met tekst.* Leiden: Brill.

----. 1904. *Inleiding tot de geschiedenis der Nederlandsche taal.* Culemborg: Blom en Olivierse.

MAPPING LIBRARY RESOURCES IN DUTCH STUDIES
THROUGH THE CONSPECTUS

Martha L. Brogan
University of Minnesota, Minneapolis

The academic library profession has a long tradition of responding to two conflicting forces: local autonomy and national interdependence.[1] The demand for self-sufficiency is usually promulgated by faculty who expect to have their teaching and research interests satisfied by the collections at their local institutions. Indeed, academic librarians involved in collection development pride themselves on not merely fulfilling, but anticipating, the needs of faculty. Further, the gravity of research libraries, in particular, has been measured by both the breadth and depth of coverage in their stock. A library's national rank has often been determined primarily in terms of the number of volumes it holds. These factors led research libraries to strive for – if not to attain – comprehensive collections.[2]

At the same time, limited acquisitions budgets have always forced librarians to practice a degree of selectivity in building collections. While the encyclopedic library may have been an ideal, it has never been a budgeted reality in recent times, except in the case of narrowly defined specialized subject collections. As a consequence, at least since the Second World War, research libraries – including the Library of Congress – have embarked on various cooperative projects at a national level to mitigate local inadequacies.

J. Michael Smethurst, Director General of the British Library's Humanities and Social Sciences Division, identifies two requirements that must be satisfied in order to promote resource-sharing: (1) "realistic and reliable guides to the scope of the collections in the major libraries in the system" and (2) "knowledge of their priorities for future acquisition expenditure in particular subject areas."[3] The "Conspectus" meets these conditions.

The Conspectus, which derives its roots from the word "to perceive" or "to make conspicuous," provides a means to survey the composite strengths of library collections on a national level. It is an inventory, available both in printed form and interactively online, which describes the existing collection strengths and the current collecting interests of libraries. It is a subjective, qualitative tool, usually based on the perceptions of those librarians or bibliographers who have nurtured the collections in various subject areas at their local institutions. In this regard, the Conspectus differs from other collection evaluation methods, such as the National Shelflist Count based strictly on title counts held by an institution in each division of the Library of Congress (LC) classification scheme.[4]

The Conspectus was conceived in 1979 as a means to encourage resource-sharing by systematically describing collections at four major U.S. research libraries: Stanford, Yale, New York Public, and Columbia. It was adopted in 1980 as a principal program of the Research Libraries Group (RLG), a non-profit consortium which numbers 36 members today. In 1983, the 108-member Association of Research Libraries (ARL) chose the Conspectus as the tool for its North American Collections Inventory Project (NCIP).[5] The Canadian Association of Research Libraries (CARL) and the National Library of Canada endorsed the Conspectus in 1985.

By the mid-1980s the Conspectus had become a national standard for describing library collections. It now includes collection descriptions of RLG libraries, the Library of Congress, and selected ARL libraries, including Indiana University, Notre Dame, Purdue, University of California system, and the University of Virginia. The Conspectus is an evolving tool and presently contains records from about one-third of the major U.S. research libraries. Notable exclusions, particularly for those interested in Dutch studies, are the University of Illinois, Texas, Chicago, and Harvard.

Today, the Conspectus is also being adopted in Western Europe. The British Library has already completed an inventory of its collections using the Conspectus instrument, and the results of its findings appear alongside those of U.S. research libraries in the online version of the RLG Conspectus. The Conspectus has also been completed in Scotland and Sweden; is underway in France; and is under discussion in the Netherlands.[6] Thus, in less than a decade, the Conspectus has expanded from an informal descriptive tool used by four U.S. research libraries to an international instrument used as a standard for describing collections.

The Conspectus uses a scale ranging from zero to five to describe a library's collection strength in some 7,000 subjects in 22 broad fields derived from the Library of Congress classification scheme. In brief, a rank of "zero," identifies a subject area "out of scope" and _not_ collected by the library. "One" specifies a "minimal level" collection in which few works are acquired. "Two" is used for "basic information" collections which offer an introduction to the subject, but are not of sufficient depth to satisfy advanced undergraduate, graduate, or independent study. "Three" denotes an "instructional support" collection that might adequately sustain undergraduate and _most_ graduate instruction. According to the Conspectus manual, a level 3 collection "includes a wide range of basic monographs, complete collections of the works of more important writers, selections from the works of secondary writers, a selection of representative journals, access to appropriate non-bibliographic databases, and the reference tools and fundamental bibliographical apparatus pertaining to the subject." "Four" signifies a "research level" collection that can support dissertation and independent research. Level 4 collections are extensive, include pertinent foreign language materials, and retain older materials for historical research. Finally, "five" represents a truly "comprehensive" collection in which a library attempts to acquire "all significant works of recorded knowledge, in all applicable languages." Level 5 is reserved, by necessity, for well defined and limited subject fields, such as those represented in a "special collection."[7]

Codes are assigned for both "existing collection strength" (ECS) and "current collecting intensity" (CCI) to allow for change over time in collecting policies. In other words, it is possible for a library to rate its collection on the "Dutch language," 1/2, as indeed the University of Minnesota has, to indicate that its existing collection is at a minimal level, but that its current collecting policy has been upgraded to a basic information level. Conspectus ratings — even for existing collections — are fluid, and may be revised at the discretion of the local institution.

Core indicators are used along with language codes to mark the prevailing languages represented in the collecting area. The following codes are used to indicate the language coverage:

E — English language material predominates. Little or no foreign language material is in the collection.
F — Selected foreign language material included in addition to the English language material.
W — Wide selection of material in all applicable languages. No programmatic decision is made to restrict materials according to the language.
Y — Material is primarily in one foreign language. The overall focus is on collecting material in the vernacular of the area.[8]

In conjunction with provisions for brief notes, the language codes permit a more refined definition of the collection level. For example, the Library of Congress identifies its "Dutch language" collection as a 4/3W, noting that textbooks are at level 3 while scholarly works and dictionaries are at level 4. This means that although LC has an existing research collection, it currently collects at an instructional support level in a wide array of languages.

Using Dutch studies as a case study, the Conspectus informs us at the aggregate level about subject areas which are adequately represented among research libraries in this country. It also exposes those areas which are "endangered subjects" — where only one or two libraries are collecting materials at a research level, or in certain instances, at an instruction support level. Libraries that accept "primary collecting responsibility" (PCR) for a subject area, agree to maintain their collections at the highest level within the partnership. Subjects with "PCR" assignments represent areas for which scholars might be concerned about our collective responsibility to preserve library support.

As is the case for any interdisciplinary study, collection data relevant to Dutch studies is spread across a number of subject areas. There are 22 broad subject fields represented in the Conspectus, ranging from agriculture to technology. Materials specifically pertaining to Dutch studies can be found in seven of the 22 divisions. The areas are: art and architecture; cartographic materials; education; government documents; history; law; and linguistics, languages, and literatures.

Although the Library of Congress classification scheme, from which the Conspectus derives its structure, provides great depth for subjects relevant to the Low Countries, the Conspectus typically relies on very broad subject categories. For example, Dutch literature is treated as a whole (LC class: PT5001-5980) despite the fact that the class itself is broken down into fine detail according to genre, historical period, and even individual authors. Or to cite another example, constitutional history of the Netherlands is simply identified by LC class JN5703, while the class dealing with the Netherlands itself ranges from JN5703 to JN5999 and covers historical periods, treatises, government structure (executive, legislative, and judiciary) and political parties. Further, many interdisciplinary subjects such as social anthropology, women's studies, and political economy defy a simple class approach and are not identified through the Conspectus framework for the Netherlands. From the area specialist's perspective, and unless the library has provided a note, it is difficult to judge subjects in-depth or to ascertain how thoroughly different authors or chronological periods are covered. The Conspectus, holding true to its etymological roots, provides only a broad overview.

With these limitations in mind, what can be learned about Dutch studies' collections from the Conspectus? In the seven divisions with pertinent information, there are a total of 47 subtopics relevant to the Low Countries - half of these are found in the history category which contains by far the most detailed data pertinent to Dutch studies. Linguistics, languages, and literatures, and art and architecture follow with six subdivisions in each. Cartographic materials and government documents are represented by four subdivisions. The history of education in the Netherlands and Belgium is identified by one subdivision. Finally, foreign law collections for Belgium, Luxembourg, and the Netherlands are rated in three separate subdivisions.

For the three core areas of art and architecture, history, and linguistics, languages, and literatures, the first has the most research level collections. Among the 38 libraries with Conspectus data recorded in art and architecture, 30 indicate existing or current collecting patterns at the research level for Dutch paintings (LC class: ND631). Eighteen libraries specify research collections in Dutch Renaissance or Baroque art; nine in 18th-century, ten in 19th-century, and seven in 20th-century Dutch art (all in LC class: N6911-6925); and eleven in Dutch architecture (LC class: NA1131-1173). In brief, it appears that Dutch art and architecture are well represented and maintained by a variety of research libraries.

The indicators for the area of Dutch language and literature are not so reassuring. In this instance, a somewhat different set of 38 libraries reveals that only seven have existing or current collections at a research level for either Dutch language or literature.

Upon closer examination only four of the seven, namely, Berkeley, UCLA, Columbia, and the British Library, indicate stable retrospective and current research collecting patterns. The Library of Congress and the University of Michigan both show a reduction from research to instructional support levels across these subjects, while New York Public Library shows a downgrading of two levels from research to basic information collections. The fields of Dutch language and literature (LC classes: PF1-979 and PT5001-5980) are considered "endangered" and Columbia has been assigned "primary collecting responsibility" to assure their future viability.

Table 1: Conspectus Data for Dutch Language and Dutch Literature for Collections at Level 4[9]

LINGUISTICS, LANGUAGES, AND LITERATURES – GERMANIC LANGUAGES AND LITERATURES (EXCEPT ENGLISH) PCR:NYCG
Dutch Language

PF1-979

UC Berkeley	4/4	
UCLA	4/4F	
LC	4/3W	Textbooks level 3; scholarly works, dictionaries level 4.
Michigan	4/3	
Columbia	4/4F	
NYPL	4/2F	
British Library	4/4F	

LINGUISTICS, LANGUAGES, AND LITERATURES - GERMANIC LANGUAGES AND
LITERATURES (EXCEPT ENGLISH)   PCR:NYCG
   Dutch Literature

                                                 PT5001-5980

UC Berkeley	4/4
UCLA	4/4F
LC	4/3W
Michigan	4/3
Columbia	4/4F
NYPL	4/2F
British Library	4/4F

   The outlook for the other subdivisions in the language and literature area is even bleaker. Among U.S. libraries, only the New York Public indicates an existing collection strength at the research level for Frisian language and literature (LC class: PF1401-1558) or Flemish language (PF1001-1184). Primary collecting responsibility for Frisian has been assigned at the instructional support level only to Berkeley. No "PCR" assignment has been made for Flemish language, an obsolete class, but presumably it will be covered by Columbia's responsibility for Dutch language. Columbia has also been assigned responsibility to maintain research level collections for provincial and local Dutch literature. Alongside the British Library, Columbia is the only library which professes to collect at level 4 in this subject. Meanwhile, Berkeley has been assigned responsibility for Flemish literature since 1830 (LC class: PT6000-6471) - an area for which only four libraries, including the British Library, affirm research collections.

   To summarize, it is evident that for the area of language and literature, researchers can expect to rely almost solely on Columbia and Berkeley. The Library of Congress and Yale remain consistent at level 3 for most of the areas. Meanwhile, the New York Public Library appears to have targeted this area for reduction, moving from level 4 to level 2 in all subjects. It is heartening to note that the British Library rates itself as a stable 4/4 for each of the seven subdivisions in language and literature.

   Among the 23 subject subdivisions for history, Stanford, Yale, Berkeley, the Library of Congress, Princeton, and the British Library attest to numerous research level collections. These collections are supported by a strong line of level 3 collections at such institutions as the University of Iowa, Northwestern, Dartmouth, Rutgers, Columbia, and Brigham Young. Princeton and Brown appear to be regularly upgrading their history collections from level 3 to level 4, while Minnesota, Michigan, and Cornell register a decline from level 3 to level 2 in several subjects. New York Public Library indicates constant research collections for Belgian history, but registers a downgrading from level 4 to level 2 for Dutch history. None of the history subdivisions is considered sufficiently "endangered" to warrant assigning particular institutions "primary collecting responsibility."

The note fields are particularly rich for the history subdivisions and often provide useful information about the collections. For Belgian history, Cornell notes that it collects in "French, Flemish, and some English"; also, "mainly the big cities: Brussels, Bruges, and Antwerp." Northwestern comments that "the library makes very few accessions of materials in the Flemish language." And Stanford frequently comments on the strengths of the Hoover Institution when these indicators vary from its other collections. For example, Stanford registers a 3/3F for the history of Holland (LC class: DJ401), but notes that Hoover acquires "internal history of World War II, including the German Occupation at 4/4F."

All of this data is accessible interactively via computer and its usefulness will increase as more libraries here and abroad add their Conspectus ratings to it. Presently, it is possible to search the database by combinations of 15 different indexes. The indexes include broad subject division phrases, such as art and architecture, as well as specific subject phrases like Benelux Economic Union. A keyword index combines the division, category, and subject indexes, thereby allowing for greater flexibility in retrieving relevant material. Boolean logical operators - and, or, not - can be used to extend or limit search commands. A search by keyword for "Netherlands or Belgium or Flemish or Dutch" will retrieve all Conspectus records categorized at any level in these subjects. Records are also indexed by existing collection strength, current collecting intensity, and primary collecting responsibility. A summary of the "PCR" assignments for Dutch studies appears below:

Table 2: PCR Assignments

Subject	LC Class	Institution	Level
Dutch language	PF1-929	Columbia	4/4F
Dutch literature	PT5001-5980	Columbia	4/4F
Dutch provincial & local literature	PT5901-5980	Columbia	4/4F
Flemish literature since 1830	PT6000-6471	Berkeley	4/4
Frisian language & literature	PF1401-1558	Berkeley	3/3
History of Education - Netherlands. Belgium	LA800-829	LC	4/4W
Maps - Surinam. Dutch Guiana	G5260-5264	Santa Barbara	3W/3W 4/4 Topo

A search can be limited to retrieve only those institutions with a current collecting intensity of level 2, for example. Or the search can be set to identify the records belonging to a particular institution or set of institutions. It is possible to extract, for example, only British Library records on any given subject.

The Conspectus has engendered "verification studies" – expertly constituted literature lists used to review duplicate and unique holdings in a given subject among libraries and to confirm the Conspectus code assignments.[10] Nine verification studies have been carried out on a variety of subjects, ranging from Swiss history to agricultural economics. A library is expected to have a certain percentage of titles from the bibliographic tool in order to validate its Conspectus rank as a level 3, 4, or 5 collection. Verification studies attempt to quantify and render objective the Conspectus indicators. In the case of Dutch literature one might suppose, for example, that even a minimal level collection should hold all of works listed in the new edition of *Books for College Libraries*.[11] At the instructional support level, King's and Wintle's new *The Netherlands* bibliography might be used as a yardstick for certain subject areas.[12]

At the local level, the process of completing the Conspectus may be one of its greatest assets. In conducting this exercise, the librarian is required to analyze systematically the scope of the library's collection in a certain subject area. It also provides a flexible means of manipulating and comparing local records, in essence, a collection development policy in machine readable form.

At the institutional level, the Conspectus may be used to identify library materials for preservation treatment, to establish budget priorities, to communicate with new faculty, to document grant proposals, or to support accreditation reviews. Several libraries are creating an institutional database from the Conspectus that contains all local records. The database may be enhanced and annotated with faculty research interests, corollary course offerings, acquisitions budgets, or shelflist title counts.

Nationally and internationally, the Conspectus provides a common framework in which to assess and compare collection resources. It forms the basis for cooperative agreements in acquiring, cataloging, making accessible, and preserving library materials.

NOTES

[1] The author gratefully acknowledges the editorial advice of Mariann Tiblin, University of Minnesota.

[2] For elaboration consult: David H. Stam, "Collaboration Collection Development: Progress, Problems, and Potential," *IFLA Journal* 12 (1986): 9-19.

[3] J.M. Smethurst, "Resource Sharing and Conspectus in the British Library," *Liber News Sheet* 21 (1987): 26.

[4] See Joseph J. Branin, David Farrell, and Mariann Tiblin, "The National Shelflist Count Project: Its History, Limitations, and Usefulness," *Library Resources and Technical Services* (Oct./Dec. 1984): 333-342.

[5] Articles about NCIP are contained in: Association of Research Libraries, "NCIP: Means to an End," in *Minutes of the 109th meeting: October 22-23, 1986* (Washington, D.C.: ARL, 1987): 6-35.

[6] In the Netherlands, librarians are discussing how the Conspectus structure coincides with the existing national online union catalog (PICA). The Royal Library is considering the feasibility of entering Conspectus codes directly into the national bibliography for each new title listed. For elaboration see the report: UKB - Samenwerkingsverband van de Universiteitsbibliotheken, de Koninklijke Bibliotheek en de bibliotheek van de Koninklijke Nederlandse Akademie van Wetenschappen, "Coördinatie van de Collectievorming: Methodiek en Realisering," in Voortgangsrapport UKB - Begeleidingscommissie Coördinatie van de Collectievorming, (Maart, 1987): 1-73. Available from the Secretariaat UKB, p/a Bibliotheek der Rijksuniversiteit, Postbus 616, 6200 MD Maastricht, Nederland.

[7] Jutta Reed-Scott, *Manual for The North American Inventory of Research Library Collections* (Washington, D.C.: Association of Research Libraries), January 1985.

[8] See note 7 above.

[9] Table 1 was downloaded directly from the RLG online Conspectus.

[10] See James Coleman, "Verification Studies: Design and Implementation," *College & Research Libraries News* (July-August, 1985): 338-340.

[11] *Books for College Libraries*, 3rd edition, (Chicago: American Library Association, 1988).

[12] Peter King and Michael Wintle, *The Netherlands*, World Bibliographical Series, (Santa Barbara: Clio Press, 1987).

DUTCH, FLEMISH, AND FRISIAN MATERIALS
AT BERKELEY: COLLECTIONS AND ACCESS

James H. Spohrer
University of California, Berkeley

In 1868, when the Library of the University of California was established, it is interesting to note that the only volume among its 1,036 titles to deal with a Dutch subject was an English translation of the *Ethics* of Hugo Grotius.[1] Now, 120 years later, the Dutch collection at Berkeley contains over 150,000 volumes, making it one of the largest among United States research libraries, and indeed one of the most significant in the world outside the Low Countries. The objective of this article is to describe the history and present state of collecting activities for Dutch, Frisian, and Flemish materials at the Library of the University of California, Berkeley, and to give an overview of that collection's strengths and special characteristics. In addition, I will be discussing online remote access to the catalogues of the collections, and providing directions for individual users outside Berkeley to dial up the catalogues using a personal computer and modem. For purposes of economy in what follows, the term "Dutch Collections" at Berkeley will refer to the entire body of material in all languages relative to the Netherlands and its historic geographical components, to Friesland and Flanders, and also to literary and linguistic works related to those areas, unless otherwise specified. It does not, however, refer to the extraterritorial expansion of Dutch culture into the Far East, although this material is indeed collected on a large scale in Berkeley's South/Southeast Asia Library by other area specialists.

Despite the relative recentness of Berkeley's founding, its collections of Dutch materials in the humanities and social sciences are generally considered to reflect a breadth and depth which are unusual among U.S. research libraries. In speaking of the unique characteristics of Berkeley's Dutch collections, and in particular of their rapid growth, there are four principal factors which can be said to distinguish its acquisition practices for materials from the Benelux countries. The first is the Library's historical policy of placing a high priority on serial acquisitions, as a way of building the collections systematically with material of relative currency and practical usefulness for scholarly research. The second important factor is the extensive network of exchange agreements maintained with academic institutions and research centers in all the Benelux countries, which provide a breadth and depth of materials generally unavailable through commercial acquisition practices. A third factor is Berkeley's strong special collections in Dutch, built chiefly through the acquisition of particular private collections at specific points in the Library's history. The final factor behind Berkeley's strong Dutch collections is its aggressive program of securing current commercial imprints from the Low Countries, maintained over many consecutive decades of collecting activity. Let us look at each of these factors individually, and the collections they have produced, in some detail.

When Berkeley's Library was being established, its first Librarian, Joseph Rowell, was faced with the task of building a library which, in as short a time as possible, could enable Berkeley faculty and students to produce research of major significance. A key element of Rowell's approach was the notion that materials of great immediacy would tend to promote research and publication at the University, and he therefore determined that the best method for building a research library quickly was to concentrate on creating strong serials collections, which would then form the basis for the Library's future growth. Consequently the bulk of the Library's acquisition activities in its formative years centered around the establishment of a strong serials program in support of the entire spectrum of the institution's teaching and research functions. Faculty members at Berkeley and librarians at the country's most prestigious universities were consulted for their recommendations, and vast resources were dedicated not only to the establishment of current subscriptions but also to the purchase of complete backfiles of journals whenever available. This emphasis on serial publications has continued to be the hallmark of the Berkeley collections up to the present day, and thanks particularly to the generous support of California's citizens in those early years, the university at Berkeley has been able to build the second largest serials collection among U.S. university libraries, numbering nearly 100,000 active subscriptions, of which more than 5,500 titles constitute the core of the Dutch collections.[2] These serials subscriptions are particularly rich in Dutch literature, linguistics, and history, but they span the entire field of the humanities and are also quite strong in philosophy, political science, sociology, the auxiliary sciences of history, art history, music, and the history of science. The goal of Berkeley's Dutch serials collecting has been to create an outstanding body of resources in all the humanities disciplines for which teaching or research are currently in progress at Berkeley.

A second important component of Berkeley's collecting strategy was Rowell's policy of establishing agreements for the exchange of research materials with scholarly societies around the world. This policy has culminated in the development of formal exchange agreements with over 4,200 institutions worldwide, of which more than 160 are located in the Netherlands, Belgium, and Luxembourg.[3] Our exchange partners include most of the college and university libraries (both public and private) in those countries, as well as the various Royal Societies and their branches, the national and regional libraries, a multitude of specialized public research institutes, and a wide variety of private research organizations and foundations as well. In return for subscriptions to some of the more than 60 journals and monographic series published by the University of California and available for exchange, our Benelux partners supply us with a wide selection of materials on virtually every aspect of the social fabric of the Low Countries. With partnerships ranging from the Académie Royale des Sciences, des Lettres et des Beaux-Arts de Belgique, to the Zeewetenschappelijk Instituut in Ostend, Berkeley's libraries collect Dutch language materials from our partners running the gamut from mainstream academic titles to ephemeral publications on virtually any subject imaginable.

These exchange agreements produce thousands of volumes each year for the Library's collections, mostly in the form of serials (around which the agreements are structured) but also in the form of significant numbers of institutional monographs and dissertations, which are still collected selectively. For many decades Berkeley's library had comprehensive dissertation exchange agreements with many of the leading universities in the Low Countries, but collecting was sharply reduced in 1985 following the decision of the Center for Research Libraries to assume cooperative collecting responsibility for foreign dissertations.[4] Now Berkeley's Main Library collects Benelux dissertations only in the humanities and social sciences, concentrating on only the most substantive ones, and those which most closely correspond to the Library's overall collection development policy.

By 1900 the basic outline of the Library's exchange program was in place, and the plan to build the serials collections was well underway. But even with a strong exchange program and a commitment to building first rate serials collections in Dutch materials, it would have been impossible to create an adequate university library in the humanities and social sciences without a significant effort to collect retrospective monographs, and in particular to extend the scope of collecting to the earliest period of book production in the Netherlands. That is the reason why the third factor in the creation of Berkeley's Dutch collections, the purchase of particular private collections of Dutch materials at specific points in the Library's history, is so important. One of the most significant of these purchases was the acquisition of the library of Karl Weinhold in 1904.[5] Weinhold was a peripatetic professor of Germanic philology in the latter part of the 19th century, living and teaching in many of the capitals of central Europe, and compiling an outstanding collection of nearly 10,000 volumes in all areas of Germanic studies, distinguished by large numbers of incunables, rare items, and first editions. His range of interests was extremely wide, and in addition to many priceless works on the history and literature of the German language he also collected heavily in Dutch linguistics, and most particularly in Frisian, a subject which held a special interest for him. Weinhold's collection was added virtually integrally to Berkeley's Library and transformed it almost instantly into one of the major institutional holders of Germanic materials in the United States. Moreover, the presence of the Weinhold material made the campus a magnet for researchers in Germanic philology, and was the impetus for the creation of a broad-based instructional program in the Germanic languages which went beyond simply teaching German as a foreign language or German literary studies, and which eventually included teaching the Dutch language, its literature and history, Dutch linguistics, dialectography, the history and culture of the Low Countries, and a small but important specialization in Frisian linguistics. Naturally, too, the Weinhold collection had an influence in the subsequent building of the Germanic collections, and its strong component in Dutch literature proved a firm foundation for future collecting activity in that area.

The next important acquisition of Dutch materials occurred in 1912, when the Library received a gift from Mrs. J. L. DeFremery of 500 volumes relative to Dutch general and local history, many of which were distinguished by their fine parchment or leather bindings.[6] These formed the basis for subsequent collecting in the history of the Low Countries, and Dutch history is now one of the important strengths of Berkeley's Germanic collections.

Berkeley's third major acquisition of Dutch materials took place in 1938, when it purchased the private library of Konrad Burdach, Germanist and bibliophile, consisting of over 16,000 volumes focussing on the languages and cultures of the Germanic peoples.[7] Burdach's library also contained many rare and valuable items relative to the Netherlands and Flanders, and strengthened Berkeley's medieval and Renaissance Dutch holdings immeasurably. Also in 1938 the Library purchased the collection of Otto Bremer, numbering nearly 8,000 volumes and yielding even richer resources in 17th- and 18th-century Dutch linguistics, phonetics, phonology, and etymology, as well as Dutch and Flemish literature.[8] The Bremer library also provided additional major strength in Frisian language and literature materials, which made Berkeley's collection in this domain the most extensive of its kind outside Friesland itself.

In recent years, as the collections have grown, there has been less interest in Berkeley in purchasing large private collections, due to the likelihood of duplication with material acquired earlier. But some specialized purchases continued. In 1964 the Library acquired a large collection of Belgian government documents, many of them quite rare.[9] And in 1967 the last major purchase of Dutch material was made, with the acquisition of the library of Mr. T.W.L. Scheltema, a private collector of Dutch materials.[10] This collection of approximately 850 titles, many of which were rare or scarce, greatly improved the quality of the 18th- and 19th-century holdings in Dutch literature.

These major collections, then, provided the central core of monographic materials in Dutch and on Dutch subjects in the Berkeley Library. But numerous other large collections, such as the Kofoid library of over 40,000 volumes, given to the Library in 1941, contained significant amounts of materials relative to the Low Countries even though the collections themselves were of a more general nature.[11]

In addition to books and periodicals, Berkeley's library has also acquired significant collections of Dutch cartographic materials. One such acquisition occurred in 1877, when Adolph Maillard, a personal friend of Joseph Bonaparte, King of Spain, gave his collection of 186 military maps of Belgium to the Library.[12] And the largest such acquisition took place in 1972, when the valuable cartography collection of Alfred H. DeVries was purchased.[13] Among its 780 volumes and 400 maps are many extremely rare and valuable items, such as the twelve-volume *Grand atlas* of Jan Blaeu, printed in Amsterdam in 1663 and one of the only three known copies in North America. This is one of the most beautiful and ambitious works of 17th-century Dutch cartographic printing and represents a high-water mark in the history of Dutch publishing.

One very interesting and valuable set which was purchased for the collections in 1976 is the Dutch clandestine press collection of 198 rare monographic titles published by the Dutch resistance movement during the German occupation from 1940 to 1945.[14] This is the largest collection of these fascinating works in the United States and joins the outstanding collections of the Universities of Leiden and Amsterdam and that of the British Library as an invaluable resource for the study of the resistance. It forms the centerpiece for Berkeley's extensive collecting activity in materials relating to modern Dutch history. And in 1987, the Library received a stunning gift from a major figure in modern Dutch literature: a signed copy of Cees Nooteboom's *Tekens tegen het Wit*, one of only seventy copies printed of this unique work. And even now, gifts of Dutch materials from both public and private sources continue to reach the Library on a regular basis, and are carefully evaluated for inclusion into the collections.

These three elements, then, of actively soliciting exchange relationships with partners in Luxembourg, Belgium, and the Netherlands, of investing heavily in serials subscriptions, and of making periodic major acquisitions of private collections and unique items, have combined to create a sound basis for Berkeley's Dutch collections. But these three factors alone would not have been sufficient to create Dutch collections of scope and depth sufficient to meet the scholarly needs of an active and growing Dutch academic program, and so the final element in the building of Berkeley's Dutch collections has been its commitment to a systematic program of acquiring current Dutch commercial imprints. The Library acquires over 2,000 volumes per year from the Dutch-speaking countries of Europe in the social sciences and humanities through this method, in addition to those obtained via other avenues such as gifts or exchanges. Selection is based on a thorough review of all Dutch-language publishing in appropriate fields through weekly or monthly consultation of the various national bibliographies. Additionally a series of approval receipt plans for such fields as Dutch-language literature, Neerlandica, and Frisian materials assures a regular and timely flow of materials from the Low Countries. The Frisian approval plan, for example, provides the Library with one copy of each title published by the Fryske Akademy in Leeuwarden, and similar contracts provide coverage for other subjects of special interest to Berkeley researchers.

These then are the particular ways in which Berkeley's Dutch, Flemish, and Frisian collections have acquired their unique characteristics. What are some of the special strengths of these collections, and how do they compare to those at other institutions which collect collect similar materials? As Martha L. Brogan's article, "Mapping Library Resources in Dutch Studies through the Conspectus," points out, the Research Libraries Group Conspectus project provides an approximate but relatively accurate means of evaluating collection strength in many academic disciplines. Berkeley's participation in the Conspectus is predicated by its Collection Development Policy Statement, or CDPS, created in 1980 and currently undergoing its first complete revision. The CDPS is the authority for all book collecting at more than 25 libraries in the Berkeley Library system, since it gives a numerical collecting strength for each of over 2,000 separately described subjects which comprise the Library's collecting universe. Berkeley's collecting level for Dutch history and the history of the Low Countries in general is "4W," which means that it collects at the research level in all appropriate languages for those subjects.[15] Similarly the Library's collecting level is 4W for Dutch-language literature from all historical periods, and for Dutch linguistics (including Flemish and Frisian), for works on art history in the Low Countries, for Benelux political science, and for a wide variety of other humanities and social science disciplines for which the intellectual contributions of the Low Countries are of significance.[16] And, as mentioned earlier, the South/Southeast Asia Library is an important national resource for Dutch materials relative to the East Indies, although its Dutch collecting is carried out independently of that done to develop the main Dutch collections themselves. Similarly, Dutch collecting in anthropology, architecture, music, and a host of other major disciplines is routinely carried out in Berkeley's branch libraries for those fields.

To summarize Berkeley's collecting strengths, then, it would be accurate to say that Berkeley has built and continues to build research collections of the first magnitude in Dutch literature of all periods, Dutch linguistics, and the history of the Low

Countries, and it moreover collects extensively in Dutch for the entire spectrum of humanities and social science fields which are incorporated in the University's curriculum. Through the foresight and dedication of those who created its exchange program, the Library enjoys excellent relations with and receives many valuable materials from dozens of scholarly institutions in the Benelux countries. And thanks to the clear vision and persistence of Joseph Rowell, the campus possesses a serials collection of Dutch materials which is unsurpassed in the United States. Taken together, Berkeley's collections of materials in Dutch and on Dutch subjects constitute a major national resource for Netherlandists, and one which is increasingly in demand as it is made more accessible.

How can researchers learn the specific content of Berkeley's Dutch collections, short of actually going to the campus to consult its catalogues? There are several ways to get at least part of the picture. One of them is the printed catalogue of Berkeley's holdings through 1963, which can be found in many U.S. academic libraries. Another is the National Union Catalog (which many of you may know as Mansell), which shows many of the scarcer items in Berkeley's catalogues. A third partial listing is provided by the computer network of the Research Libraries Group, but it must be understood that the RLIN online catalogue, the Research Libraries Information Network, is only one of several bibliographic utilities which Berkeley uses to catalogue its collections, and that consequently RLIN cannot be considered a reliable guide to the totality of Berkeley's holdings. Fortunately, there is an easier way for researchers to find materials amid this plethora of catalogues, and it is now possible for readers with a personal computer and modem to dial directly into the computer system which manages Berkeley's online catalogue. There is no charge for this service, other than communication costs accrued in the process, and there are no limitations on the availability of the service at the present time. The Library's online catalogue is called GLADIS, and though it will eventually include records for all of the materials in all campus libraries, at the present time it is systematically complete only for items accrued since 1977. Complete conversion of the Library's catalogues to online format is expected to take a minimum of five years.

GLADIS has been operational in Berkeley since 1984. It is a locally-developed system which includes a circulation system and an interface with the Library's computerized acquisition system and its serials system, allowing users to find materials which are on order, at the bindery, or in process, as well as those which have been catalogued and are ready for use. Readers who are unable to come to the Library can configure their personal computers to communicate with GLADIS, and can dial the appropriate Library telephone number which will connect them to its remote user ports.[17] The searching protocols are mnemonic and based on natural language, allowing users to find materials by personal or corporate author, exact title (or truncation of exact title), series, controlled-vocabulary subject headings, and a variety of alphanumeric and numeric identification codes such as Berkeley call numbers, International Standard Book Numbers, Library of Congress card numbers, and so forth. Keyword and Boolean searching are planned for future implementation. The catalogue contains fully- and briefly-catalogued material as well as recently received material awaiting cataloguing, and soon users will be able to see titles on order as well. Records for serials show complete holdings and plans are presently being implemented to display detailed serials check-in records for information on missing and claimed issues, not-yet-published titles, and items which are unavailable because they are being bound. Eventually the catalogue will contain all holdings for the Main Library, the Undergraduate Library, and the 41 specialized libraries on campus. There is no fee for dial-up access to the Berkeley catalogues, but remote users must pay the cost of long-distance telephone charges in connecting to GLADIS. The system is available 24 hours per day, and downloading of records is authorized for personal users.

That, then, is an overview of the Dutch collections at Berkeley, as well as a glimpse of the Library's methods of extending access to its catalogues to readers outside the Bay Area. I am grateful for the opportunity to provide this sketch of our resources for Netherlandists, and would like to extend a sincere invitation to all to visit the Library and to use its remarkable resources in Dutch, Frisian, and Belgian materials. We welcome scholars from other institutions and hope that many will have the occasion one day to see and use these collections in person.

NOTES

[1] Dora Smith, "History of the University of California Library to 1900." M.A. Thesis (University of California, 1930), 21, Appendix I, leaf (8).

[2] Association of Research Libraries, *ARL Statistics*, (The Association, 1986-87), 40.

[3] Joseph W. Barker, "A Case for Exchange: the Experience of the University of California, Berkeley," *Serials Review* 12:1 (Spring 1986): 63.

[4] Center for Research Libraries. *Handbook* (The Center, 1987): 23-28.

[5] Kenneth G. Peterson, *The University of California Library at Berkeley, 1900-1945* (University of California Press, 1970): 24.

[6] Audrey E. Phelps, *Guide to Special Collections: University of California, Berkeley, Library* (Scarecrow, 1973): 35-36.

[7] Ibid.: 1-22.

[8] Ibid.: 19.

[9] Ibid.: 13.

[10] Ibid.: 125.

[11] Peterson: 32.

[12] Phelps: 87.

[13] Ibid.: 36.

[14] Frank Brechka, "Underground Literature from the Netherlands," *CU News* 31:3 (13 May 1976): 1-2.

[15] University of California, Berkeley. Library. *Collection Development Policy Statement* (The Library, 1980): 14.

[16] Ibid.: 44, 52, 70, 89-90, etc.

[17] (415) 642-7400 for 1200 baud; 642-6870 for 1200 baud with Racal-Vadic modems; 642-9721 for 300 baud.

ACCESS TO DUTCH STUDIES MATERIAL IN THE ENGLISH LANGUAGE: THE CLIO PROJECT

Michael Wintle
University of Hull, Hull

Introduction

In this presentation I shall be trying to do two things more or less simultaneously: in the first place, I shall discuss the general problem of obtaining access to printed material on a specific subject (in this case, Dutch Studies), and secondly, I shall recount some of the salient points regarding the collection and processing of the materials which make up one specific bibliography on the Netherlands. This was the Clio bibliography, which was prepared by Peter King and myself at the Centre for Modern Dutch Studies in the University of Hull, and was published by the Clio Press early in 1988. It is my intention to use the practical project to illustrate the general heuristic issue of where and how to find books and papers on almost any aspect of a small but well documented country like the Netherlands.

The Remit from the Publishers

At the end of 1984 Peter King and I were approached by Clio, an Oxford-based firm of publishers, with a request to consider compiling the volume on the Netherlands in their World Bibliographical Series. This series was of course known to us, and although neither of us had or has any pretensions to professionalism in the field, we had both done bibliographical work in the past. The project was attractive to us in that it would help us in building up the reputation of the Centre for Modern Dutch Studies at Hull. Furthermore the compilation would probably function complementarily with a project we were about to take on in our teaching program, namely a one-year taught MA in area studies on the Low Countries. Many of the areas in which we would need to do new work for the Clio project would also need investigation for the new degree course, and thus work could be combined.

The Clio editors have a very long and very precisely worded shopping list of do's and don't's to which they insist their compilers keep. They are producing a very large series, at present of more than 100 volumes, one on virtually each country in the world, and a high degree of uniformity of layout and approach is demanded. The bibliography was to be selective, annotated, aiming to provide (and I quote from the remit) 'an interpretation of that country which will express its culture, its place in the world, and the qualities and background that make it unique.' We were told to write for the informed and motivated general reader, and in particular for people planning a long Dutch sojourn, and for librarians seeking to improve their stock on the Netherlands. We were to include about 1000 titles, the great majority of which were to be in English, and which should be generally available, either from booksellers or from libraries. We should stick fairly closely to a provided list of about 35 chapters, covering all aspects of Dutch society, and there were very strict rules about forms of bibliographic notation and presentation. There was also to be a very comprehensive index, containing all titles, authors, places, concepts, themes, and names that were mentioned anywhere, either in the citations or in the annotations. That was the gist of the remit; we blithely agreed to submit our MS in later part of 1987, three years on.

Setting up the System

At this point we began to take the project seriously, for it was necessary to set up a system into which data could be dumped over the next 2 1/2 years, more or less in the normal course of our researches in the Centre, before we progressed to sorting and processing the raw data in the last six months or so of our contract period. This is in fact exactly what happened. It is true that we spent 10 days in early 1987 in the Netherlands working intensively on the project in various libraries and other repositories; but apart from that, and of course some 'gap-filling' in the final closing stages, we devoted very little time exclusively to collecting data. We decided at the start on our version of the chapter list, and found we needed to make special adjustments to suit the case of the Netherlands, including sections on drainage and reclamation, the colonies, ethnic minorities, Rotterdam harbour, and horticulture. We divided the chapters between us equally, retaining joint responsibility for a few general subjects like periodicals, directories and bibliographies. I ran a few pilot programs in a database package to identify basic needs, and we agreed to use 12 fields to record our data, including of course author, title, publication information, and the like. We both set up card indexes divided into the chapter headings we had established, and scribbled the data we needed (publication details and a comment) of titles we came across on cards, just dropping them into the file-box for future processing. Some of the data, when convenient, we entered directly onto computer disc, either mainframe or micro. In other words, the system was set up for random searching in the general subject area, and we had ensured that the data would be recorded in at least approximately the correct format.

The Research

Despite the impression I have given of the project being a light-hearted if properly organised part-time hobby, there were of course periods of intense and even systematic research, and I want now to say a few words concerning both the sources and the criteria we employed in that research. The most important sources were the bibliographies which are listed in the chapter on bibliography in the published volume itself: it is the final chapter, containing 44 entries, and 16 cross-references to bibliographical works cited elsewhere in the book. These tend to be subject bibliographies, and vary greatly in quality (our list is by no means exhaustive). The most useful general one for our purposes was probably Walter Lagerwey's *Guide to Netherlandic Studies*, despite being unannotated and now rather dated (1964). Other very important sources in specific areas were the indexes of certain English-language periodicals, notably *Dutch Crossing* (for language and literature), *Delta* (for virtually everything, but only to 1974), and *Planning and Development in the Netherlands* (for politics and the social sciences). The standard Dutch bibliographical tools were also useful, notably the *BNTL (Bibliografie van de Nederlandse Taal- en Letterkundewetenschap)*, and the excellent *Bibliografische Attenderingslijsten voor Docenten Neerlandistiek in het Buitenland*, published by the Bureau voor de Bibliografie van de Neerlandistiek in the Royal Library complex in The Hague (since 1986). These and other standard Dutch tools, like Brinkmans, do require a reading knowledge of Dutch. A very useful source indeed was the *Bibliographia Neerlandica* compiled by Morel and Mollema in 1962, which lists foreign language books on the Netherlands from 1940 onwards, and is continued first in *Het Nederlandse Boek in Vertaling*, and then in the periodical *Ons Erfdeel* (again requiring some Dutch). We also wrote to all and visited many of the Dutch government ministries in our search: most were very helpful indeed, especially the Ministry for Economic Affairs. We made frequent reference to the British Library printed catalogue, notably on such matters as government publications and legal affairs, and indeed to such listings as *Books in Print* and *British Books in Print*. Finally mention should be made of the Brynmor Jones Library, which is Hull's University Library. Over the past 12 years we have been building up a substantial collection on Modern Dutch Studies there, and although only a small portion of the collection is in English, it is very often a serviceable starting point for a literature search. This is of importance to researchers in Dutch Studies far beyond the world of Kinston-upon-Hull and Humberside, for the Brynmor Jones Library's entire stock is accessible through a GEAC computer catalogue to anyone who has access to the JANET network which links all British campuses. JANET is one of the British equivalents to BITNET, and can also be accessed from other countries. Once having gained access to the computerized catalogue, the on-line system allows sophisticated searching by any number of entrants, including keywords.

As to the criteria we used in the selection, they were very varied. Firstly, it must be emphasized that, although a thousand or more titles seems a great deal, when it comes down to an individual chapter, we were looking at an average chapter size of 30 titles, which is hardly scratching the surface when one is looking at an area such as History, or Art. In some areas we had to be so rigorous in our selection that many perfectly good works were excluded simply because there was no room. For this reason in the main, we made very little mention of literary translations. Further criteria were a recent publication date wherever possible, reliability and quality (this was of course a subjective judgement, and the reason why most of the annotations in the book are so friendly and favourable!), and availability. This last is important: we made it a rule that nothing would go in, even if it had rave reviews, unless we had seen and touched it ourselves. This excluded many references we had found to semi-official publications and privately published or cyclostyled papers. After all, if we had not been able to find them, how could we expect our readers to?

In the introduction to the book, Peter King and I made the point that the nature of the country itself tended to determine the extent of printed material about certain subjects, and so this also formed a passive criterion in our selection. The fact that subjects such as flora and fauna, sports and pastimes are thinly represented is not surprising, since there is little in these areas which other European nations do not share with the Dutch, and thus very little is written on these subjects in English. The fact that there is a flood of material on every aspect of government work and planning is explained by the gross overcrowding in the country. The emphases on the particular attributes of the Dutch economy, the Dutch political system (post-*verzuiling*), and land drainage are all explained by the nature of the country itself: indeed it was a specific part of our remit from the publishers to allow this to occur.

In the final stages, we had to reduce our data from about 5,000 titles to about a thousand titles to fit the publisher's requirements, and we attempted to re-employ these criteria which we had used in the initial collection over a period of two years or more. I believe that we have been reasonably successful, but I would freely admit that much of the selection took place at least partly on the basis of the personal tastes and competences of the compilers, namely, Peter King and myself. King is a specialist on the literature and art of the Low Countries, while I am a socio-economic historian. Our fields of expertise are undoubtedly better represented than some others, and we cannot deny that in certain areas our knowledge amounts to little more than that of the interested layman. On the other hand, we are both members of the Centre for Modern Dutch Studies at the University of Hull, which consciously concerns itself with *all* aspects of life in the Low Countries. The Clio volume remains a bibliography based on a personal selection by two biased and opiniated individuals, only partly able to use objective citeria in the selection process. But despite its warts and all (and there are plenty of them), I think we have produced a serviceable tool, at least for the investigator who does not have the use of Dutch.

FAMULUS77

Finally it is appropriate to say a little about the more technical side of processing the data. With this side of the project, with which (incidentally) Peter King was not involved, I can say that I was delighted. There was some initial work in investigating the correct package, but the result was submission on time, and more-or-less camera-ready copy instead of a shoe-box full of dogeared filecards. We used FAMULUS, a package widely available on most university mainframes.

The FAMULUS package is a database program specially tailored to bibliographical needs. It has been around since the late sixties, and is thus a bit long in the tooth: a more recent package like CAIRS would probably have done very well, but CAIRS is not available in a version for Hull's ICL mainframe. You might well protest that bibliographical work, and indeed most private database work, is probably best done on an IBM PC-type machine with a hard disc. True, but have you got one of your own on your desk? I haven't. Nor do I have access to enough hard-disc space on a public-access machine to store my data without it being very vulnerable to malicious hacks and benign fools. The mainframe has other advantages: with large databases the speed of the programs when run on the VME handling system is impressive; they are more or less instantaneous, even when running complicated sorts through 5000 cases. Printing out large files is very fast and cheap. Terminals are available. Disc space is not a real problem. I have had a great deal of bibliographical data on the mainframe for some time, and was looking around for a new system. Someone suggested FAMULUS. Added to this was the commission from Clio, with its strict instructions about the format of the manuscript, with comprehensive indexing according to rigid and extensive guidelines. This was obviously computer work: the task by hand would be near-hopeless. So I borrowed a copy of the FAMULUS77 manual.

FAMULUS77 was created in the mid-eighties (77 stands for Fortran77, not 1977!) to rationalize all the developments and extensions which had modified the original package since the late sixties. The basic concept is very similar to most mainframe packages for playing around with data: crude data is read into a systems file inside FAMULUS, and then can be manipulated, altered, sorted, indexed, and generally messed about with by a suite of 10 main routines, as follows: Edit, Galley (prints), Index, Sort, Key (part of indexing), Kwic (an index option), Merge, Multiply (splits up fields), Ossify (makes a portable version of a systems file), and Sort. When you have sorted out your data, corrected it, selected the parts you want to print out today, indexed it, or whatever, you can have it written to a file, for line-printing or for transfer to another machine for high-quality printing. The output from the system comes in one of four basic formats (with all sorts of optional parameters and variables within each), called Tagged (includes the fieldnames), Catalogue (the smart version), Columns (tabular format), or Compact (minimal space). So if you are using the package for bibliographical data, you take along your list of references, or stack of dogeared file cards, with publication details, brief notes, and anything else you want. You can have up to 4096 bytes (characters) per card, case or (as FAMULUS calls it) 'citation'. You feed this all in and end up with a neatly formatted reading list, a list of references at the end of an article or book, or in my case, a comprehensive national bibliography, arranged by subjects in chapters, with full cross-referencing and indexing.

In order to help illustrate the package, it may be useful to run through what I did with my data. As with any database, you must decide your data fields (author, title, date, number, comments, notes, keyword, whatever), give them labels, and stick to them. You can have up to 25 (I had 12). No need to add empty ones for luck: it is very easy to add them later. Having decided roughly which 1200-or-so titles were going into the final selection process, I had these keyed into ordinary datafiles on the mainframe, and used the Edit program in FAMULUS77 to feed them into a systems file. I then sorted the citations according to chapter, author's name, title, and several other variables, simply instructing the program to sort first on field 3 (which was the chapter number), then on field 7 (author's name), and then on field 9 (title). It was easy to check for duplicates, and to select in or out various citations according to what I had decided to include (authors beginning with B, books which appeared before 1973, whatever). I spent quite a lot of time, which eventually proved to be well worth it, on determining exactly how the alphabetical sorts should treat numbers, spaces, punctuation, dipthongs, diacritics and the like: FAMULUS has a highly sophisticated set of controls for such things. Once I had finalized the 1025 titles I needed for the project, and had got them into the order and shape I wanted, I started the indexing.

I had never done any indexing before with bibliographies, but found the FAMULUS77 system very powerful and very useful. The publisher had specified that I needed to index four different concepts: authors/editors, book titles (not periodicals), keywords or subjects, and the editors of books in which cited essays appeared. This required running four different index programs, which produced four different sets of output which I then merged into alphabetical order. The FAMULUS output was quite near to the format specified by the publisher, and it was easy enough to tidy it up with an editing macro. I sent off a substantial stack of line-printout to the publisher, who expressed his warm approval of the presentation of the data and especially of the thoroughness of the index. Then I transferred the lot, main listing and index, to seven 5 1/4' floppy discs on an IBM PC-type machine, and sent them off to the printer, who fed them into his typesetting machine. This for me was the most satisfying part of the whole operation: manuscript to publication in two months flat. Proofreading was veritably relaxing.

There are of course some things about FAMULUS77 which do not please. It will not index more than one thing at a time; its printing formats are limited; mainframe handling systems are fast and reliable but an unpleasant environment for the non-buff; inputting and editing are easier with a proper word-processing facility. On the other hand, there are ways round all these things. The package is available and free to university staff, and the manual is reasonably well written and intelligible. I also use the package for other bibliographical work, for research referencing, for cataloguing lecture slides, and the like. It would certainly do for things like mailing lists as well, though the advantage of the mainframe is its speed with huge files – larger than most mailing lists. Whether it would handle prosopographical analyses and other such data uses I rather doubt: it is best for books and similar items.

Conclusion

This article has tried to use autobiographical confession to provide insights into the various steps of gaining access to materials on Dutch studies in the English language, and of processing that data when it has been collected. Our claims for the resulting book are modest: it is a rough guide and a selective introduction to a vast field, which in any individual specialism can do little more than scrape the surface. There is certainly not the slightest claim to any form of comprehensive coverage. But in our defence I can also say that I find my own students in Modern Dutch Studies increasingly interested in using it, despite the ability of most of them to read Dutch, and I also find that telephone and written enquiries from all manner of people from within and without the university world are quite often answered by a quick skim through the index of 'the Clio'. If it becomes as useful to others as it is becoming to the compilers themselves, then our objectives will have been substantially achieved.

REFERENCES

P.K. King and M.J. Wintle, *The Netherlands*, World Bibliographical Series (Oxford, Clio Press, 1988).

Walter Lagerwey, *Guide to Netherlandic Studies: Bibliography* (Grand Rapids, 1964).

Bibliografie van de Nederlandse Taal- en Letterkundewetenschap (The Hague, 1975-).

Bibliografische Attenderingslijsten voor Docenten Neerlandistiek in het Buitenland (The Hague, 1986-).

P.M. Morel and A.M.P. Mollema, *Bibliographia Neerlandica* (The Hague, 1962).

Famulus 77, Version 2.3, User Manual (Edinburgh, 1985) [Programme Library Unit, Centre for Applications Software and Technology, University of Edinburgh, 1 Roxburgh Street, Edinburgh EH8 9TA United Kingdom].

RECONSTRUCTION OF A DISFIGURED DUTCH HISTORY PAINTING

Mary Ann Scott
University of Denver, Denver

Some seventeenth-century Dutch paintings have been mistreated.[1] Unknown dealers, presumably intent on creating more marketable images, and collectors uncomfortable with seemingly offensive or unattractive details, have disfigured many works by cutting, overpainting, adding false signatures, and in other ways altering the artists' original compositions. The famous genre scene with two women and a man (before 1655, Berlin-Dahlem, Staatliche Museen Preussicher Kulturbesitz) by Gerard ter Borch (1617-1681) was known as *Parental Admonition* by the eighteenth century because it was believed to have represented a father chastising his daughter. We now know that the male figure in this painting originally held a gold coin, which was later overpainted. Before the removal of that crucial detail, the subject could have been properly interpreted, according to ter Borch's original intention, as a brothel scene with the man offering payment to the standing woman in exchange for sexual favors.[2] Another genre scene by ter Borch in Berlin (*The Cello Player*, c.1675, Berlin-Dahlem, Staatliche Museen Preussischer Kulturbesitz), representing a pair of female musicians, wears the overpainted features of a woman, an alteration that occurred sometime before the late nineteenth century. An old copy informs us that ter Borch originally painted a man at the clavichord. X-rays suggest that the artist himself probably replaced the man's features with those of a matronly woman. That detail was later repainted with the features of a younger woman in the late nineteenth century.[3]

Among other infamous repaintings is Frans Hals's *Portrait of Verdonck* (c.1627, Edinburgh, National Gallery of Scotland) whose sitter was correctly identified as the braggart of Haarlem when the National Gallery of Scotland discovered that the detail of the hat and wine glass were later additions painted over the presumably offensive details of an ass's jawbone and the figure's unruly hair.[4]

Less well known is a dark tavern scene by Cornelis Bega (1631/32-1664) in Bordeaux (Musée des Beaux-Arts, c.1658-1660) depicting a hostess seated on the lap of a coarse peasant. Up until 1981, when the painting was restored, the background was a flat area of thin brown varnish. During cleaning, the detail of a pair of copulating figures within the bedframe at left became visible prompting the museum to relegate the work to storage. Based on an old copy from 1830 which shows the erotic passage already covered, we know that Bega's scene wore overpaint for at least a century and a half.[5] The fate of Bega's work recalls that of a genre scene by Frans van Mieris (1635-1681) and of a barnyard scene by Dirck van den Bergen (c.1640-c.1690). In both Mieris' *The*

Inn Scene (1658, The Hague, Mauritshuis) and Bergen's *The Bull* (Oberlin, Allen Memorial Art Museum), a pair of copulating animals was dramatically transformed into a single docile creature when the upper animal (dog or bull) was visually hidden by overpaint.[6]

Seventeenth-century Dutch paintings have not only suffered from removal of paint and the addition of disfiguring overpaint, as these representative works demonstrate. Numerous works have also been cut. As one example among many, the now vertical painting of *The Liberation of St. Peter* by the workshop of Abraham Bloemaert (1564-1651) in Cincinnati (Cincinnati Art Museum, c.1625) was once the left half of a horizontal composition which showed at right the fleeing figures of the angel and St. Peter.[7] I believe that in the case of the Cincinnati painting, however, the apparent damage could instead have been purposeful alteration of the composition by Bloemaert himself intending to create a less manneristic, and more Caravaggesque image under the influence of his student, the Caravaggiste Honthorst.

Paintings like the one in Cincinnati present special problems since we cannot always ascertain the artist's original conception. The possibility of an artist's own modification of his primary idea appears as well in the most recently encountered example of dramatic alteration, a newly discovered history scene (1641, Denver Art Museum, on loan from the Robert Appleman Family) by the Amsterdam artist Claes Moeyaert (c.1590/91-1655), who was one of the so-called Pre-Rembrandtists. The Colorado collector Robert Appleman purchased the work in c.1970 from an establishment known as "La Granja" in Mexico City. Its earlier provenance is unknown, and it does not feature in Astrid Tümpel's valuable catalogue on Moeyaert.[8] She now knows the work and, based on a photograph, accepts it as by him.[9]

The painting is large, measuring 183 x 231 cm, and represents a scene from the Euripidean drama, *Iphigenia in Tauris*. Before an imaginary background of classical buildings, the artist depicted Iphigenia, who was an enforced priestess made to officiate at bloody sacrifices in honor of Artemis. The goddess' temple and cult statue are visible at upper right. Unknown to Iphigenia is the fact that the two latest victims (the figures standing left of her) are her long-lost brother, Orestes, and his companion Pylades, neither of whom she recognizes. According to the Taurians, the presence of the shipwrecked Athenians has desecrated the cult statue which can only be cleansed with their blood. Iphigenia decides that since the youths are from Athens, she might spare one so that he could carry a message to Orestes whom she presumes is still in Greece. Orestes, for his part, fails to recognize his beloved sister because he presumes her dead. The moment selected is the one in which Pylades attempts to restrain Orestes from offering himself as the sole sacrifice. The equestrian figure at left must be King Thoas who, in Van Mander's account, plays a larger role than he does in Euripides' original version.[10] The exotic setting, melodramatic figural representation, and bright coloration are typical for Moeyaert.

When exhibited in 1985, the Denver painting displayed freshness of execution and homogeneous craquelure in the foreground.[11] The sky, however, was an unattractive area of thick, blue-green overpaint. In 1986, the conservator Carl Grimm, from the Western Center for the Conservation of Fine Arts in Denver, removed several layers of overpaint, primarily in the sky.[12] He also removed the original glue lining and a more recent lining made with Elmer's glue, and relined the canvas. During this process it became evident that, although the pigment of the important foreground area remained stable, a considerable amount of original pigment had been roughly scraped off the sky. Most unexpected, however, was an enormous loss in the shape of a classical column near the center of the composition, providing a vertical wedge between the principal figures, Iphigenia and Orestes. Faint diagonal lines within the column indicated that it had been painted with spiral reliefs of the Trajanic type. X-radiographic study and chemical analysis of the pigment in the area of the column showed that it was consistent with Moeyaert's surrounding layer of paint, and therefore that Moeyaert did paint the column. Indeed, he separated the clouds to allow space for what is now an unreadable figure atop it. That Moeyaert himself did not cover the column was indicated by the awkward articulation of the colonnade painted over it in orangish paint uncharacteristic for him.

Further evidence that the column might have been part of Moeyaert's original idea is the possibility that it served a symbolic purpose, that is, a visual reference to Orestes as the "pillar of the family" since Iphigenia speaks of him in those terms in her "deathly dream" of Agamemnon's destroyed palace.[13]

Prior studies have demonstrated the popularity of classical motifs among the Pre-Rembrandtists.[14] We know that Pieter Lastman, who strongly influenced Moeyaert as Tümpel has shown, and whose own version of the subject in Amsterdam (Rijksmuseum) directly inspired Moeyaert's painting, topped a column with an alligator in his painting, *Joseph Selling Corn in Egypt* (1612, National Gallery in Dublin).[15] Among Moeyaert's other works, the column motif appears in a lost variant (1647, formerly Los Angeles, with Joseph M. B. Guttman Galleries), where the figure atop it is a bull, and in a preliminary sketch (Berlin, Kupferstichkabinett, Staatliche Museen Preussischer Kulturbesitz) for the Denver work.[16] The drawing has been cropped through the crucial detail of the figure atop the column, another example of damage. We might be able to ascertain Moeyaert's intentions for the figure if a copy of the painting or a reproductive print after it were to surface.

More than other such reconstructions, the restoration of the Denver work proved to be exceedingly difficult. The area to be inpainted was exceptional in size and prominently positioned. Mostly destroyed were details of the spiral frieze. Since no original paintings by Moeyaert with Trajanic columns were readily available to Grimm, he, probably like Moeyaert himself, turned for inspiration to Lastman. A slide of Lastman's painting in Dublin with its large, centrally placed column, projected onto the Denver painting, helped to suggest the contours of the missing spiral reliefs. Rather than fabricating misleadingly precise details, however, Grimm merely suggested their forms. Also following sound conservation practice, he used removable materials, filling losses with thin acrylic paint, and relining with a reversible synthetic adhesive.

Viewers will see what they will in the figure which is now a mysteriously unreadable object formed from the connected dots of surviving original pigment. Moeyaert himself may have altered his figure. One may read both the foreshortened wings of a bird, perhaps symbolizing Jupiter, and a seated human figure, perhaps Minerva, both of whom are mentioned in the drama. The irresolution of this important detail adds to the provocative nature of the reconstruction which cannot really be complete until we learn what Moeyaert originally placed there. In the meantime, the Denver work joins the growing list of dramatically altered Dutch paintings.

NOTES

[1] This article is being published posthumously. Professor Scott died unexpectedly in October, 1988, not having been able to provide the photographs which were to accompany the text. The editor hopes that she has done justice to Professor Scott's manuscript and that the text is clear despite the absence of illustrations.

[2] S.J. Gudlaugsson, *Geraert Ter Borch*, vol. 1, The Hague, 1959, 96-97.

[3] Ibid., 161.

[4] Seymour Slive, *Frans Hals*, vol. 1, New York, 1970, 81; P.J.J. van Thiel, "De betekenis van het portret van Verdonck door Frans Hals," *Oud Holland*, vol. 94, 1980, 112.

[5] Mary A. Scott, *Cornelis Bega*, Doornspijk, forthcoming from Davaco, cat. no. 11.

[6] Otto Naumann, *Frans van Mieris, the Elder*, vol. 1, Doornspijk, 1981, 104, 107. Wolfgang Stechow (*Dutch Landscape Painting of the Seventeenth Century*, New York, 1980, 7) noted that

some paintings were altered further by additions like the figures at the right in Jacob van Ruisdael's painting *Waterfall* in the Toledo Museum of Art.

[7] Existing copies and versions of the same scene, most given to Honthorst, in the collection of R. E. Baron van Dorth van 't Medler, Vorden, in the Schloss Museum, Anholt, in the Bayerische Staatsgemäldesammlungen, Munich, formerly with A. Nystad in Lochem, and on the French art market in 1978, indicate the probable appearance of the Cincinnati work before it was cut (M. Scott, *Dutch, Flemish, and German Paintings in the Cincinnati Art Museum: Fifteenth through Eighteenth Centuries*, Cincinnati, 1987, 15-19, and n. 21).

[8] Astrid Tümpel, "Claes Cornelisz. Moeyaert," *Oud Holland*, vol. 88, 1974, nos. 1-2, pp. 1-163, and no. 4, pp. 245-290.

[9] Personal conversation, June 1987. The painting could be identical with one on the art market in Nijmegen in 1816, Tümpel cat. no. 171.

[10] Whether Moeyaert drew upon Euripides directly is still undecided since the dramatist's works were first translated into Dutch only in 1666. According to Eric Jan Sluijter (*De 'heydensche fabulen' in de noordnederlandse schilderkunst, circa 1590-1670. Een proeve van beschrijving en interpretatie van schilderijen met verhalende onderwerpen uit de klassieke mythologie*, diss., Leiden, 1986, 55, and 393, nn. 6, 7), rather than Euripides' drama *Iphigenia in Tauris* directly, a more likely source for such subjects is Carel Van Mander's *Wtlegghingh op den Metamorphosis Pub. Ovidii Nasonis* in *Het Schilder-Boeck* (Haarlem, 1603-1604, fol. 103v). I will discuss iconographical details of the Denver painting in an upcoming issue of *Mercury*.

[11] The painting was exhibited in a small show called "Colorado Collects" at the Denver Art Museum in 1985.

[12] I am grateful to Carl Grimm for including me in the numerous and lively debates that attended the reconstruction. Deep appreciation is also due Robert Appleman who financed my research trip to the Rijksbureau voor Kunsthistorische Documentatie in The Hague and the Courtauld Institute in London.

[13] Lines 50-56, *Iphigenia in Tauris*, *Euripides II* in the series *The Complete Greek Tragedies*, ed. by David Green and Richmond Lattimore, Chicago, 1969.

[14] Christian Tümpel in Sacramento, E. B. Crocker Art Gallery, *The Pre-Rembrandtists*, by Astrid and Christian Tümpel, with Wolfgang Stechow, 1974, 27-152; and Albert Blankert et al. in

Washington, D. C., National Gallery of Art, *Gods, Saints, and Heroes*, 1980.

[15] Tümpel cat. no. 170.

[16] Ibid., and fig. 255.

BUITENPARTIJEN: GARDENS OF LOVE OR GARDENS OF LUST?

Kahren Jones Arbitman
The Frick Art Museum, Pittsburgh

Picnics in seventeenth-century Holland were not the kind of casual affairs we think of today. Rather, the *buitenpartijen* depicted by early seventeenth-century Dutch artists were elegant festivities attended by the Dutch elite. Several authors, myself included, have undertaken iconographic investigations of these parties, and often our conclusions about their meanings conflict.[1] The ambiguity arises, so it seems, from the variety of sources which feed the genre, for the simultaneous use of such disparate artistic prototypes as gardens of love on one hand, and scenes of the prodigal son on the other, has led those of us interpreting these paintings down different garden paths. Some viewers would disallow any symbolic or allegorical interpretations for these works, preferring to see them only as generic outdoor parties which reflect Holland's prosperity during its Golden Age. Given the tenor of the times, this assertion - at least on one level - is understandable. Equally undeniable, however, is the recognition that artists included at these festivities many motifs with longstanding symbolic associations.

In some cases, the question of whether an artist intended moralistic or allegorical implications for his painting can be answered by examining the painting's prototypes. One garden party, in particular, contains such clear references to moralistic prints and emblems that a specific meaning must underlie its seemingly realistic veneer (fig. 1). This painting, *Garden Party Before a Palace*, now in the Mauritshuis, is an early work by Esaias van de Velde, and one in which he made little attempt to disguise his borrowings from paintings, prints, and emblem books.[2] Esaias's use of sources that - as we shall see - denounce the wickedness of the idle rich and the vanity of worldly things, should allow us to draw conclusions about the artist's intent for his painting. And this could suggest possible interpretations for less obvious paintings by Esaias's contemporaries which contain similar subjects and motifs.

On the surface, Esaias's painting is indistinguishable from other garden parties produced in and around Amsterdam during the first quarter of the seventeenth century. Its general compositional arrangement, as well as many of its specific motifs, are standard fare in *buitenpartijen* by Dirk Hals, Willem Buytewech, and David Vinckboons. Signed and dated 1614, Esaias's panel was painted when he was noticeably under the influence of the latter artist.[3]

Esaias was twenty-seven when he painted his Mauritshuis panel, and his relative youth may account for his strong reliance

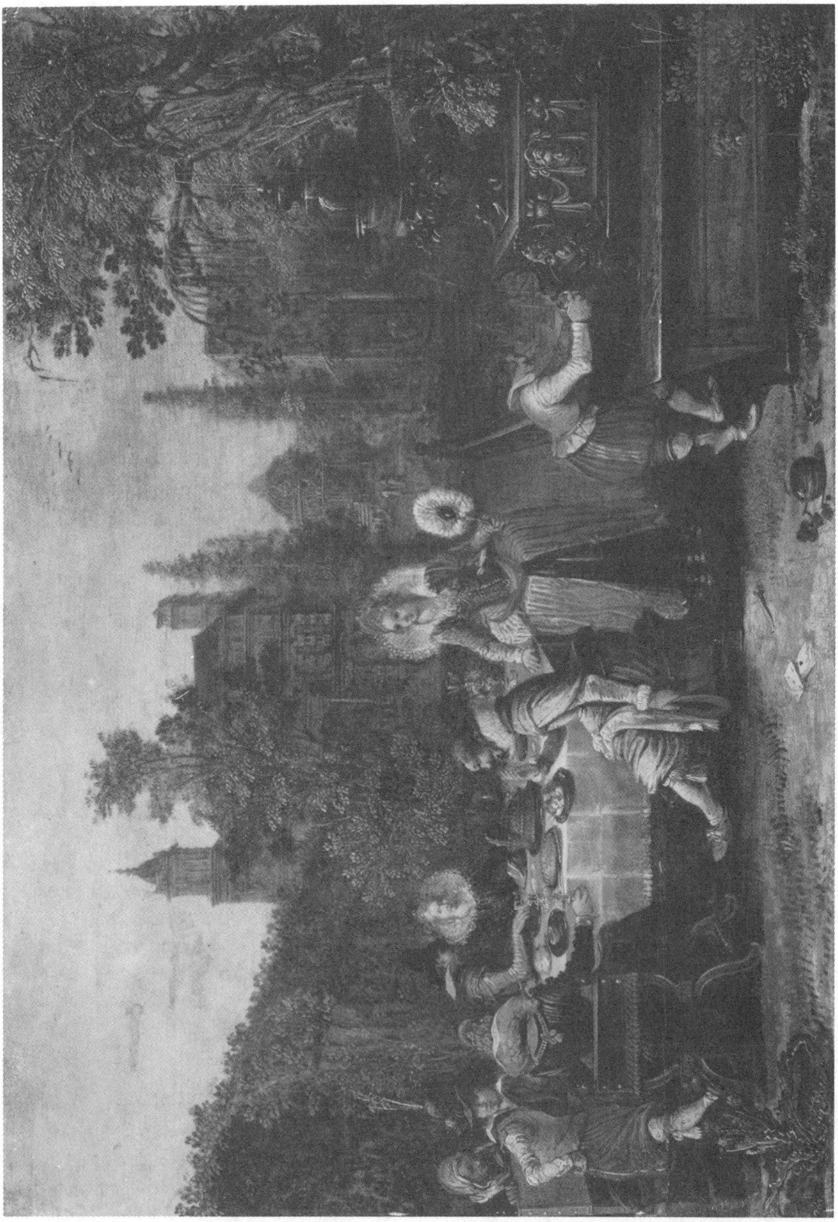

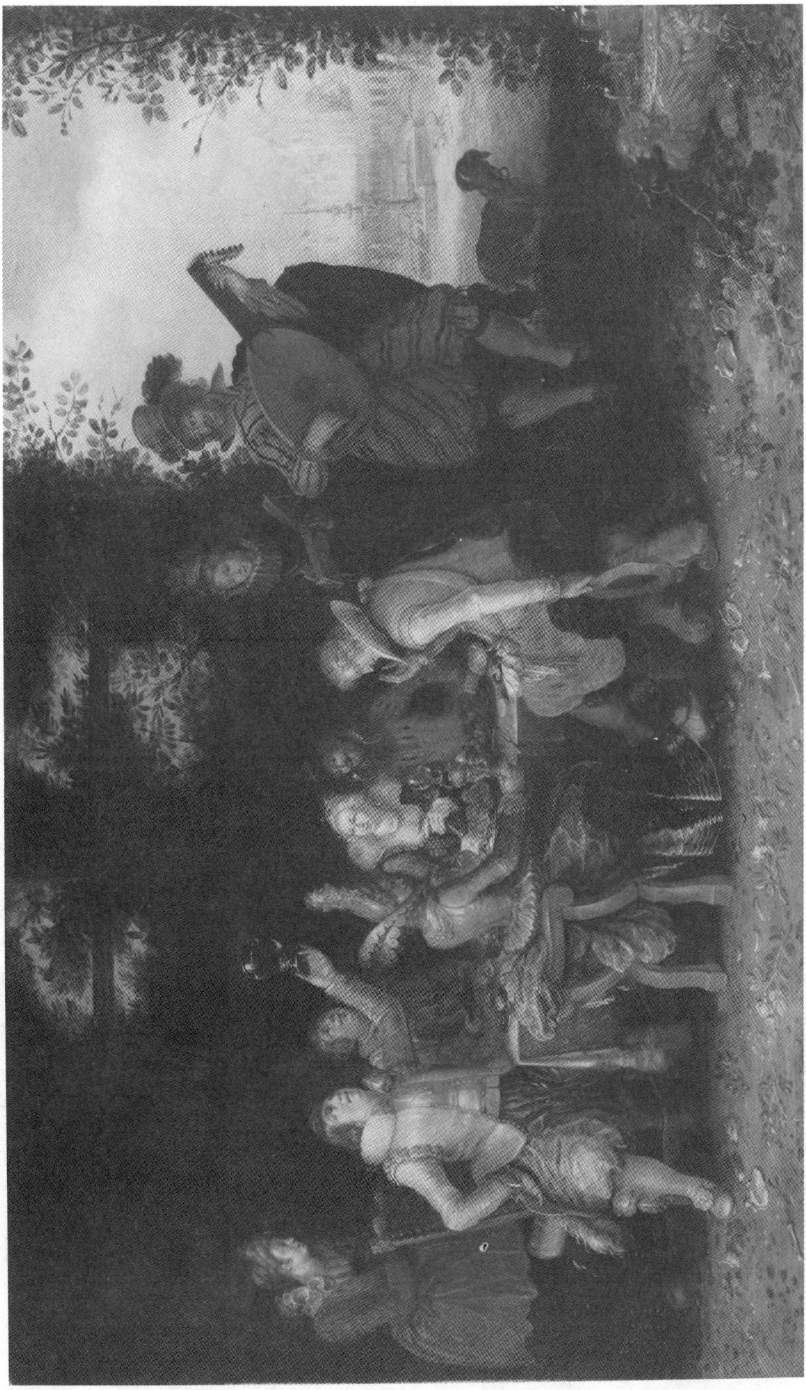

Cedite PYRAMIDES, et splendida MAVSOLÆA.
ROMVLIDVM Parvis extructa palatia saxis.
Æmula regifsis surgunt genialibus hortis.
Fontis aquam rigido fundit DYCTINNA metallo:
Sub Jove regali celebrant convivia luxu.
Et personati ducunt ad plectra choreas.
Parsque coronatis decurrunt flumine cymbis:
LAZARVS ast avidi patitur jejunia ventris.

on other artists for so many of its figures. For example, he borrowed the seated man at the corner of the table with his hat in his left hand from a painting by Vinckboons now in Copenhagen (fig. 2).[4] Furthermore, Vinckboons's woman seen from behind, whose skirt falls through the open back of her Savonarola chair, also appears in Esaias's painting.[5] She shows up in garden parties attributed to Buytewech and Dirk Hals as well.[6]

The simultaneous appearance of this figure in the art of Esaias and his contemporaries is particularly noteworthy when their prototype is revealed to be a moralistic print. In 1606 Jacob Matham engraved a depiction of *Lazarus Starving While the Rich Man Feasts* after a design by Sebastiaen Vrancx (fig. 3). In the print, the rich man's outdoor banquet takes center stage while the emaciated figure of Lazarus is relegated to the background. The print's importance for Esaias's composition is immediately evident. To the left of both print and painting sit figures at a banquet table. A multi-level fountain and palace with prominent spires fill the background of each, while tall cypresses flank a deep plunge into space which ends with a domed garden pavilion. Esaias's lady in the Savonarola chair appears in Matham's engraving; she also must have been the model for Vinckboons, Buytewech, and Dirk Hals.

The question here is whether the print's implied moral damnation, directed at those who ignore the starving Lazarus, is present in Esaias's painting which is based on it, but which leaves out its operative factor - Lazarus. Given the tradition of symbolic associations in a great many Dutch genre paintings, it is likely that Esaias is here warning against the excesses that would lead to an enternity in Hell.

Additional evidence supports this conclusion, for the source of the painting's main character, the prominent woman who stands to the right of the banquet table wearing an elaborate costume and carrying a feathered mirror, is the engraved emblem of *Superbia* which first appeared in the 1596 edition of *Emblemata Secularia* by Johann Theodor de Bry (fig. 4).[7] De Bry's *Superbia* differs somewhat from the usual depictions of this deadly sin, and these differences could have prompted Esaias to choose it as his model. Normally *Superbia* prints do not stand alone, but are part of a series of *Seven Deadly Sins* and include allusions to the fate which awaits those whose pride had caused their fall from God's grace. An example of a popular engraving of *Superbia* is Pieter van der Heyden's print after Pieter Bruegel the Elder. The engraving's inscription emphasizes the spiritual ramifications of Pride: the Latin, "Those who are proud do not love the gods, nor do the gods love those who are proud," and the Flemish, "Pride is hated by God above and at the same time, God is reviled by Pride."[8] In the same vein, an engraving of *Superbia* by Hendrick Goltzius includes a background vignette of the fall of Lucifer to underscore the Biblical derivation of the subject.[9]

GLORIA TOTIVS RES EST VANISSIMA MVNDI 8

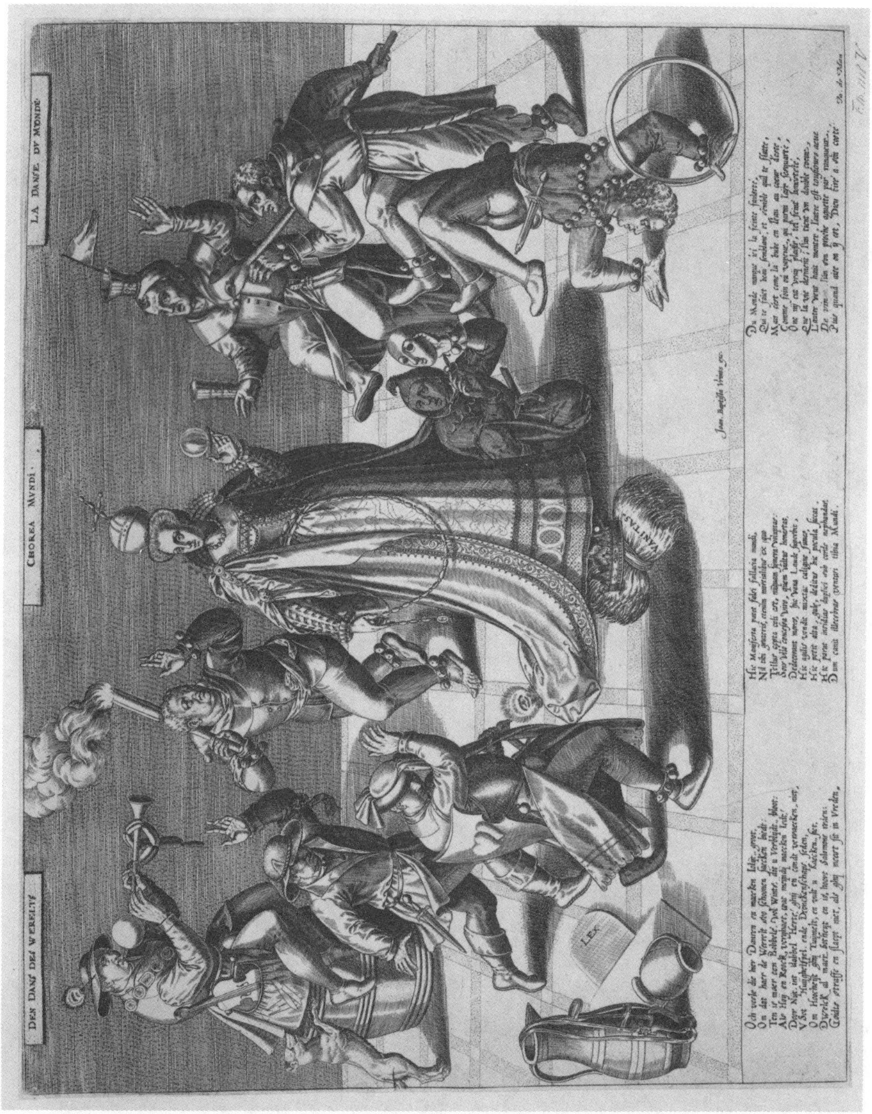

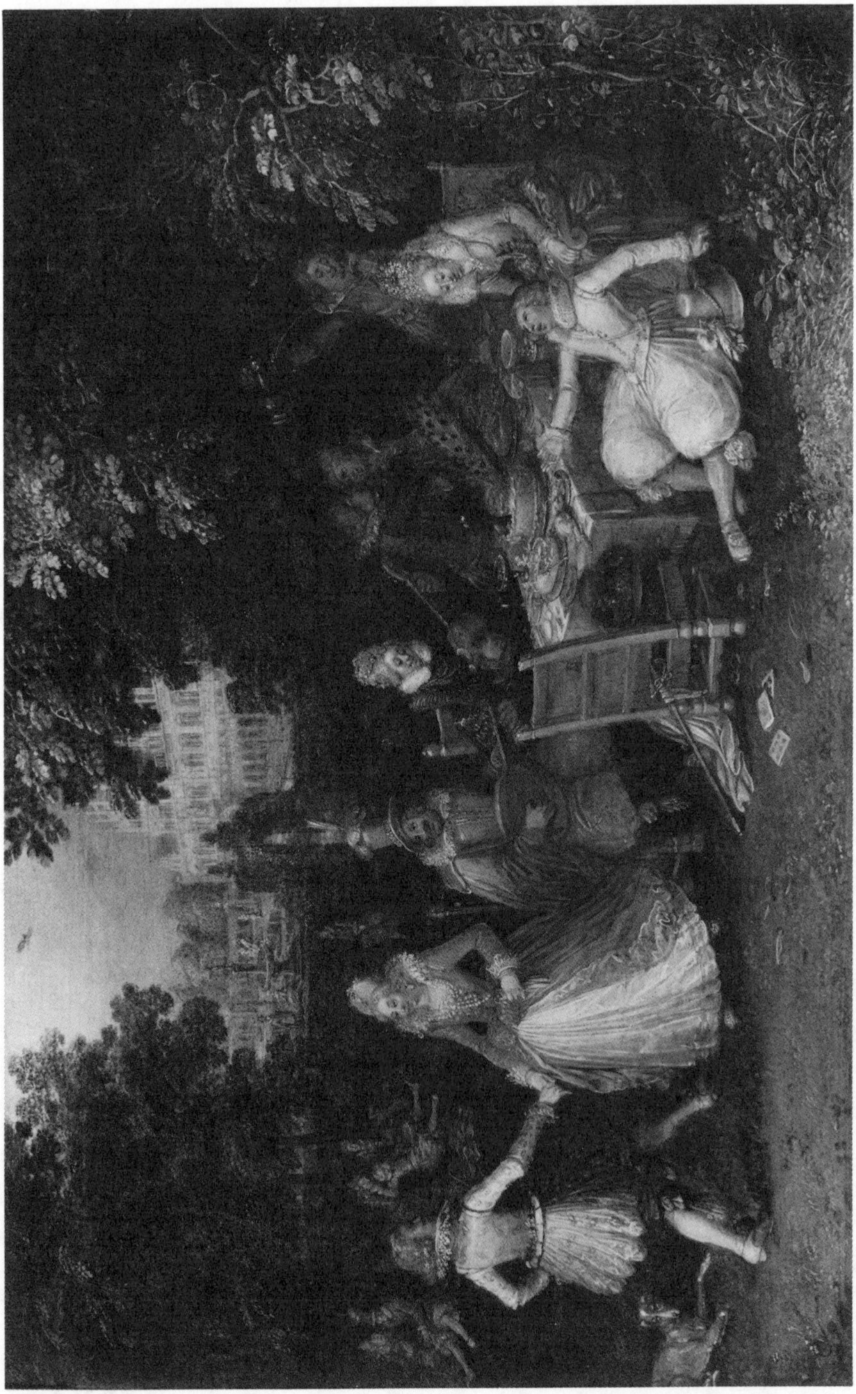

De Bry's emblem, on the other hand, emphasizes worldly vanity and temporality; Pride reigns, as she does in Bruegel's and Goltzius's examples, but this deadly sin is not reinforced with Biblical associations. In addition, the globe the woman wears on her head alters somewhat her identification. Rather than being strictly a personification of *Superbia*, she represents *Vrouw Wereld*. Her sphere of influence now encompasses more than a single deadly sin, for Lady World has been proven to represent "the beautiful and seductive personification of all vice and lust."[10]

A *Lady World*, similar to the woman in De Bry's emblem, appears in an engraving after Pieter Baltens of *The Dance Around the World*, a popular print which exists in several versions (fig. 5).[11] In Baltens' engraving, the woman is surrounded by wildly dancing personifications of various sins. Dancers appear in De Bry's emblem as well, but they have moved to the background, where they have joined other revelers beneath a pergola. De Bry's merrymakers, whose festivities appear to have progressed to the raucous stage, are oblivious to the unmistakable reminders of temporality which surround them: the prominent winged hourglass, vanishing smoke, falling rose petals, and short-lived bubbles. The ultimate fate of these carousers can be found in the left background, where the skeletal figure of Death rides a racing chariot and mows down his victims with a scythe.

De Bry's easy combination of lust, vanity, and retribution in a single garden party setting must have appealed to Esaias. In his Mauritshuis painting, Esaias maintained *Superbia*'s central position while bringing forward the background pergola and fountain to frame the painting. The party guests have also moved their festivities to the forefront. At the same time, Esaias left aside De Bry's obvious symbolic trappings; the hourglass, smoking urn, and falling petals are gone. The message they imparted is not lost, however, for although *Lady World*'s tresses are no longer crowned with a distinguishing globe, references to her lusty nature continue. The deck of cards, cut to reveal the ace of hearts, ripe melon, and crone who leans over the young dandy's chair all allude to illicit love and lust.[12] As in De Bry's emblem, this haughty lady oversees the worldly vanity about her. Dissipation and excess continue unabated, as revealed by the sumptuous feast which barely fits onto the banquet table and the tall wine glasses, large enough to ensure the drunkenness of anyone who empties them. Thus, although the Grim Reaper no longer makes his chilling appearance, Esaias is nonetheless warning the viewer against worldly excesses which lead to damnation.

The larger question is, of course, whether similar paintings without such clearly defined sources, contain moralistic messages. A case in point is David Vinckboons's *Garden Party* of c.1610 in the Rijksmuseum (fig. 6). A decade ago Eddy de Jongh pointed out the appearance of many of the standard attributes of vice, lust, and temporality in this painting, as well as the connection between this composition and a Vinckboons drawing of *The Prodigal Son Dissipating His Inheritance*.[13] However, neither he, nor most of those writing after him, would unequivocally assert that this painting carries a clear warning against the excesses it portrays.[14] Perhaps paintings like Esaias's *Garden Party Before a Palace*, which makes little attempt to disguise its sources, will give art historians more confidence when dealing with Dutch *buitenpartijen*, and we will at last be able to agree about what is going on in these gardens of earthly delight.

NOTES

[1] See, among others, Peter C. Sutton, et al., *Masters of Seventeenth-century Dutch Genre Painting*, ex. cat. Philadelphia Museum of Art, Philadelphia, 1984, pp. xxvii-xxx; E.L. Goodman, "Rubens' Conversatie à la Mode and the Tradition of the Garden of Love," unpub. diss., Ohio State University, 1978, pp. 29-53; E. de Jongh, *tot Lering en Vermaak*, ex. cat. Rijksmuseum, Amsterdam, 1976, pp. 123-125 and 273-275; and Kahren Jones Hellerstedt, *Gardens of Earthly Delight*, ex. cat. The Frick Art Museum, Pittsburgh, 1986, pp. 44-47 and *passim*.

[2] The Mauritshuis painting is one of ten garden parties accepted by George Keyes as painted by Esaias, see *Esaias van den Velde 1587-1630*, Doornspijk, 1984, cat. nos. 59-66 and 68-69. The painting is not in good condition; Dr. N.C. Sluijter-Seijffert, curator of the collection, informs me that it is rather heavily overpainted.

[3] Although no archival evidence verifies a student/teacher relationship between Esaias and Vinckboons, the parallels between the artists's works make such a connection likely.

[4] The painting in the Statens Museum for Kunst, Copenhagen is discussed by Korneel Goossens, *David Vinckboons*, Antwerp and The Hague, 1954, fig. 51. The connection between this painting and Esaias's Mauritshuis panel was already noted by Goossens, p. 97. A copy of the Vinckboons painting, monogrammed and dated 1622, was formerly in the art market, see *Antiek*, April, 1974, p. 780.

[5] She appears in many of Esaias's paintings beginning with the 1614 panel and continuing throughout his career. See Keyes, as in note 2, cat. nos. 69, I, VII, IX, and XII.

[6] The woman appears in the two Vinckboons compositions cited above in note 5. For the Buytewech see Gernsheim 39292. The Hals painting, formerly on the art market in New York, is

discussed and illustrated in Hellerstedt, as in note 1, cat. no. 20.

[7] See *Emblemata Saecularia. Kulturgeschichtliches Stamm- und Wappenbuch*, Frankfurt, 1596, emblem no. 2; copy in the Bodleian Library. The second edition of this book was published in Oppenheim in 1611 with twenty-two additional plates; copy in the Koninklijke Bibliotheek, The Hague. At the time of the second edition, the numbers were altered to reflect the addition of the new emblems: *Superbia*, numbered 2 in the 1596 edition, was renumbered 18. Johann Theodor de Bry's 1596 book was, itself, an enlargement of *Emblemata Nobilitatis Stamm- und Wappenbuch* by the artist's father, Theodor de Bry, published in Frankfurt in 1592 and 1593; copy in the Rijksprentenkabinet, Amsterdam. The *Superbia* image appears in a reversed engraving attributed to Crispijn de Passe I, see Hollstein's *Dutch and Flemish Etchings, Engravings and Woodcuts ca. 1450-1700*, Amsterdam, 1974, XVI, no. 300 ad., p. 81.

[8] Translations are from Ludwig Münz, *Bruegel: The Drawings*, London, 1961, cat. no. 132.

[9] See for illustration Walter L. Strauss, *The Illustrated Bartsch*, New York, 1980, III, no. 85 (32).

[10] See Sutton, as in note 1, p. 263. For a discussion of the motif see E. de Jongh, "Vermommingen van Vrouw Wereld in de 17de eeuw," *Album Amicorum J. G. van Gelder*, The Hague, 1973, pp. 198-206.

[11] Hollstein, I, no. 7, attributes the design of the Dutch version, published by Joan-Baptista Vrints, to Pieter Baltens (called Custodis). The reversed German version, published by DC (Dominicus Custos), Baltens' son, is illustrated by De Jongh, as in note 10, fig. 2. Both the De Bry and Baltens engravings of *Vrouw Wereld* are discussed by De Jongh, as in note 10, pp. 199-200.

[12] For these various figures and staffage as symbols of vice and lust see, among others, Sutton, as in note 1, cat. nos. 104 and 108; Keyes, as in note 2, p. 82; and *Die Sprache der Bilder*, ex. cat. Herzog Anton Ulrich-Museum, Brunswick, 1978, cat. no. 8.

[13] De Jongh, as in note 1, cat. no. 72. In the same entry De Jongh used a later edition of De Bry's *Superbia* to illustrate the possibility of moralistic intent behind a number of Vinckboons's details, including the peacock pie.

[14] See also Sutton, as in note 1, cat. no. 121.

IDENTIFICATION OF FIGURES

Fig. 1.   Esaias van de Velde, *Garden Party Before a Palace*, 1614, Mauritshuis, The Hague.

Fig. 2.   After David Vinckboons, *Garden Party*, Statens Museum for Kunst, Copenhagen.

Fig. 3.   Jacob Matham, after Sebastiaen Vrancx, *Lazarus Starving While the Rich Man Feasts*, 1606.

Fig. 4.   Johann Theodor de Bry, *Superbia*, 1596.

Fig. 5.   After Pieter Baltens, *The Dance Around the World*.

Fig. 6.   David Vinckboons, *Garden Party*, Rijksmuseum, Amsterdam.

NEW VISTAS ON NETHERLANDIC LANDSCAPE AND THE NATURAL WORLD

Anne W. Lowenthal
New York

The subject of this session has recently inspired two important exhibitions: one called "Dutch Landscape, The Early Years," at the London National Gallery in 1986, investigated pioneer figures in Haarlem and Amsterdam in the first half of the seventeenth century. An even more ambitious exhibition, "Masters of 17th-century Dutch Landscape Painting," could be seen at the Rijksmuseum in Amsterdam in the fall of 1987, then at the Boston Museum of Fine Arts, and finally at the Philadelphia Museum of Art. Each exhibition was accompanied by a hefty catalogue with scholarly essays, and symposia offered further opportunities to assess the material.[1] Thus, the genre of landscape has taken its turn in the spotlight, and we have scrutinized it from present critical perspectives. I believe the most useful role I can serve here is to review some of the ideas that have emerged from these discussions, providing a context, *ex post facto*, for the two papers just presented. The emphasis will be on seventeenth-century Dutch landscape, although, of course, strictly speaking the topic extends back two centuries and down to the Southern Netherlands as well.

We continue to follow the old paths into Netherlandish art, and specifically, here, Netherlandish landscape, by tracing influence from artist to artist, tracking down sources, and outlining stylistic development. But while such issues remain important, for the most part they have lately yielded to another one – interpretation. And the question of how to interpret images has been rephrased. Can we rid ourselves of twentieth-century baggage and reconstruct sixteenth- and seventeenth-century experience? Can we understand how images were perceived in their own time?

For twenty years now, ever since Eddy de Jongh published a little book called *Zinne- en minnebeelden in de schilderkunst van de 17de eeuw*, we have been trying to understand the relationship between texts and images in Dutch art.[2] In that book, De Jongh illustrated an emblem from Jan Hermanszoon Krul's *Minnebeelden*, of 1634, and found in it a key to understanding such paintings as Vermeer's *Letter* in the Rijksmuseum.[3] The lemma reads "Though you are far away, never out of my heart," and the text continues, "The boundless sea, with waves that disappear, my loving heart does sail 'twixt hope and fear. Love is like a sea, a lover like a ship," and so on. Thus, De Jongh reasoned, the seascape on the wall behind the lady and her maid is not simply a fortuitous household item but is a clue to the contents of the letter – a love letter – and consequently to the meaning of the painting. Thus, De Jongh argued for what we might call a one-to-one connection between a text, the poem – in other cases an inscription on a print – and a textless image, a painting. Although he was not the first to interpret pictures in this way, he was the most articulate and persuasive spokesman for the approach, and he opened the floodgates. As if trying to regulate them, De Jongh became increasingly cautious in his own work, and he remains so today. In a Boston lecture, "Mountains in the Lowlands," he recently questioned whether it was possible to pin down meaning in Dutch depictions of mountains, given the vast range of literary and visual "associations" that play around them. For example, if we compare Aelbert Cuyp's *Landscape with a Rider and Peasants* (The Marquess of Bute, on loan to the National Museum of Wales, Cardiff)[4] with Jacob van Ruisdael's *Waterfall with a Castle and a Hut* (Cambridge, Mass., Fogg Art Museum, Harvard University),[5] we discover Italianate and Scandinavian landscapes, the former with gentle peaks veiled in a golden haze, the latter with brooding crags. Do these different types carry definable meanings?

Having opened a Pandora's box, De Jongh now finds hope of valid interpretation only in rigorously controlled method: attention to all meaningful elements within a picture, careful documentation of sources, a tight relationship between visual motif and putative source, cohesion among various elements within the picture, and so on.[6]

In a catalogue essay called "Toward a Scriptural Reading of Seventeenth-Century Dutch Landscape Paintings," Josua Bruyn has emerged as De Jongh's most controversial current follower. Bruyn argues that one can "read" a given landscape painting by making connections between its important motifs and textual sources. Thus, he argues, Rembrandt's *Landscape with a Stone Bridge* (Amsterdam, Rijksmuseum),[7] for example, would have been recognized as a visual metaphor for the pilgrimage of life. The main motifs are a carriage pausing at an inn in the shadows, at left; in the middleground, directly illuminated by the sun, a lone traveler with a staff over his shoulder approaching a bridge; and a fence, several old trees, and a church at right. Using scriptural and other sources, Bruyn concludes, "Therefore, whosoever should bypass the sinful tavern, the picture implies, and reach death by way of Christ's bridge, is assured arrival at the church visible to the extreme right; it must be supposed that the latter means salvation, as in De Gheyn II, van Goyen, and so many others."[8]

At the other end of the spectrum from De Jongh's and Bruyn's analytical method lies an effort to discover essential meaning in the aesthetic, expressive character of Dutch landscapes. In a lecture on Rembrandt as landscapist, David Freedberg found a key to understanding in Constantijn Huygens' poetry.[9] Comparing works like the *Ice Scene near Farm Cottages* (Cassel, Staatliche Kunstsammlungen),[10] and a drawing of a *Sunny Landscape with a Farmhouse* (Amsterdam, Rijksprentenkabinet) with Huygens' poems, Freedberg found in both the visual and the verbal a similar urgency, directness, and earthiness, objective correlatives for the rugged strength of nature herself.

Seymour Slive pleads for a similar response to the landscapes of Jacob Ruisdael, such as his *Landscape with a Stone Bridge* (Philadelphia Museum of Art). Interestingly, several elements of Rembrandt's *Landscape with a Stone Bridge* are repeated there: a solitary traveler traversing a bridge, having passed what appears to be a shrine, and heading toward a church spire in the distance. Even if we can determine that the meaning of these motifs is the same in both cases, the expressive effects - and thus the works of art as wholes - are worlds apart. And so, Slive argues, a simple reading of motifs - bridges, travelers, churches - sells them short. Only when we vicariously move through these landscapes, immersing ourselves in their motifs and their moods, do we do justice to their haunting power.

Even Ruisdael's *Jewish Cemetery* (Detroit Institute of Arts)[11] conveys its conspicuously symbolic message of death and rebirth not only by means of fallen trees and saplings, tombstones, ruins, and a rainbow, but also with evocative contrasts of dark and light, a palette rich in earth tones, and dynamic pictorial rhythms. Freedberg and Slive did not seek to limit artistic import to the purely aesthetic, but rather to redress an imbalance they believed had resulted from overly analytical interpretations.

Let us now knit this session into the context of these ideas. In discussing an outdoor merry company, a seascape, and a still life, our speakers focused only tangentially on landscape, but they did address problems of interpretation, of central interest to us here.

Kahren Arbitman bases her interpretation of Esaias van de Velde's outdoor garden party on his choice of sources. She argues that when Esaias adopted a visual motif, the meaning it had carried in its earlier context came with it. Thus, the feasting company is not simply a group of privileged Dutch folk making merry. Van de Velde's dependence on such moralizing prints as Matham's *Lazarus and the Rich Man*, where didacticism is explicit, turns it into a warning against indulgence. That warning is underscored by the prominent presence of the woman with the fan - a reminder of Superbia.

Arbitman's approach is close to that of Bruyn. She reads the painting by setting up equations between individual motifs and meanings these same motifs had carried in other contexts. This approach is workable if one can integrate such equations into a coherent conception of the work of art as a whole. Arbitman offered an important step to such an integration. I find sufficient congruence between the sources she adduces and the painting in question for the connections she draws to be persuasive. I should add that her view that naturalism like that of Esaias is loaded with implication beyond appearance now seems indisputable.

We can move beyond Arbitman's iconographic analysis to pose other questions about the painting. What does the young servant washing glasses at right contribute to the meaning? Is there a pointed comment here about virtue in the servant class? Might he signify cleansing, thus purification – an antidote to the dissipation at left? The metaphor of water as spiritual purge figures in the emblematic literature, and even on the narrative level that makes sense.[12] And returning to our landscape theme, might the tall cypresses be reminders of mortality? Since pre-Christian times they have been associated with death, because of their dark foliage and their failure to spring up from the roots once cut.[13] An even larger question: Why is the scene set outdoors? What does the worldly setting contribute to meaning?

There remains the question of how seventeenth-century viewers would have experienced the picture. Assuming they recognized the meanings we have uncovered, how did they react? Did they in effect decipher the picture, reading from one motif to another? Or was their response more ruminative, more expansive?

I would argue for the latter reaction. Esaias here uses a syntax common in Dutch painting, embedding a moral plea within a dazzling material seduction. He appeals to his viewers' delight in sensory pleasure – delicious food and drink, fine tableware, and elegant clothes. Indeed, he engages his viewers via the picture's visual beauty. And once he has our attention, once we savor the colors, the juicy painting technique, once we imagine enjoying the pleasures he spreads before us, he appeals to conscience. Beneath the surface lie the dangers of Pride, Gluttony, and Lust – but, as I have suggested, there is an alternative. We can wash our hands of such seductions. Significantly, the artist does not preach, and he does not take sides. He is more clever than that, leaving the choice to us.[14]

Typically, the appeal to conscience is *sotto voce*, yet that was enough to remind the viewer of the consequences of indulgence or poor judgement. The depiction of sensuous revelry made a vigorous assault on the senses, appealing to the passions, which resided in the second soul, according to the then current tripartite conception inherited from the ancients. But once the passions were engaged, the effects of the work of art could reach the highest soul, the seat of understanding and will, there to instruct through reason.[15] And the voice of reason could whisper.

Lawrence Goedde's paper directly addresses the question of how earlier viewers perceived meaning, offering an interpretive tool that is consistent with the kind of reflective approach I have just described.[16] Goedde has shown that seventeenth-century artists and writers exploited the rhetorical device of *ekphrasis* for what he calls "engaged empathic viewing," for entering a painting's world. *Ekphrasis* offers another means of "reading," an image, leading the viewer closely through a vicarious experience of what is depicted. Such a reading might involve discovering a motif laden with overtones, like Van de Velde's lady with a fan, or Porcellis's overcanvassed vessel, or Bosschaert's worm-eaten leaves. But musings on individual motifs were absorbed within an expansive reaction with room for varied responses and moments of reflection.

In effect, Goedde presents a rhetorical basis for the kind of engaged viewing I have described as consistent with seventeenth-century principles. The artist seizes the viewer's attention, *tot lering en vermaak*, for instruction and pleasure. Oudaen's poetry makes that clear. As Arbitman, Goedde, and many others agree, similar didactic intent pervades images.[17] But, as Goedde puts it, "moral lessons were regarded as implicit and accessible, not in a process of reading detail by detail as though the image were a hieroglyphic pattern of symbolic units, but as an organic part of the subject and expression of the picture."

At a remove of three centuries, we have of course lost a natural, organic connection with these images, and it is that to which we aspire. We cannot hope to track precisely an earlier viewer's experience. But we can hope to map the range of possibilities open to him. In search of these possibilities, we need to approach works of art expansively, integrating the emblematic and the aesthetic, the didactic and the sensuous, doing our best to place images in the cultural matrix that produced them.

Each of the approaches under review here is admirable in its own way; each opens up a vista on Netherlandish landscape. The vistas might seem mutually exclusive, but let us hope that taken together in successful measure, they will converge on a view of the era that intrigues us all.

NOTES

[1] Christopher Brown, *Dutch Landscape, The Early Years: Haarlem and Amsterdam* 1590-1650, London, The National Gallery, September 3 to November 23, 1986. Peter C. Sutton, *Masters of 17th-Century Dutch Landscape Painting*, Rijksmuseum, Amsterdam, October 2, 1987, to January 3, 1988; Museum of Fine Arts, Boston, February 3 to May 1, 1988; and Philadelphia Museum of Art, June 5 to July 31, 1988. Symposia were held in Boston on March 12, 1988, and in Philadelphia on June 11, 1988. Seymour Slive reviewed *Masters of 17th-Century Dutch Landscape Painting* in *The Burlington Magazine* 130 (1988): 395-398.

[2] De Jongh's book was published by the Nederlandse Stichting Openbaar Kunstbezit and Openbaar Kunstbezit in Vlaanderen in collaboration with the Prins Bernhard Fonds, 1967.

[3] Ibid., 49-55.

[4] *Masters of 17th-Century Dutch Landscape Painting*, 302-304, cat. no. 25.

[5] Ibid., 450-451, cat. no. 85.

[6] De Jongh's lecture on "Possibilities and Limits of Interpretation of Genre," given in connection with the exhibition "Masters of Seventeenth-Century Dutch Genre Painting," at the Philadelphia Museum of Art, March 24, 1984, set forth these principles.

[7] *Masters of 17th-Century Dutch Landscape Painting*, 426-429, cat. no. 76.

[8] Ibid., 97.

[9] "Rembrandt as a Landscapist: Inventor Novissimus in Depingendo Rure," given in Boston on March 12, 1988.

[10] *Masters of 17th-Century Dutch Landscape Painting*, 429-432, cat. no. 77.

[11] Ibid., 452-456, cat. no. 86.

[12] See, for example, E. de Jongh, et al., *Tot Lering en Vermaak*, Amsterdam, Rijksmuseum, 1976, p. 195, fig. 48a, illustrating an emblem from Bartholomeus Hulsius, *Emblemata sacra, dat is, eenighe geestelicke sinnebeelden. . .* , 1631.

[13] George Ferguson, *Signs and Symbols in Christian Art* (New York: Oxford University Press, A Galaxy Book, 1966), 30.

[14] I have advanced an argument for this structure in other paintings also. See Anne W. Lowenthal, "The Debate on Symbol and Meaning in Dutch Seventeenth-Century Art: Response to Peter Hecht," *Simiolus* 16 (1986): 188-190; and idem, "Lot and His Daughters as Moral Dilemma," *The Age of Rembrandt: Studies in Seventeenth-Century Dutch Painting*, ed. Roland E. Fleischer and Susan Scott Munshower, Papers in Art History from The Pennsylvania State University, 3 (1988): 12-27.

[15] For further discussion of this conception, see H. James Jensen, *The Muses' Concord: Literature, Music, and the Visual Arts in the Baroque Age* (Bloomington: Indiana University Press, 1976), 15, 66-68.

[16] See Lawrence O. Goedde, "A Litte World Made Cunningly: Dutch Still Life and Ekphrasis," in *Still Lifes of the Golden Age: Northern European Paintings from the Heinz Family Collection*, Washington, National Gallery of Art, 1989, 35-44, wherein

Goedde develops the same thesis presented in the paper under discussion.

[17] For more on didacticism in Netherlandish art, see Anne W. Lowenthal, *Joachim Wtewael and Dutch Mannerism* (Doornspijk: Davaco Publishers, 1986), 18-19, 56-61.

A FEMALE FAUST: *MARIEKEN VAN NIEUMEGEN*

Johanna C. Prins
Columbia University, New York

Marieken van Nieumegen[1] is a fascinating play, which lends itself to approaches from a wide variety of disciplines. It has a clearly defined historical background, it mirrors many of the religious and philosophical convictions of its time, and it uses various poetical devices to present its story. Although there have been plenty of discussions and disagreements about several points (textual, formal, and others), this article refers to them only as they turn up on the way. I merely wish to share with readers who are not necessarily medievalists some of the many interesting aspects of this play.

First, briefly, an outline of the plot: Marieken is a young woman who lives with her uncle, Sir Gijsbrecht, two or three miles outside Nieumegen. As the play starts the uncle sends her to town for shopping. He urges her to stay overnight at her aunt's house rather than return after sundown "Want die boeverie der wereld is menigerhande" 'There are lots of scoundrels in this world' (44). But when Marieken turns up at the aunt's house she is greeted with abuse and slanderous accusations, and refused hospitality. In fear and despair she leaves town and prepares to spend the night under a hedge, calling for sympathy, whether from God or the devil; she does not care which.

Of course the devil jumps at this invitation. He appears in the guise of a one-eyed young man named Moenen and offers friendship, help and protection. If she will accept his friendship he will teach her the seven *Artes Liberales*. He also offers wealth, but Marieken is much more interested in learning. The invitation "Oft gi met mi verzamen wilt in jonsten" 'If you will become close friends with me' (195) has clear erotic implications, but the sexual element of the relationship is not stressed except in Marieken's confession. Moenen's only condition is that she must no longer cross herself and must give up her name because "Marieken es voor mi een onbekwaam woord" 'Marieken is for me an uncomfortable word' (274). But for Marieken this is incomprehensible and out of the question, and they finally settle on the compromise that she will retain the first letter of her name, and now be called Emmeken.

Emmeken and Moenen travel to Antwerp, and settle in a tavern. Their journey takes about a week, in which time Moenen teaches Marieken the Liberal Arts and all the languages of the world, but this is not shown on stage. In Antwerp Marieken attracts attention by her beauty and demonstrations of her learning, including recitation of a *Refrein* in the fashion of the Chambers of

Rhetoric. At the margins of the crowd Moenen stirs up drunken fights and homicides, thus collecting a harvest of souls for Hell.

Marieken is aware of the evil done for her sake, and suspects Moenen's identity, but she feels it is too late to stop, and also enjoys the pleasures of their life. After about six years she persuades Moenen to return to Nieumegen to visit her uncle and friends. They arrive on *ommegankdag* (day of the procession of Our Lady) and, much to Moenen's chagrin, witness a performance of *The Play of Masscheroen*. In this play Masscheroen, Defender of Lucifer, complains to God that His divine justice is much more lenient towards humans than towards the fallen angels. As God responds to Masscheroen's long list of human sins the Virgin Mary delivers a fervent plea for grace and mercy. Just as Moenen had feared, the play awakens Emmeken's remorse and urge to repent. In a rage, he picks her up, flies high up in the sky and drops her to the ground. Miraculously, she survives and is found by her uncle, who was in the audience and manages to chase Moenen away with a conjuring prayer.

Marieken and her uncle now go on a long journey searching for the proper penitence. The bishop of Cologne feels unqualified to deal with such horrendous sins, but finally the Pope commands her to have three iron rings attached around her neck and wrists. When the rings will fall off she will be forgiven. She withdraws in a convent of Penitents in Maastricht, and after twenty-four years an angel appears in a dream and takes off the rings. An Epilogue notes that she died about two years later, that the rings were hung above her grave and can still be seen there. (Unfortunately for the modern reader, this convent no longer exists.)

So far the story of *Marieken van Nieumegen*. The text as we have it appeared in an early printed book, probably from 1516. It is mostly dramatic in form, interspersed with short pieces of narrative prose. There is also an English version in prose only, dating from about the same time. The relationship and interdependence of these two texts have, of course, aroused a great deal of discussion, but we will not discuss that here.

As I mentioned, this story is connected in many ways with the world of its time and with ours. Let me start with the historical context. The Prologue sets the events in a very specific timeframe: "At the time when Duke Arend of Gelre was imprisoned at Grave by his son Duke Adolf and his companions, there lived, three miles from Nieumegen, a devout priest named Sir Gijsbrecht, and with him lived a pretty young maiden named Marieken, his sister's daughter, whose mother had died. This forementioned maiden kept house for her uncle, faithfully and dutifully taking care of his needs." Arend or Arnold van Egmond, Duke of Gelre and Count of

Zutphen (1410-1473) had some disagreement with the Burgundians. Philip the Good tried to appoint Arnold's son Adolf as *Ruwaert*, 'governor,' and Adolf imprisoned his father Arnold and forced him to abdicate (in 1465). But later (in 1471) Charles the Bold restored Arnold in function and imprisoned Adolf.

This is not merely a casual historical remark, which incidentally offers some basis for dating the play, but politics also play an important role in the plot. Sir Gijsbrecht's concern for Marieken's safety is partly based on the discord and unrest in the area, and when Marieken arrives at her aunt's house the latter is in a particularly bad mood because she has been quarreling with some neighbors about the political events of the day. In fact, the aunt's political fervor is so violent that it makes her also an easy target for the Devil. While Marieken and Moenen are traveling to Antwerp the plot briefly shifts back to Nieumegen and Sir Gijsbrecht's concern over his niece's failure to return. When he visits his sister to inquire after Marieken, the aunt merely repeats the slanderous remarks that she made to the niece before. After Sir Gijsbrecht's visit, news arrives of the turning of political events (in 1471), which has freed the old Duke and imprisoned the young one. This unleashes a great fury in the aunt and she declares herself ready to call on all devils for help. Immediately, the devil appears, encourages her rage until she cuts her own throat, and carries off her soul to Hell. We note that the aunt's appeal to the Devil, in itself, is not so different from Marieken's, earlier in the play, but the results are very different, as we will see later.

Not only history and politics, but also the details of daily life in the play are true and realistic. Moenen promises to teach Marieken the seven Liberal Arts: "rhetorijke, muzijke,/ Logica, grammatica ende geometrie,/ Aristmatica ende alkenie." "Alkenie" is probably Alchemy, taking the place of the traditional Astronomy, but this may be a deliberate confusion for comic effect. Marieken would also like to learn "Nigremantie," noting that her uncle practices that with great effect, but Moenen advises her that this is an art with more risks than profits, and she yields readily. He is understandably reluctant to teach her a skill that would give her control over him.

The Rhetorical element in the play is often seen as one of its flaws, although this prejudice is beginning to disappear. Besides the *Refrein* recited by Marieken (discussed extensively by Van Dijk, 31-2) there are several "embedded poems," passages where the rhyme scheme changes from the simple rhymed couplets. As far as I know it has not been noted that especially the two embedded rondels are extremely effective in their context. In the confrontation between Sir Gijsbrecht and his sister the repetition of the line "Eilazen, zuster, gi beguut mi" 'Alas, sister, you treat me like a fool' (348, 351, 354) becomes a litany expressing his distress in the face of her ravings. The second rondel is a dialogue between Moenen and Marieken, after the latter has expressed her longing to return to Nieumegen. Here the repeated line is Moenen's "Emmeken, uw bede ontzegge ik u no" 'Emmeken, your request I will not deny' (648, 651, 654), and the effect is highly ironic. Immediately after this emphatic show of compliance he explodes into an aside cursing Sir Gijsbrecht, who has protected Marieken and curtailed Moenen's evil by his prayers.

As a depiction of common daily life, the scene in the Antwerp tavern is completely natural and realistic, with two young men first discussing Marieken's good looks and, so to speak, already reserving her for their own use; later they are suitably impressed by her intellectual accomplishments.

Interesting also is the performance of the "wagon-play" of Masscheroen. Wagon-plays were fairly common in England, but not well known in the Low Countries. Even rarer, in medieval drama, is the phenomenon of a play within a play. *The Play of Masscheroen* itself is known from Jacob van Maerlant's *Merlijn* and from a fourteenth century poem (Debaene, 16).

Perhaps the most attractive and realistic element of the play is the character of Marieken. Female protagonists are not very common in medieval literature, and Marieken is an attractive heroine to identify with: bright but naive in the beginning, gregarious and a bit of a show-off in the tavern scenes, and sincerely and deeply remorseful after seeing the play. In the Faust tradition she seems to be the only woman. This has been connected with the emancipation of Dutch women and their active part in the intellectual life of the sixteenth century. Lucy de Bruyn, in her fascinating *Women and the Devil in Sixteenth-Century Literature* quotes a report by a Venetian ambassador on "the freedom women at Antwerp enjoyed and that much of their time was spent in dancing, singing, the playing of musical instruments, in addition to their complete management of domestic affairs without their husbands' control" (5). In our text Marieken is the one who settles the bill at the tavern when she and Moenen return to Nieumegen.

On the one hand, then, Marieken represents a reality of social conditions in the Low Countries at the time, on the other hand she provides an especially close connection with the Virgin Mary, who plays an important part in *Masscheroen* and in human history.

Thematically, *The Play of Masscheroen* is the heart of *Marieken van Nieumegen* because its subject is God's grace and man's redemption. The complaint of Masscheroen about God's lenience towards mankind serves to emphasize His grace above all. In spite of the innumerable examples of human misbehavior listed by Masscheroen, Mary will continue to remind Christ of his own redemptive incarnation through her body, and Christ will promise that those who repent will be forgiven. The crucial role of Mary as mediator between God and man is reflected in the many collections of miracles of Mary (of which the legend of *Beatrijs* is one of the highlights), and in the increasing cult of Mary, especially from the twelfth century onward. As Moenen remarks when he asks Marieken to change her name:

> Marieken es voor mi een onbekwaam woord;
> Bi eender Marieen ik ende mijn gezelschap zulk grief hebben,
> Dat wi nemmermeer dien naam en zullen lief hebben.
> (274-6)
>
> Marieken is for me an uncomfortable word;
> Through one Mary I and my kind have such grief,
> That we will never like that name again.

He is referring here to God's words to the serpent in Genesis 3:15, "And I will put enmity between thee and the woman, and between thy seed and her seed; it shall bruise thy head, and thou shalt bruise his heel." Since the early churchfathers Origen and Irenaeus this prophesy was seen as referring to Christ who, as a second Adam, came to undo the damage done by the Serpent to mankind. Parallel to this Mary became the second Eve, undoing the damage done by the disobedience of the first Eve.

The final difference between man and the fallen angels, the subject of Masscheroen's complaint, is that the angels sinned of their own accord, while mankind was seduced by the Serpent. But man's fall is inextricably linked with Christ's redemption. As long as these two events remain connected, the general world view is essentially un-tragic. On this point a comparison between *Marieken* and Marlowe's *Doctor Faustus* is revealing. In both plays devils appear on stage as real people, and in both plays human beings make a pact with the devil.

The belief in witches and devils exists throughout the Middle Ages, and increases in the sixteenth century. As De Bruyn notes in her book on *Women and the Devil in Sixteenth-Century Literature*, this is a time of great upheaval both in learning and in religion, and "the general decline in religious fervour and stability gave rise to greater fear and superstition, which, at times, took on alarming proportions" (3). Attacking witchcraft, as was done by a papal bull by Innocent VIII in 1484, and by the publication of the so-called *Malleus Maleficarum 'The Witch Hammer*,' of Hendrik Kramer and Jacob Sprenger in 1487, in many ways only made the problem more serious by acknowledging its existence and proportions. The two plays, *Marieken van Nieumegen* (1516) and *Doctor Faustus* (circa 1590), are at the opposite ends of the tumultuous sixteenth century, and comparison shows how essentially medieval Marieken is next to the Renaissance Faustus.

Watching the play of Masscheroen instantly awakens in her the recognition of her sin and the need to repent. So instantly, in fact, that we know that she has always retained, however tenuously, a connection with her faith just as she has retained the M of Mary in her name. Despair briefly appears when she fears that she is doomed forever, but these thoughts are briskly dismissed by the uncle's words "'t En es niemand verloren dan die hem verloren geeft" 'No-one is lost except who give himself up for lost' (952). Faustus' tragic failure, on the other hand, is not so much his sinful life or his pact with the devil, as his failure to believe in the possibility of forgiveness and mercy.

Yet for all its medieval quality *Marieken van Nieumegen* can also be seen to reflect, more generally, the history of salvation, as Hans van Dijk shows in his article in *Dutch Crossings* of April 1984. Listing the many connections between Marieken and the Virgin Mary - the name, Moenen's oblique reference to Mary, the aunt's casting doubts upon Mariken's virginity - Van Dijk notes that "Mariken's behaviour links her not only with Mary but also with Eve. Does not Mariken's first conversation with Moenen remind us of Eve's conversation with the serpent? In both cases a woman is tempted by the devil and in both cases the matter is settled by the promise of knowledge. In this way Mariken's fall evokes the Fall from paradise. Similarly, just as Eve brought misery on mankind, so Mariken brings misery on the people of Antwerp" (33). In this way, Van Dijk argues, the crucial events in Marieken's life are, in the play, connected with "turning points in the history of God's intervention in man's life on earth." Her fall echoes the fall of man, her conversion is caused by Mary's words in *The Play of Masscheroen* in which she evokes Christ's redemption. But as Marieken represents one part of mankind, so the gruesome end of the aunt shows us the other possibility for mankind, and serves as a warning to those who do not repent.

Although Van Dijk presents his argument with great caution and urges further study, I personally find him very convincing, and I would like to conclude with one more quotation: "For mankind this [i.e., Marieken's final redemption after her long penance] is an eschatological promise which gives hope to those who follow Mariken's example. Seen in this light, *Mariken van Nieumeghen* is the story of the salvation of a particular human being, but it is also about the possible salvation of any human being, and perhaps even about the future salvation of mankind" (34).

NOTES

[1] The most easily available text is Debaene's edition. All quotations are from this edition, and English translations are my own. Debaene has adjusted the spelling somewhat, and this has caused some discrepancies between quotations from his edition

and those in Van Dijk's article. The play was translated into English by Ayres. Further bibliographical references can be found in Debaene's edition and in Van Dijk's article.

WORKS CITED

Ayres, Harry Morgan. *A Marvelous History of Mary of Nimmegen* . . . translated from the Middle Dutch by --, with an introduction by Adriaan J. Barnouw. Den Haag: Nijhoff, 1924.

Bruyn, Lucy de. *Women and the Devil in Sixteenth-Century Literature*. Tisbury: The Compton Press, 1979.

Debaene, Dr. L. ed. *Marieken van Nieumegen* ingeleid en van aantekeningen voorzien door --. Vijfde druk bezorgd door Dr. D. Coigneau. Den Haag: Nijhoff, 1980.

Dijk, Hans van. "Mariken van Nieumegen" *Dutch Crossing* 22 (April 1984): 27-37.

The Malleus Maleficarum of Heinrich Kramer and James Sprenger translated with Introduction, Bibliography and Notes by Rev. Montague Summers. (1928) New York: Dover, 1971.

MAX HAVELAAR: A ROMANTIC NOVEL FOR SOCIAL FLUIDITY

Gary L. Baker
University of Minnesota, Minneapolis

Max Havelaar, written between the 10th of September and the 13th of October, 1859, is the first literary work ever published by Eduard Douwes Dekker (Multatuli). Jacob van Lennep, a poet and editor himself, called Dekker's manuscript a masterpiece and aided in the publication of the text, which appeared in May 1860 in the J. de Ruyter publishing house. There is a large amount of secondary literature dealing with the work of Multatuli, who is regarded as one of the most important Dutch writers of the 19th century. The novel Max Havelaar: of de Koffij-veilingen der nederlandsche Handelmaatschappij is considered to be his most accomplished work. The importance accorded this work is due to its combination of expository and fictional contents as well as its unique structure. Multatuli, like few authors before or after him, struck a rare harmony between form and intention in this particular work. However, the anti-linear approach to his subject matter has sparked much discussion, some of which expresses doubt that Max Havelaar is even a novel.

Is the structure of Max Havelaar novelistic or not? This is a question that has been posed repeatedly. D.H. Lawrence maintained: "As far as composition goes, it is the greatest mess possible."[1] Peter King discusses the literary situation in the Netherlands at that time and explains that Multatuli could not have used any Dutch novel from the 18th or 19th centuries as a model. He goes on to interpret the work as an "anti-novel."[2] Garmt Stuiveling, in an article entitled "De inzet van de moderne literatuur in Nederland," considered the text's structure to be unique and the most important aspect of its contribution to modernity in Dutch literature.[3] Even Multatuli himself felt it necessary to address the form of his work within the text itself: "Ik vraag geene verschooning voor den vorm van mijn boek, . . . die vorm kwam mij geschikt voor ter bereiking van mijn doel."[4] The author explicitly tells the reader that he chose a form to suit his intention and vice versa. An investigation of both form and content will demonstrate in what manner Max Havelaar is indeed novelistic and how its form is intended to reach a certain social, political, and historical goal.

Certainly, a novel with such a structure had never before appeared in Dutch literature. Analyzing the composition of this text, one believes to perceive an organizationally impaired product. The reader must practically become an archivist in order to read Havelaar without frustration. One must peruse its contents and follow the stories as must the family Droogstoppel, Rosemeijer, and the literary mediator Ernest Stern. The reader is invited into the book to have dessert at the Rosemeijers, "die in suiker doen," (p. 22) or the Havelaars, to hear the stories being read by Stern or told by Havelaar. S/he is often addressed and actually remains involved throughout the text. E.M. Beekman therefore evaluates the book as a type of letter - a "praatbrief" - which means the recipients of the story are addressed directly.[5] This collection of texts is a presentation to the reader from which the recipient may take as s/he wishes: ". . .het is eene staalkaart; bepaal uw keuze, ..." (p. 172). Thus, the reader becomes a text-participant because subjective engagement of and intellectual reflection on the text is an essential task induced by form and style.

The novel's literary composition and its intrinsic desire to communicate with the reader invite its interpretation in light of German romanticism. One of the leading thinkers and writers of this literary epoch, Friedrich Schlegel, wrote: "Which travelogue, which collection of letters, which autobiography would not be a better novel for one who reads them in the romantic sense. . . ."[6] Reading in the romantic sense requires a type of subjective participation of the reader where s/he must ontologically transform the text into a personal story. Moreover, the text must be presented such that it may become part of the recipient's personal experience and thereby part of her/his consciousness. *Havelaar* lends itself well to this type of reading. The romantic aspect of *Havelaar* permeates the interaction of form, content, and reader.

German romanticism gave rise to the notion that the novel was the genre with the greatest possibilities for poetic and progressive materials, because it could include a constellation of several literary forms: "Indeed, I can scarcely visualize a novel but as a mixture of storytelling, song, and other forms."[7] Various forms within a form make it possible for a work to be read over and over again and always offer something new. Since *Max Havelaar* consists of letters, documents, poems, stories, anecdotes, fairy tales, essays, and notes, it presents an appearance of incompleteness. In Schlegel's famous fragment number 116 he states: "The romantic kind of poetry is still in the state of becoming; that in fact, is its real essence: that it should forever be becoming and never be perfected."[8] No form can offer more subjective freedom of interpretation and remain incompletely complete than a collection of fragments. Because the contents are preserved in their fragmentary form they can be subjectively completed with each new reading. Such a completion of the text requires the reader to become subjectively involved in its contents. In *Max Havelaar* the reader is called upon to employ her/his intellectual and emotional faculties so that the story becomes an intricate part of the reader's subjective makeup. Since romantic poetry, as Schlegel writes, "is a progressive, universal poetry,"[9] both the romantic notion of engaging the text and progressivity are valid for *Max Havelaar*. Progressive, in the romantic sense, means perpetually maturing, never taking solid form, and thus never congealing. This romantic progressivity pertains to the thematic level of the reader/text relationship as well as to the formal level of the text itself. For *Max Havelaar* it implies being historically based while remaining ahistorical, set in definitive time while being timeless. As D.H. Lawrence stated: "When there are no more Drystubbles, no more Governor-Generals or Slimerings, then *Max Havelaar* will be out of date."[10] Which novel then could be more romantic than one consisting of fragment upon fragment, including the diversity of many genres and human discourses? In this sense, *Max Havelaar* is a prime example of a romantic, i.e., novelistic piece of literature.

It is clear from the beginning of *Havelaar* that Dekker knew works by the German author Gotthold Ephraim Lessing. In the "Onuitgegeven Tooneelspel" (p. 2), one finds the situation in which a man named Lothario is unjustly accused of murder but proven beyond all doubt to be innocent. During the trial the judge repeats continuously: "Gij moet hangen" (p. 2). The alleged murder victim arrives in the courtroom to prove Lothario's innocence and give him an excellent character reference besides. Lothario says: "Gij hoort het, regter, ze zegt dat ik een braaf mensch ben, . . ." (p. 2). The judge then sentences him on other grounds: ". . . , hij moet hangen. Hij is schuldig aan eigenwaan" (p. 2). This ultra-rationalistic exercise of power represented in the command "You must hang" invariably echoes the dogmatic judgement of the patriach against Nathan in Lessing's "dramatic poem," *Nathan the Wise*: "All one! The Jew must burn."[11] In *Nathan the Wise*, as in Multatuli's piece, Nathan and Lothario are not only innocent, but portrayed as intrinsically virtuous human beings as well. However, the petrified system - be it religious or judicial - is not flexible enough to recognize this fact. The "unpublished play" actually defines the underlying issue of the whole *Havelaar* novel - well-intentioned individual against rationalistic and dogmatic system. Thus, while the form remains timelessly fluid, we are confronted with contents that expose social stagnation as an inflexibility disproportionate to the flexibility of the form.

The system, as portrayed in *Havelaar*, perpetuates a condition where traditional Christian values of love and human ideals become interpreted in pure economic and instrumental terms. On the one side stands Lessing's patriarch, together with Multatuli's "regter," Droogstoppel, the Reverend Wawelaar, the Governor-General, and Slijmering. They represent the petrification and solidification of middle-class Dutch society by means of religion and economics. The symbol of its congealed state is Droogstoppel's incessant repetition of his address. He has an almost psychotic propensity to affirm his identity to the reader. It is as if he fears floating from the earth's surface at any moment: "-ik ben makelaar in koffij, en woon op de LAURIERGRACHT, No 37,-" and "Ik zeg: *waarheid en gezond verstand*; daar blijf ik bij" (p. 3). This "Ik ben" and "Ik blijf" is the petrification of which we are speaking and Droogstoppel's personal defense against dreaded *dweepzucht* or *Schwärmerei*. Droogstoppel's initial criticism of Sjaalman (i.e., Havelaar in Holland after his demise), and that which activates his suspicion the most, is: "Hij wist niet hoe laat het was" (p. 13). Droogstoppel needs place, time, and nomenclature in order to feel psychologically, socially, and politically secure. Since Sjaalman does not know how late it is, wears a scarf instead of a jacket, and obviously has no money, he deserves no identity, and therefore remains an object of Droogstoppel's derision throughout the novel. For Droogstoppel, Sjaalman obviously does not belong to the right class or have the proper faith. But Sjaalman is also not stagnant.

During the initial encounter between Sjaalman and Droogstoppel the reader experiences the latter's abuse of religion: ". . . hij scheen niet in goede omstandigheden te verkeeren, en ik houd niet van arme menschen, omdat er gewoonlijk eigen schuld onder loopt, daar de Heer niet iemand verlaten zou, die hem trouw gediend had" (p. 10). Wawelaar and Droogstoppel, like Lessing's patriarch, represent the perversion of religious values in their dogmatic perceptions of them. Droogstoppel uses religion as a weapon against threatening and suspicious outsiders or anybody who does not think as he. For example, his son Frits must pay money into the church coffers for criticism of Reverend Wawelaar. That was his punishment. Droogstoppel often interrupts Stern's readings in an attempt to set him and the reader ideologically straight. During one such intervention Droogstoppel contributes his debased views on religion and economics:

> Ik sta verbaasd over Wawelaar's doorzigt in zaken. Want het is de waarheid dat ik, die stipt op de godsdienst ben, mijne zaken zie vooruitgaan van jaar tot jaar, en Busselinck & Waterman die om God noch gebod geven, zullen knoeijers blijven hun leven lang. . . . Onlangs is gebleken dat er weer dertig millioenen zuiver gewonnen zijn op den verkoop van produkten die door de heidenen geleverd zijn, en daarbij is niet eens gerekend wat ik daarop verdiend heb, . . . Is dat nu niet alsof de Heer zeide: "Ziedaar dertig millioenen ter belooning van uw geloof?" Is dat niet de vinger Gods die den booze laat arbeiden om den regtvaardige te behouden? . . . Staat er niet dáárom in de Schrift: bidt en werkt, opdat *wij* zouden bidden, en het werk laten doen door het volk dat geen 'Onze Vader' kent? (p. 183)

The real antagonist in the book is then a mentality and not Droogstoppel himself. He is merely the embodiment of it. The utter perversion of religiously based values has produced a class of people with no heart. This is the class Multatuli desires to affect and consequently change.

Other congealing aspects of society are its narrowing field of interest and instrumental judgements on areas of study. The greatest contrast between Havelaar and Droogstoppel is obvious in the latter's lack of appreciation for the cases, testimonials, and essays in Sjaalman's "vervloekte pak" (p. 182). The list of contents covers four pages and includes many humanistic and scientific subjects. Droogstoppel finds little there that interests him and only lays articles concerning coffee to the side for future reference. In this example, Multatuli has demonstrated Havelaar's universality in order to present the one-dimensional thinking of middle-class Dutch society and of the Dutch government more crassly. Multatuli shows how much the middle-class sliced away from its image of the world as Droogstoppel cuts piece after piece from Sjaalman's package. Middle-class modes of thought are much too narrow; that is one of Multatuli's most important projections. Multatuli demonstrates how the injustice in Java persists because of this home-grown mentality. He therefore begins the novel with Droogstoppel. He introduces the source of injustice and corruption in Holland while demonstrating its manifestation in the East Indies. The problems found on the islands could be at least partially solved with a loosening of the bourgeois perception of life at home. Thus, the same is valid for people like Slijmering and the Governor-General, who import such views into the Indies while exporting riches for Holland.

The configuration of the Havelaar-Sjaalman-Multatuli character is then similar to Nathan in methods of bringing about change. Like Nathan, Havelaar too is in favor of the fluidity or movement of stagnant society. The most important words of Havelaar's speech to Duclari and Verbrugge are: "Natuur is beweging . . . stilstand is de dood. Zonder beweging is geene smart, geen genot, geene aandoening" (p. 110). However, movement itself is not enough, the story and/or history must be the essential element of movement. Havelaar mentions waterfalls as being unimpressive phenomena, maintaining "Zij *zeggen* mij niets" (p. 109). Buildings speak somewhat more loudly to him because they are "bladzijden uit de geschiedenis" (p. 109). Duclari believes to detect a contradiction in Havelaar's philosphy and reminds him that waterfalls move. Havelaar retorts: "Ja, maar zonder *geschiedenis*. Zij bewegen, maar komen niet van de plaats" (p. 110). Although Havelaar is speaking about art and nature here, the social overtones cannot be denied. Both Nathan and Havelaar use stories – the opposite of a formalized education – to spur on social movement. Middle-class stagnation is indeed death – a figurative death-state in Holland, literal death in the colonies. Thus, storytelling becomes a type of education meant to keep the mind and heart open and not inculcate them to dormancy. Just as Nathan explodes religious dogmatism with his parable of the three rings, Multatuli hopes to discharge a heartless society out of its sleepy and self-contented state with his stories. This is the implicit link between form and intention (*doel*) in Multatuli's novel. In a truly romantic fashion, stories are utilized as fluidizing agents against the congealing aspects of society.

To be sure, *Max Havelaar* contains both doleful and delightful stories. One thinks here of the fairytale of the Japanese sculptor and the several ballads and poems contained in the text. The central story, of course, is the tale of Saïdjah and Adinda. But to what extent are the stories really accessible to the reader? The theme of *Havelaar* is much like the type described by Schlegel: ". . . that is romantic which presents a sentimental theme in a fantastic form."[12] "Romantic" refers to the genre itself, i.e., the novel; "fantastic" is the adjective of fantasy, meaning imaginative and original. "Sentimental," however, does not refer to the feelings aroused by human interest stories and trivial literature: "It is that which appeals to us where feeling prevails and . . . not a sensual but a spiritual feeling. The source and the soul of all these emotions is love, and the spirit of love must hover everywhere invisibly visible in romantic poetry."[13] The ultimate congealing of society is a critical lack of this type of sentimental feeling. Multatuli demonstrates this by juxtaposing the marriages of the Havelaars and the Droogstoppels. The former is clearly filled with love, and therefore an exception, while the latter is an economic convenience, and thus the rule. (As an essay in Sjaalman's package - "Over de prostitutie in het huwelijk" (p. 25) - insinuates, even marriage vows can be economically perverted.) An initial and natural feeling of love provides access to the progressivity inherent in the stories. Therefore, a willingness to progressivity is that which the reader must bring to the text. That which s/he fetches out of the novel are then progressive messages. The elder Droogstoppels are surrounded by this sentimental feeling but do not possess it themselves. Their son Frits, for example, digs about in the package for poetry. At one point he finds a sad poetic story and reads it for Luise Rosemeijer, causing her to cry (pp. 16-22). Their daughter Marie is also affected by the package; she refuses to read the Bible at breakfast one morning (pp. 180-181). And the fact that Stern is German, composes romantic poems - a textual connection to German romanticism - and is in charge of presenting pieces from the package is certainly no coincidence. It is also important to learn from Droogstoppel that Ernest Stern "schwärmt" (p. 22).

Droogstoppel's greatest and longest lament about the effect of Sjaalman's package on his family comes just before the reading of the tale of Saïdjah and Adinda. Droogstoppel is not interested in hearing it for the same reason Luise Rosemeijer wishes to, because "er van liefde zou inkomen" (p. 180). The author/mediator explains that this particular story is not for everybody and hopes: ". . . dat, wie gezegend is met blankheid en de daarmeê zamengaande beschaving, edelmoedigheid, handels- en Godskennis, deugd; -die blanke hoedanigheden zoude kunnen aanwenden op andere wijze dan tot nog toe ondervonden is door wie minder gezegend waren in huidskleur en zielevoortreffelijkheid" (pp. 178-179). All racist overtones aside, Multatuli is expressing hope that the sentimental feelings discussed above are somewhere at hand amongst his readers. With the introduction of this tale into the finer circles of Dutch society we experience the commencement of Multatuli's self-proposed errand, i.e., telling the story of oppression and exploitation of the Javanese people to those who could halt it but choose to perpetuate it. Thus, Multatuli demonstrated how, through a novelistic form of storytelling, sentimental feeling can be probed to fluidize petrified and stagnant aspects of society.

NOTES

[1] D.H. Lawrence, introd. *Max Havelaar: Or the Coffee Auctions of the Dutch Trading Company*, by Multatuli, trans. Roy Edwards, afterword E.M. Beekman (Amherst: University of Massachusetts Press, 1982), p. 12.

[2] Peter King. *Multatuli*. Twayne's World Author Series 219 (New York: Twayne Publishers Inc., 1972), p. 42.

[3] Garmt Stuiveling. "De inzet van de moderne literatuur in Nederland," *Levenslang* (Amsterdam: Huis aan de Drie Grachten, 1982), pp. 67-68.

[4] Multatuli. *Max Havelaar: of de Koffij-veilingen der nederlandsche Handelmaatschappij*, ed. G. Stuiveling (Amsterdam: G.A. van Oorschot, n.d.), p. 236. All further references to this work occur in the text.

[5] *Max Havelaar: Or the Coffee Auctions of the Dutch Trading Company*, p. 373.

[6] Friedrich Schlegel. "Dialogue on Poetry," trans. Ernst Behler and Roman Struc, *German Romantic Criticism*, The German Library 21 (New York: Continuum Publishing Company, 1982), p. 110.

[7] "Dialogue on Poetry," p. 108.

[8] Friedrich Schlegel. "Athenaeum Fragments," in *Friedrich Schlegel's Lucinde and the Fragments*, trans. and introd. Peter Firchow (Minneapolis: University of Minnesota Press, 1971), p. 175.

[9] "Athenaeum Fragments," p. 175.

[10] Lawrence, p. 15.

[11] Gotthold Ephraim Lessing, *Nathan the Wise*, trans. Bayard Quincy Morgan (New York: Frederick Ungar Publishing Co., 1955), p. 98.

[12] "Dialogue on Poetry," p. 106.

[13] "Dialogue on Poetry," p. 106.

ASPECTS OF MYTH IN FERDINAND BORDEWIJK'S *KARAKTER*

Augustinus P. Dierick
University of Toronto, Toronto

Ferdinand Bordewijk's 1938 novel *Karakter* has been a perennial favorite with the Dutch reading public, and was for a long time required reading for high school and university students. The novel's popularity is not hard to explain. Many a young and not so young reader may find an intense interest in the career of Jacob Willem Katadreuffe, the illegitimate son of the bailiff Arend Barend Dreverhaven and his servant girl Joba Katadreuffe, from working class beginnings to the respected position of lawyer in one of the major law offices of Rotterdam. A kind of *Bildungsroman*, that is to say, a novel in which especially the psychological and moral development of a young person is stressed, *Karakter* holds the reader's interest thanks to Bordewijk's firsthand knowledge of the milieu into which Katadreuffe ascends, and because of the subtle and differentiated psychological states in which his hero finds himself in various stages of his career. Linguistically and structurally quite accessible, and hence almost ideal reading for young persons involved in the process of growing up and defining themselves, the seemingly straightforward novel has nevertheless been the subject of a number of varying interpretations, which suggests that major ambivalences and a problematic message lie under its deceptively smooth surface.

Two major foci can be distinguished in all critical discussions of the novel. There is first the conflict between Katadreuffe and Dreverhaven, i.e., between father and son. Throughout the novel, Dreverhaven plays the role of obstacle in the path of Katadreuffe's career. After Joba refuses to marry Dreverhaven, because of her feeling of shame for having been subjected by him to what almost amounts to rape, Dreverhaven turns up on a number of occasions in Katadreuffe's life, always at a crucial stage in his studies or career, always as a force opposing the smooth social ascent of the young man. As director of a finance company he lends the young man money on two occasions, only suddenly to call his loans and thereby forcing Katadreuffe to declare himself bankrupt. He opposes Katadreuffe when the latter applies to be admitted to the bar, but is finally thwarted in his designs, and must admit defeat. Yet, somewhat surprisingly, in a final confrontation between Dreverhaven and Katadreuffe, the father now prides himself on having forced the son to show his true mettle, and therefore on having contributed to, rather than having prevented the son's career and triumph. In view of this rather abrupt turnaround it is no wonder that many critics see a difficulty in assessing the novel's constellation of characters and their relative roles.

A second focus is provided by the progress of the hero himself. Disciplined to the point of being a fanatic: this is how Katadreuffe has often been characterized. His single-minded efforts lead him away from the working class background provided by his mother (whose refusal to marry Dreverhaven has condemned her to a life of poverty with pride) and towards a goal which at the time the novel was written could hardly have been called anything but a pipe dream for someone with Katadreuffe's background. Along the way, many pleasures are sacrificed by the hero, including those of the flesh. Even the temptations of genuine love have to be overcome, in order that the single important goal in life remain clear and visible. The rise of Katadreuffe acquires overtones of tragedy, it has been argued, and the triumph at the end of the novel is mingled with an acute sense of lost opportunities.

Given the ambiguity of the role of Dreverhaven, and given the ambiguity of the novel's ending, it is not surprising that one perspicacious critic, Helbertijn Schmitz-Küller, has argued that Bordewijk's intention and the end result are in disharmony. In a letter to Victor van Vriesland of March 26, 1946, Bordewijk had written: "Of my novels, large and small, I think I may say: a vice, or an exaggeration of a virtue, although not without a certain degree of impressiveness, leads in the end to disaster" (quoted in Schmitz-Küller, p. 201). Quoting this letter, Schmitz-Küller argues that the catastrophe and the sense of tragedy to which Bordewijk refers are not successfully conveyed because the novel remains ambivalent about its heroes and their qualities. There is both admiration and rejection in the two main figures of the novel: in the case of Dreverhaven, his "vices," i.e., his violent character and his cruelty to those who are the target of his legal powers (as bailiff) and his private power (as landlord of a slum tenement in the heart of a working class district of Rotterdam) are not only never really condemned, but in fact described by Bordewijk with great relish. Schmitz-Küllers concludes, therefore, that in reality Bordewijk was an admirer of the kind of powerful individual represented by Dreverhaven.

Along the same lines, Katadreuffe's "exaggeration of a virtue," by which we are to understand the single-minded pursuit of his goal, and its attendant iron discipline (Marcel Janssens speaks of the "terror of discipline" [Janssens, p. 47]), is called into question only at a very late stage of the novel, almost as an afterthought. Faced with this ambiguity, Schmitz-Küller suggests that Bordewijk in the final analysis had more admiration than contempt for the exaggerations of discipline: "Discipline, self-discipline. Not in the least in the thirties loaded concepts. It looks as if Bordewijk was very much aware of its dangerous sides, and therefore aimed in his novels to lead them to catastrophe. The admiration with which he described them, however, and the feeble power of conviction which is given to the intended catastrophe, form an intriguing contradiction" (p. 202).

A further "intriguing contradiction" must be mentioned at this point. As I suggested, *Karakter* has generally been seen as standing in the tradition of the realistic sociological and psychological novel. Marcel Janssens, however, has drawn attention to the emotional tensions which run counter to the superficially "cool" observations which Bordewijk applies to his heroes. Janssens calls Bordewijk a "psychorealist" and compares his style to that of Gerard Walschap. Expressionism and *Neue Sachlichkeit* seem to be indicated in the presentation of the "essential" characteristics of the heroes, and in the economy of presentation. The depiction of character in Bordewijk is not, Janssens argues, "realistic-rational" but "visionary" (p. 49); the characters acquire a "monumental greatness" which he situates in the domain of the "mythical," and he quotes with approval P. H. Dubois' reference to Jeroen Bosch as a stylistic parallel to Bordewijk.

How are these ambiguities of "message," i.e., content, and of style to be reconciled? I believe the various interpretations just presented can at least be brought into closer contact with each other if we pursue an idea which Janssens suggested, but did not work out, namely by looking at the novel from the point of view of myth. In fact, I believe that we are dealing in this realistic-grotesque novel with a transposition – from the domain of "real" myth to the domain of everyday life – of two narrative myths, namely that subsumed under the father-son conflict, and that of the quest. Seeing the novel in terms of these two narrative myths will not only explain, I believe, the apparent contradiction which Schmitz-Küller has indicated, namely that between intention and execution, but also the problematic nature of style to which Janssens refers. Both can be made less puzzling if we see *character* primarily as a function of *structure*.

There are some superficial factors which would suggest that a consideration of *Karakter* in terms of myth might not be inappropriate. Bordewijk wrote the novel in 1938, after a pause in his creative output. Recently, however, P. H. Dubois has shown that the main themes and ideas contained in *Karakter* were already present in a novella which Bordewijk published in instalments in the weekly *De Vrijheid* between 14 June and 20 September, 1928 (Dubois, p. 75). This means that the novel's true germination took place at the end of the twenties. These, however, are the final years, in Germany at least, of the movement of Expressionism. Janssens is therefore quite right in pointing to stylistic features which resemble those of Expressionist prose. But there is an even more compelling factor which suggests that Expressionism is involved: the conflict between father and son, between the older and younger generations had been a central theme of German Expressionist drama and prose. It is not at all impossible that Bordewijk's earlier novella (whose title *Dreverhaven en Katadreuffe* suggests that Bordewijk saw his story from the beginning in the light of a confrontation rather than a simple linear development of his young protagonist) was conceived under the influence of the Expressionist movement.

A major stylistic and structural feature of all of Expressionism was the tendency to abstract, and to a certain extent to distort, reality. Particularly in the Expressionist drama, characters were often given a mere generic appellation, such as "the father" or "the son" or "the beggar." These reductions to a single function were intended to convey the "essence" of a character, his or her "function" not primarily in the external world, but in the world depicted on the stage. To underline this function, certain "realistic" or "naturalistic" features were suppressed, and others emphasized. Often a single character trait, or a striking gesture or tick sufficed for the role. These stylistic features of Expressionism were intended to focus the action of the story on the main theme, on the timeless-timely of conflict and resolution. I believe that Bordewijk, consciously or subconsciously, employed these techniques in his novels, particularly in *Karakter*. The reduction of Katadreuffe to a single virtue (exaggerated to the point of, at least in the end, becoming a vice) and of Dreverhaven to a single vice (in the end, because of Bordewijk's own ambiguity vis-à-vis the powerful individual, turning into a kind of virtue) results not only in what Janssens calls a "situational" presentation (a few scenes, a few highlights, always dramatic and full of tension), but in the quality of myth. In the conflict of father and son we have a true myth, going back to the most remote antiquity (Chronos, Zeus); we remember its revival, in *psychological* terms this time, in the writings of Freud (again a seminal influence on German Expressionism!); and we recognize its enormously productive integration into the myth of the New Man, the destroyer of the old, in German Expressionism itself. Mythical, psychological, or sociological (we think of Mitscherlich's *Society without the Father* and all forms of anarchy, where Brotherhood takes precedence over Patriarchy), the father-son conflict *is* mythical by its very nature.

But Bordewijk did not simply trust the myth to convey its own mythological dimensions. He consciously aimed for myth in the *presentation* of his two primary characters. Of these, Dreverhaven is by far the most striking. Many critics have called attention to the way in which Dreverhaven is presented in the novel. Certain features or characteristics are constantly reiterated. Repetition is indeed one of the most effective devices used to characterize Dreverhaven. Whenever he appears on the scene (and we have the feeling that it is indeed a *scene in the theater* on which he appears) a description of his clothes accompanies his appearance. His handwriting is on several occasions called "cyclopic" and dark, almost demonic. His physique is animal-like, his hands are hairy, his posture that of an ape. He is in fact called "a man like a beast" (p. 30). Dreverhaven seems to personify energy, and is said to be much stronger than his son, who is physically afraid of him. Dreverhaven has a strong sense of drama: he flirts with death, has little use for tenderness (he consorts with prostitutes whenever the need strikes him), and even towards the only woman who has ever meant anything in his life he shows will-power and determination, rather than understanding and love. What he admires in others is merely the reflection of that which he embodies: hence his grudging admiration for his own son's determination and the hard-heartedness of Joba. Towards people not immediately within his own circle of interest he merely shows the face of power. He has only contempt for the common man (though he is one himself) and even when in function, there is entirely too much enjoyment in following the letter of the law rather than its spirit. Towards those who are at his mercy he shows outright cruelty, even going as far as to abuse his legal authority in the furthering of private goals. On two occasions especially, once while clearing an apartment building in the Rubroeckstraat, once clearing his own building of tenants, his action is larger than life, and the scenes acquire the characteristics of the grotesque. Grotesque are also his employees, striking examples of the distorted human beings with which Bordewijk liked to people his novels and short stories.

Should all these indications not suffice to convey the image of Dreverhaven as a larger than life figure, Bordewijk, in his role as omniscient narrator is in fact not ashamed to add his own admiring and "loaded" epithets to guide the reader towards a "correct" (thought in the final analysis *wrong*) evaluation of his hero: he calls him a Caesar (p. 83) and his house a "castle" (p. 172); at other times he is likened to a man-o-war, one eye like a cannon fixing the enemy (pp. 29-30). The very first mention we have of Dreverhaven includes the remark that he has a heart of granite (p. 7).

Other important techniques seem to be borrowed directly from the Expressionist theater or film. In narrating the several encounters between Dreverhaven and Katadreuffe, Bordewijk makes use of highly effective dramatic devices such as close-ups and quasi-stage lighting. The scene describing the first time Katadreuffe goes to see his father is a striking example of this. Coming upon him from behind, seeing his father sitting at his desk, he is fascinated by the overpowering presence of this man:

> His whole attention was riveted to the man who sat there. . . . He recognized him by his hat and coat rather than by his facial features. Now he saw him as clarified through a magnifying glass, for in the high, half-dark room the man sat in the sharp light. In one corner a round stove, large as for a waiting room of a station, never blackened, red with rust, some vague office furniture here and there, dossiers, office

ledgers, a copying press, a typewriter, but especially the large desk, once beautiful, and the half-statue of the man sharply illuminated. Just as sometimes in a dark corner of a museum a single light from a window reflects on a painting, or a jewel surges up in the light of a lamp in a store window, so the statue surged up out of the toned-down darkness of the room. For a light from a hanging lamp with a green shade streamed down on it.

The son stood still and looked at the old man. . . . The eyes still were precisely in the shadow of the rim of the hat, but they were closed, their iron glint did not flash twofold from the dark.

All the devices used by Bordewijk tend to go in the direction of presenting Dreverhaven not so much as a realistic character than as a "monster." But monsters have their function in myth: they must be conquered and left behind. No heroism is possible without obstacles: the hero tests his qualities in conflict and battle, faced with a suitable opponent. The quasi-hysterical outbursts which Katadreuffe directs at his father on the first two occasions of his meeting him show he is still weak in the face of overwhelming odds. As in many fairy-tales, and in myths, the third time he triumphs over his father, and sees him cut down like a tree. Katadreuffe's bouts of hysteria echo those heard on the German Expressionist stage (Reinhard Sorge, for example); their common source is an extreme sense of frustration at the obstacles put in the path of the idealized and idealistic hero. Only, in Bordewijk the social dimension, and the revolutionary impulse of Expressionism are absent. Bordewijk's hero is not interested in the fate of humankind, or in the utopia: *his* quest can be formulated in personal terms only.

It is, for all that, no less mythical, and Bordewijk himself, in his function of omniscient author, once again provides clues as to the true nature of Katadreuffe's progress or quest. It might be argued that the opening of the novel, with the hero's birth, and the mention of the child's parents, is in the tradition of the socio-psychological novel of the 19th century, but the fact that the hero is born around Christmas time might also suggest the Christian myth, and the mention of the child's lineage and his having been delivered by caesarian section yet another myth. Similarly, in the mundane world described in the first few chapters we might nevertheless recognize from the medieval epic the motif of sloth, the hero's indolence and subsequent awakening to a life of action. Certainly the discovery of the copper plates with the names of the lawyers, affixed to the front of the law office of Stroomkoning, is in the nature of an epiphany. It is specifically referred to in the text as a vision (p. 140), and the end of the novel picks up this motif very consciously. And what about the *personnel* of the law office? Does not the name of the senior lawyer, Stroomkoning, suggest King Arthur's court, and the knights of the round table?

In Katadreuffe's single-minded pursuit of his goal, which is in the nature of a quest, it is not only his father who appears as a necessary obstacle, a "black knight" who is only defeated during the third contest of strength. There are other obstacles to be overcome, and other qualities to be developed. This is the meaning of the repeated reference to Katadreuffe's chastity. The temptations of such sensuous creatures as Miss Sibculo, or even the servant girl at his rented quarters, are easily dismissed as inappropriate and not of sufficient quality for a hero of Katadreuffe's stature (though in profane, psychological terms Katadreuffe, like so many of Bordewijk's heroes, of course simply fears sexuality).

More problematic is Katadreuffe's attitude towards the "pure love" embodied by Lorna te George. Towards her he feels a "strange fear," again *psychologically* perhaps to be explained by Katadreuffe's illegitimate birth, the problematic relationship between himself, his mother, and his father. In terms of our "mythical" interpretation, it is of course another indication that the quest is in danger of being diverted. The temptress, even though she remains but a platonic spectre, of which he is said to dream "chastely" after she has obligingly disappeared from his life, is therefore duly bypassed, albeit not without Katadreuffe's earning from his mother the qualification of being "a big donkey" (p. 236). To be sure, during his last, coincidental encounter with Lorna, Katadreuffe experiences true pain. Only once before had he been on the verge of seeing himself in terms other than those of his quest. That moment, during which the possibility of sexual and emotional fulfillment was offered to him seemed then, and in retrospect, the most important moment of his life. Now, having rejected for good any alternatives to his chosen path, he calls himself - appropriately enough - a "cowardly Leander." Not only is he, as the Greek word indicates, a "man of the people;" he also has indeed failed to answer the call of Hero to cross the stream and join her (Lorna *does* live on the other shore of the river), though he has thereby been spared the fate of drowning.

Having chosen to be a chaste, ultimately a "classical" kind of hero, though not the shining Apollo, but rather a frail but handsome Antinoüs (again a broad hint by Bordewijk, p. 182), Katadreuffe aspires to a completion which no longer lies in the domain of the human, but of the divine. His last wish is to be taken to church, so that he might incorporate this dimension too into his now almost perfected *Weltanschauung*. With his typical insouciance and utter lack of understanding for those surrounding him he expresses this wish to his Communist friend Jan Maan - a contrast figure of an all-too-human, but greatly more appealing nature.

It is at this point that the utter banality and the shabbiness of Katadreuffe's achievement become clear. His aspirations continue to preoccupy him, to be sure. But the goals which he presents to his own mind, and the kind of accomplishments of those bourgeois colleagues which he has taken as his models, now strike the careful reader as a litany of mediocre virtues and superficial, insignificant talents, arrived at to impress, to cajole, and to outsmart the competition. The *quest*, that is to say the mythical dimension which consciously and unconsciously Bordewijk has hinted at throughout the novel, by way of pervasive symbols, names, by touches of the grotesque, by borrowings from Expressionist drama and film, by use of repetition, contrast, subtle reader manipulation and by his use of language, now stands revealed as hollow, and the reader is left with an inescapable feeling of having been cheated. Since admiration and criticism are so profoundly mixed in Bordewijk's treatment of his protagonists, a fundamentally ambivalent book is the result. The positing of a mythical intent, and the analysis of some of the devices by which myth is hinted at in the text can only help to heighten our awareness of this ambiguity.

WORKS CONSULTED

1. Bordewijk, Ferdinand. *Karakter. Roman van zoon en vader.* 's Gravenhage: Nijgh & van Ditmar, 1986 [Originally published 1938]. All translations are my own.

2. Bronzwaer, W.J.M., "Bordewijks 'Noorderlicht,'" in *Tirade*, 25 (1981), pp. 419-442.

3. den Boef, August-Hans. "Over Dreverhaven en Katadreuffe," in *Bzzlletin* 10 (1981-82), nr. 96, pp. 49-50.

4. de Schutter, F. "*Karakter* van Bordewijk nog eens doorgelicht," in Nova et vet 57 (1979-80) 5 (1980), pp. 237-335.

5. Dinaux, C.J.E. "Ferdinand Bordewijk," in *Gegist bestek. Benaderingen en ontmoetingen.* 's Gravenhage: A.A.M. Stols, n.d. (1958), vol. 1, pp. 41-7.

6. Dubois, Pierre H. *Over F. Bordewijk.* Rotterdam, 1953.

7. Dubois, Pierre H. "Bij een 'onbekend werk' van Bordewijk," in Bordewijk, F., *Dreverhaven en Katadreuffe.* 's Gravenhage: Nijgh & van Ditmar, 1981, pp. 75-79.

8. Dubois, Pierre H. and N. Funke-Bordewijk. "Angst en vervreemding bij F. Bordewijk" [Interview], in *Literama* 15 (1980-81), pp. 203-209.

9. Dupuis, Michel. *Ferdinand Bordewijk.* Brugge: Orion and Nijmegen: Gottmer, 1980.

10. Janssens, Marcel. *Tachtig Jaar na Tachtig. De evolutie van het personage in de Nederlandse verhaalkunst van Couperus tot Michiels*. Leiden: A.W. Sijthoff, 1969.

11. Lukkenaer, Pim. "Karakter als zelfverminking: Wereld en tegenwereld in Bordewijks crisisroman," in *Bzzlletin* 10 (1981-82), nr. 96, pp. 38-43.

12. Schmitz-Küller, Helbertijn. "Kwestie van Karakter," in *Voor H.A. Gomperts bij zijn 65ste verjaardag*. Amsterdam, 1980, pp. 196-202.

13. van Zanen, L. "Recente uitgaven van Bordewijk; Fantastische vertellingen en Dreverhaven en Katadreuffe," in *Literair paspoort* 33 (1982), nr. 296, pp. 191-196.

THE OCCUPIED MIND: REMEMBERING AND FORGETTING SOME RECENT EXAMPLES IN DUTCH LITERATURE

Jolanda Vanderwal Taylor
University of Wisconsin, Madison

The stage for the investigations at hand is set by the description of an intellectual game played by Umberto Eco, a major contemporary literary theoretician: "The problem was to establish the principles of a technique and of a rhetorical art – and therefore principles of a process that was artificial and institutable at will – that would permit one to forget in a matter of seconds what one knew"(Eco, p. 254). This line of inquiry is interesting because at first blush it appears that the entire notion of narrative is based on our ability to remember. However, I hope to show in this article that Eco's concerns are of central importance to some recent fiction.

Although the Occupation remains a standard theme in Dutch literature as the experience of World War II fades into history, one might expect its literary treatment to change its focus from the experience of that period to the memories of those experiences and their implications for the survivor. Thus one productive approach to recent Dutch fiction set in this period involves its reading as an investigation of and discourse on the nature and function of memory – specifically, the memory of the survivor, from "Lived Time" to "Remembered Time" in the midst of the Present Time.

The persistence of emphasis on the war extends into the realm of shared idiom in language: the Dutch term referring to those times maintains the definite article (*de oorlog*), and the persistence of expressions such as *Dat heeft-ie van de oorlog overgehouden*, (to refer to a nervous tic) or *Die heeft de oorlog niet meegemaakt* (said of a person who does not clean his or her plate), testifies to the depth of its influence and may suggest how central the image of the war's privations and wounds is to Dutch thinking. The frequency with which recent fiction is set in the war years is another indication that it still fulfills a function in Dutch consciousness.

"The War" may serve various functions as a fictional setting. It has been used successfully to provide ready-made adventure, or the threat of real danger – as it does in the novels considered here. Moreover, it is a productive fictional focus for the articulation of ethical dilemmas; by nature of its "Pastness," by receding into "history," it provides an arena for the investigation of personal culpability, the "sins of the fathers": "Daddy, what did *you* do during the War?" – or, "What did you *omit* doing?" This article posits that some recent Dutch fiction adds to this list of thematic uses of "The War" an explicit investigation into the emotional, congnitive, and social roles of memory.

One of the best-known recent novels which considers the effects of World War II upon its survivors is Harry Mulisch's 1982 novel *De aanslag*, which deals both with a protagonist's wartime experience and with the relationship between memory and that character's attempt to come to terms with his experience – or, to *avoid* doing so. Marga Minco's *De glazen brug*, published four years later, (one might say: *as if* in response) is strikingly similar in structure and theme. Minco provides a provocative example of the shift in emphasis which I wish to illuminate here. Up until the publication of *De glazen brug*, of course, Minco was best known to Dutch readers as the author of her earlier World War II novel *Het bittere kruid*, which tells the tale of a young Jewish woman who escapes as her entire family is arrested by the Nazis and taken to concentration camps. The narrative ends just after the end of the war, as it becomes clear that the main character is indeed the sole survivor in her family. Minco's newer "war novel" *The glass bridge* (which we will consider here) does not omit the wartime story of survival in the midst of death, but continues the narrative to a point many years beyond the end of the war and considers the effects of the remembered experience on a protagonist's postwar existence.

Both Harry Mulisch's *De aanslag* and Marga Minco's *De glazen brug* have here been chosen as two exemplary recent examples of novels which use both the "history" and personal history of the second World War in the Netherlands as their setting. However, their initial distinction lies in the location and identification of the protagonist's suffering. I will offer a brief analysis of each of these works, which focuses on the role of memory, and then interpret these findings in light of Umberto Eco's essay on memory arts.

Minco's presentation of a Jewish main character sets the novel in the context of the experience of the primary group of those persecuted and exterminated under the Nazi regime, whereas Mulisch presents the case of a purportedly "normal," apolitical protagonist – a child – and his entirely Dutch family. They are unlikely targets for violence and persecution during the Occupation – a conventional family caught up in and destroyed by the random violence and mayhem of war.

But apart from the ethnic differences between the main characters, the two works under consideration here exhibit striking similarities in structure and theme which allow for productive comparison. A few of these similarities include single protagonists who escape death at the hand of the Nazis while their entire families perish, an experience of love and comfort in the midst of tragedy which is mediated through members of the

Resistance — a love which will strongly mark their respective future romantic entanglements, the loss of these lovers, and finally the central function of the memories of these events in the lives of the protagonists after the war's end.

Mulisch's narrator tells the story of Anton, a young boy whose life is forever altered by a single apparently random event. The narrator takes pains to present the boy, and in addition, his entire family as innocent and ignorant of the events which lead to the catastrophe. As the Steenwijk family is quietly playing a game of *Mens erger je niet*, the Chief Inspector of Police, a collaborator and reputed torturer named Fake Ploeg, is liquidated near their home by members of the Dutch Resistance. The Steenwijks watch in horror as their neighbors move the body and deposit it in front of their home. The Nazi response to the murder is to burn down the *Steen*wijks' house, and kill its inhabitants — except for the protagonist, Anton, who is saved either as the result of an oversight or perhaps because of his youth. Early on in the novel, the reader is introduced to the symbol of the stone, which serves a central interpretive function in the story. Just before the assault, Mr. *Steen*wijk refers to the origin of the word "symbol" which, he explains, is etymologically related to the concept "stones."

> Steenwijk legde zijn boek geopend naast zich neer, en even later was er niets anders meer te horen dan het stuiteren van de dobbelsteen en de stappen van de pionnen over het karton. Het was bijna acht uur: spertijd. Buiten was het zo stil als het op de maan moet zijn. (Mulisch, p. 23)

The phrase "het stuiteren van de dobbelsteen en de stappen van de pionnen over het karton" suggests a symbolic narrative device: the dice and pawns used in the game of *Mens erger je niet* foreshadow the fateful event which is just about to occur in the lives of the Steenwijks. The Dutch word for "dice" is, of course, *dobbelsteen*; throughout the book any stone or rock will signify fate to Anton. Although he will do his best to forget the events of that night, stones and rocks will continue to appear in the narrative as obstacles placed in his path. As long as he succeeds in repressing from his consciousness the memories of that evening's events, he will have migraine headaches brought on by the presence of rocks.

Dice constitute a carefully chosen symbol for Anton's experience: he views his parents' and brother's deaths as an example of essentially arbitrary fortune — a fate so inexplicable and meaningless that he blocks it out or isolates it in his memory; the narrator repeatedly indicates that he attempts to view the events of that night as irrelevant to his later life; as the previously quoted passage states: ". . . en even later was er niets anders meer te horen dan het stuiteren van de dobbelsteen en de stappen van de pionnen over het karton. Het was bijna acht uur: spertijd. Buiten was het zo stil als het op de maan moet zijn" (p. 23).

In effect, Anton attempts to believe that the entire event did happen "on the moon" where sound does not travel and signaling must be done by line of sight, that is, in a remote place and time which are unrelated to his life. In one of the narrator's many comments on the function of memory in Anton's connection with the occurrences of that night, he describes the effect of forgetting first as distancing, and then as the perception that the experiences had been dreamed:

> . . . in die vervorming van de tijd school later zijn onmacht om zijn kinderen duidelijk te maken, wat de oorlog was geweest. Zijn familie was ontweken naar een domein, waar hij zelden aan dacht maar waar op onverwachte momenten soms een flard van opdook: als hij op school uit het raam keek, of op het achterbalkon van de tram: een donker oord van kou en honger en schoten, bloed, vlammen, geschreeuw, kerkers, ergens diep in hemzelf en daar vrijwel hermetisch afgesloten. In die ogenblikken was het of hij zich een droom herinnerde, maar minder *wat* hij had gedroomd als wel *dat* hij een nachtmerrie had gehad (pp. 79-80).

Anton's refusal to remember is presented as a strategy by which he shields himself from his experience – an experience which the narrator describes as "ergens diep in hemzelf en daar vrijwel hermetisch afgesloten" (hermetic means impervious to air, and perhaps also to thoughts, in this case). Anton's sense of isolation from the experience mirrors his sense of its arbitrary character: since he cannot connect his experience to some rational construct, he cannot connect it to himself and thus he rejects it.

By contrast, in Marga Minco's novel *De glazen brug*, the catastrophic events endured during the war are presented as an expected part of life which derives from the protagonist's identity rather than conflicting with the family's ordinariness. Stella, the novel's Jewish first-person narrator, is aware at the beginning of the story that Jews are being deported and she ridicules friends who believe they will be saved because they have collaborated with the Nazis. At the end of the first chapter, the narrative discloses that Stella's safety has been compromised even at its most secure point when under the care of her contact in the Resistance; later it is said of her friend Carlo, her other Resistance contact, that *he* did *not* require anything from her but a passport photo, her fingerprint, and a signature, and that this was an improvement over her previous situation, in which she was sexually harassed (Minco, p. 9). Thus from the beginning of the story, the threat of physical and emotional danger is an unavoidable and explicitly acknowledged element of Stella's world. The book's title refers to a memory of her father in which she describes him standing alone on a bridge – Stella has been momentarily forgotten and abandoned – a scene which becomes a prefiguration of her father's death. In addition, the phrase *op het glazen bruggetje geweest zijn* means "having been in mortal danger," and this phrase accurately describes Stella's wartime experience. Note Minco's elimination of the diminuitive suffix of "bridge" in the title, so that *brug* may suggest a longer exposure to danger, preventing the impression that the phrase could refer to an isolated incident.

The protagonists of both novels being considered here fall in love with a member of the Resistance; in each case they have an experience which fundamentally changes their futures. Anton's experience consists merely of a night spent in a prison cell talking with the woman who, as he later discovers, had shot Ploeg, and for whom he apparently searches subconsciously until he marries his first wife. When he discovers what he has done – that he has married his wife in an attempt to substitute her for the unknown woman and thus tie himself to a past he rejects – the marriage disintegrates. Minco's protagonist Stella has a love affair with a member of the Resistance, which would presumably have continued after the end of the war, except that her lover Carlo is betrayed and dies at the hand of the Nazis. Stella also marries after the war and subsequently begins a series of affairs which function first to provide her with the excitement which accompanies illicit affairs (thus fulfilling a need for excitement created during the war), and more importantly, to reassure herself that the relationship with Carlo, which she has been denied by history but retains in memory, had been better. Her life is viewed as a continuation of the life she led during the war although her wartime experiences are presented as privileged over the later ones.

On the other hand, Mulisch's Anton views his postwar experience as essentially discontinuous from the events surrounding the assault. The events of that night are viewed as a mysterious and perplexing puzzle which Anton refuses to or is reluctant to solve. The present intrudes upon his hermetically sealed past and reminds him of several missing pieces. He speaks with Takes, the colleague and friend of the woman in the Resistance with whom Anton shared the prison cell the night of the assault. Takes was in love with this woman, but did not realize that she returned his affection. What Takes would like to be told is that she loved him – and she had in fact told Anton so, but Anton begs off, complaining that it happened too long ago. The reader knows what he really means: that the responsibility to report the past that he remembers brings it into the present from which Anton has sealed his memories. The events apparently lack a sense of reality, and Anton refuses to make them real.

In order to understand Anton's capacity for forgetfulness we now return to the essay on memory and forgetting by Umberto Eco, entitled "An *Ars Oblivionalis*? Forget it!" This essay provides a theoretical framework and a vocabulary with and within which we can discuss Anton's act of forgetting. A striking resonance between Eco's system and Mulisch's presentation of Anton's coping mechanism will affirm the rightness of our analysis.

Although there are types of forgetting about which little can be done, such as those arising from organic causes, Eco is interested in a different variety of forgetting: "The problem was to establish the principles of a technique and of a rhetorical art — and therefore principles of a process that was artificial and institutable at will — that would permit one to forget in a matter of seconds what one knew"(Eco, p. 254). We have mentioned earlier the contrastive differences between memory as distancing (forgetting) and as a way of recapturing the past, and the fact that the two are linked. Eco recognizes a similar linkage and begins by discussing the techniques for remembering which he finds described in various memory treatises, hoping that a reverse process might prove useful for forgetting. The techniques recommended in these memory treatises resemble those most of us were taught in grade school. It is suggested that lists of unfamiliar objects or words or stories may be memorized by mentally associating each item with an item on a list which one has already memorized, such as the alphabet. Each "item" in the list we have already memorized becomes a symbol for an object on the list of items which we wish to memorize, and thus aids the memory. A given symbol could represent a variety of items or interpretants. Therefore one needs to remember which characteristic of the symbol is symbolic of the item to be remembered. Eco states: "In order to associate Proserpina with the underworld, an art of memory must establish that the rape of Proserpina, not the fact that she is a woman, is of prime importance. The memory treatises tell us how to select these features for the image we wish to impress in our memory. . ." (Eco, p. 260). For Anton, this would not have been a difficult step. We may assume that his experience the night of the assault made a sufficiently strong impression on him, and that the dice are a sufficiently obvious symbol for arbitrariness that he would never think dice symbolic of anything else ever again. Given the gravity of the situation, it is credible that not only *dobbelstenen* but *all* stones might come to carry this meaning.

Likewise, for Minco's narrator, excitement in the generic sense, whether derived from an illicit affair or from the experience of war, is the generalized symbol of that which Stella seeks.

> Ze had genoten van de spanning, de geheime afspraken, en er zich tegelijkerijd over verwonderd dat het haar geen moeite kostte, alsof ze kon bogen op een lange routine.

Na de eerste zeven jaar met Reinier was ze weggezakt in een lusteloosheid waartegen zij geen verweer had en waaraan hij niets kon veranderen. Toen ze die eenmaal doorbroken had dacht ze niet meer zonder de opwinding te kunnen die de opeenvolgende avonturen haar bezorgden (p. 76).

In addition to providing excitement, her illicit affairs also serve to reassure her that her war experience was superior to her life in peacetime, though the two are intimately related rather than discontinuous. "Aldoor leek ze op zoek naar een ervaring die ze kon toetsen aan die ene kortstondige van lang geleden, of ze voorgoed bevestigd wilde zien dat niets daarmee te vergelijken was" (p. 76).

The proof that her experience is continuous lies precisely in the fact that she requires repeated affairs to prove to herself that her wartime experience had been unique.

Eco states that it is not really possible to actually forget something once learned, but he does explain how it is possible to confuse memories or how one can distinguish between the interpretants "apple" and "ape" when one thinks of the letter "a", which could be the symbol for both in two possible memory systems. Eco explains as follows: "Interpreting the expression in context means *magnifying* certain interpretants and *narcotizing* others, and narcotizing them means removing them provisionally from our competence, at least for the duration of the interpretation taking place" (p. 260). To return to my example, it is possible to block out certain interpretations of symbols: if I think of the symbol "a," I can reject "ape" as the interpretant if I am looking for the fruit, namely "apple."

In light of this process, we are now struck by the passages in *De aanslag* where Anton's choice of profession is explained:

Overigens waren het niet alleen negatieve redenen, waarom hij voor de anesthesie koos. Hij was geboeid door het delicate evenwicht, dat bewaard moest worden als de slagers hun messen in iemand plantten, – dat balanceren op het scherp van de snede tussen leven en dood, de zorg voor dat arme hulpeloze wezen in zijn bewusteloosheid. Hij had trouwens het min of meer mystieke vermoeden, dat een narcose de patiënt niet zo zeer gevoelloos maakte, maar dat de chemicaliën uitsluitend bewerkstelligden, dat hij zijn pijn niet kon uiten, en verder, dat zij achteraf de herinnering aan de doorstane pijn wegnamen, terwijl de patiënt er toch door veranderd was. Als zij ontwaakten, was toch altijd te zien dat zij geleden hadden (p. 111).

Anton does to patients what he has already done to himself: he "narcotizes" them, so that their pain is temporally isolated from the rest of their experience. Their (experience of) pain has changed them, but he has placed the pain within certain temporal boundaries so that they do not consciously remember it. Nearby, Mulisch states: "Ook het afgrenzende moet steeds afgegrensd worden; maar de taak is hopeloos, want alles raakt alles in de wereld. Een begin verdwijnt nooit, zelfs niet met het einde" (p. 109). Boundaries have to be continuously sealed off because the pain is still present, and a symbol such as "stone" cannot be avoided; one is continuously reminded of it. A beginning never disappears and a learned association is never forgotten; the best one can do is to seal it off, narcotize it, place it within local or temporal boundaries. As we saw earlier, Anton described his memory of the night of the assault to himself as the memory of a nightmare; not the memory of the content of the nightmare, but merely the knowledge upon awaking that one had had one, just – we may now add – as the surgery patient may know that he has undergone surgery while not remembering the painful details.

In the interest of brevity, I have presented here only a skeletal version of an investigation into the function of forgetting and into the support for it found in two recent novels. It is my hope, with Minco's narrator, that I have <u>remembered</u>. But others will doubtless be able to remind me of what I have forgotten.

WORKS CITED

1. Eco, Umberto. "An *Ars Oblivionalis?* Forget It!" *PMLA* 103 (1988): 254-261.

2. Minco, Marga. *De glazen brug*. Bert Bakker, Stichting Collectieve Propaganda van het Nederlandse Boek, 1986.

3. Mulisch, Harry. *De aanslag*. Amsterdam: De Bezige Bij, 1982.

CHILDREN, CHURCH, AND SICKBED?
THE LIVES OF DUTCH IMMIGRANT WOMEN

Suzanne Sinke
University of Minnesota, Minneapolis

> Do you remember that I wrote not long ago that the children should sit for a portrait on Sunday if J[antje] was a little better?. . . Well mother she lived exactly until then . . . oh mom when death comes we stand by so powerless, eh? When I saw that it was going wrong I told her that she was going to die, and if she knew where she was going. Without hesitation . . . she called: I go to Jesus mom. That is also the last thing we heard from her, but it was enough eh mom?. . . .[1]

Children, church, and sickbed, these are just three of the topics discussed by Dutch immigrant women in their private writings. The value of such writings for a historian comes as much from the strength of the emotions women shared as from the specific news they reported. Letters have an immediacy not found in autobiographies and seldom found in published reports. I was drawn to women's letters as source material because I wanted to know more about how migration affected women, their attitudes and their activities; also because people identify and define themselves through their choice of words.[2] This was manifested in the letters in two ways. First, the topics these women discussed reflected their relationships to the power structure of their worlds. Most often they gave details of their home lives. They wrote of family, friends, health, food, and religion among other things. Clearly they had domain over many aspects of the household. Secondly, the words women chose and the syntax they used illustrated their educational and philosophical background.[3] Specifically these features reflected how religion provided women with a language in which to write and an ideological system to order their lives.

My focus was the late nineteenth and early twentieth centuries. Within this time frame, I examined approximately 75 letters written by Dutch Protestant women to their families and friends in the Netherlands. There was no single "Dutch" immigrant woman's experience, just as there was no single "American" woman's experience.[4] Women migrants, depending on their circumstances when they arrived - e.g., marital status, age, settlement in rural or urban location, size and complexity of the Dutch ethnic group in that area - might find their situation replicating that in the "old world." Or they might face a more extensive task of cultural creation and/or recreation. Because my source materials were confined primarily to the immigrant letter collection found at Calvin

College's Heritage Hall, the variety of experience I found was more limited. These women generally lived in Protestant Dutch-American communities and came to America as adults with their husbands and children. Those who did not fit this pattern often illustrated how different life could be. The patterns in the letters overall provide clues as to how various factors affected the process of acculturation and, at the same time, demonstrate some general patterns of women's roles in Protestant Dutch immigrant communities. They cannot be considered representative of letters by Dutch-American women, but they can provide insights into important aspects of these women's lives. In this article I deal with three of these areas: family ties, religion, and gender roles.

Family Ties

The most striking feature of most of these letters by female Dutch immigrants was the prevalence of references to family and friends.

> Now you must write about your children to me if any of them are married and who is still at home. . . if you and your husband are still strong or sickly and if your children are quite healthy. . . .[5]

By exchanging news immigrants could maintain family ties despite the geographic gulf which separated them. Women reported the health, occupations, and economic status of nuclear family members, kinfolk, and various acquaintances. They wrote when they moved, when a child was born, when someone died, or simply because they wanted to keep in touch. While they expressed the desire to see family and friends, they rarely digressed into a melancholia of homesickness.[6] On specific occasions such as holidays and other family rituals, the writer might bemoan the distance separating them, but they still acknowledged the connections.

> It will be a difficult day, the 16th of June, when I know that I cannot be with you then Mother, but I hope that I will stand close by, and we will celebrate the birthday here by us at home with the thought that my dear Mother is 76 years old today.[7]

Reports of homesickness frequently accompanied requests that the relatives and friends write soon. The news from one writer could then be shared with nearby friends and family by word of mouth, or the letter could be passed on intact. Other items crisscrossed the Atlantic as well: what the immigrants requested were often items they could not get in America, from photographs to a lock of hair. According to these indications, tangible links to families were important. The reciprocal nature of gifts and requests indicated that family ties continued to operate on a material as well as emotional level. This was also true for money. Writers in America relied on relatives to send them their inheritances, and the recipients of the letters often depended on the immigrants to help them come to America.

Relatives were a migrant's link to the new world. Besides encouragement, Dutch relatives obtained advice on the journey, such as how to smuggle cigars through customs.[8] They were also assured of a place to stay once they arrived. The very real possibility that Dutch correspondents would migrate if they received favorable reports about America helped restrain immigrants from exaggerating their success. But they often sent encouraging news anyway.

Women encouraged their relatives and friends to join them if they thought the move would be advantageous economically, and in some cases socially. While both men and women received news of job prospects, opportunities to buy land, and wages in America, single women also received news of favorable marital prospects.

> There is another Dutch boy coming from Holland .... A brother of his is here with us now and it was said that 3 more boys would come from Hasselt. ... So, Mientje, you can see that several boys come but no girls. Here there are now 10 Dutch boys and 2 Dutch girls.[9]

Compared with other immigrant groups such as the Swedes, the Dutch were more heavily family oriented in their migration, meaning that relatively few young women migrated alone.[10] Still young Dutch immigrants, both male and female, found themselves involved in a marriage market that sometimes bridged the Atlantic.

This international marriage market served as a counterpart to the international labor market, assuring that the immigrant population would not only have a role in the productive sphere, but also in the reproductive sphere. Reproduction as I use it here has two components: 1) biological and 2) social. From the biological standpoint, women bore and nurtured children as well as provided for the daily needs of their families. Issues of health, food procurement and preparation, and psychological support fall under this rubric. Social reproduction includes the maintenance and recreation of society, from child socialization to foodways to organizational life. A major component of social reproduction related to religion.

Religion

The Dutch immigrant women I studied, wrote in religious terms frequently, using this medium for the expression of emotion and as a shared cultural discourse through which communication could occur. In a sense, ritualized language took the place of the rituals that these family members could not share because of geographic separation.

In writing, women were constrained by the vocabulary available to them, which was more forthcoming on certain issues than on others. The passages utilizing religious metaphors and biblical quotations often contained the most elaborate writing style in these women's letters; the syntax indicating that religion was the one area where persons might command a more formal language. Beyond stylistic implications, the passages relating to religion manifested that participation in religious bodies and home religious practice were an integral part of many of these women's lives.

Standard references to health, either to that of the writer and her family or to that of the recipient, were often paired with statements of thanksgiving: "Through the Lord's blessing we are all still quite well and we hope that you are all that way too."[11] In cases of illness or death, religion served as a primary coping strategy.

> . . . isn't it wonderful in such circumstances that we may know through grace that it is not fate but the Lord Himself who brings us these blows, that He decides are necessary for us? that He also gives us comfort with such a wonderful, blessed consolation.[12]

Other themes along these lines were that since burdens came from God, they could never be more than one could bear or that they would meet the loved one again in heaven. This resignation often bordered on fatalism, and it was not confined to incidents of death: ". . . so it goes down here in the World Nothing lasts down here. Luckily we have a better life in the future. An eternal blessed life in heaven."[13]

These immigrant women often conveyed positive reports about church participation and other religious activities within their ethnic group. Their opinions about "Yankee" religion, however, varied. Much of the variation related to the size of the Dutch-American community in their area and their degree of association with it. One woman who was part of a closely-knit Dutch community expressed her pleasure at the opportunity to attend a Dutch-speaking church; others wrote with enthusiasm about their congregation and *dominie*. Some also noted the strong social connections which the church engendered or reinforced. The importance of church connections appeared most clearly in cases of financial or psychological distress, where the church functioned as an agency of social welfare, providing funds, helping hands, and a sympathetic ear to those in need.

But not all the letter writers were enthusiastic about church participation. A domestic servant in Chicago wrote: "People tend to go to church a lot here, you are more respected if you go to church. . . . I don't go so much. I find it too warm."[14] Regardless of how warm she found the atmosphere, the young woman was distancing herself from the Dutch community, a process that culminated in her marrying an American of different descent. Her opinion about religiosity in America was not prevalent among other writers. More frequently the immigrants saw Americans as lax in religious observance: "Americans don't think much of Sunday. Even though they are such fine people, they don't pray before they eat. . . ."[15]

Religion played an important role in setting the cultural standards of which topics were appropriate for discussion. Pregnancy and birth, while important parts of these immigrant women's lives, received only brief mention, mainly notices about who was expecting or had another child. This stands in sharp contrast to a near preoccupation with health in their letters generally and with the emotions they shared on other topics.

Likewise, women tended to be circumspect, even when writing to their closest friends and relatives, concerning sexuality and menstruation. None of the letters I read referred specifically to either, though comments concerning "happy marriages" might be construed in sexual as well as other terms. A recent widow who described her relationship with her departed husband as "especially happy," provided a veiled reference along these lines: "Mornings before the children are up and evenings after they are in bed and nights, those are the most painful times."[16]

Morality, religious practice, and language, what do these aspects of immigrant women's letters illustrate? First, Dutch immigrant women often maintained their formal religious ties in the "new world." Religion served in some cases to bolster ethnicity by creating an institutional base for continuing old country practices and unifying Dutch-speaking persons, a common pattern in immigrant groups. Second, and more important, religion provided the world view and the language through which many of these writers defined their identities, expressed their emotions, and carried out their lives.

Gender Roles

The roles women held within the church were only part of a larger constellation of their activities. What those activities included depended largely on a woman's marital status and the family livelihood. The reports of everyday life indicated that young women, especially single women, recognized gender role differences in American culture, and were more strongly affected by them than older, married women, who were more likely to learn about American culture from their children. In any case, the way women evaluated the changes entailed by migration differed.

According to most commentators, a young single woman who decided to join family or friends in America made a good choice. In domestic service, the most common form of employment outside the home or family business, America was generally considered a better locale than the Netherlands.

> You can earn a lot of money here. . . . And you don't have to do anything hard. Just cooking and cleaning. . . . They aren't too particular. That is really much easier than to milk cows as you do now, and helping in the field.[17]

Wages for domestics in America were comparatively good, and their status in regard to the employer's family, if the employers were American, was more egalitarian than in the "old world." Conversely, immigrant women who sought domestics complained about how difficult and expensive it was to find household help.[18] This lack and the economic pinch that often accompanied getting established in America, meant that women who were accustomed to having domestics might have to take over certain tasks in the home or on the farm. A woman's productive activities were considered indispensable by many: "Gerrit . . . bought himself a piece of property, but does not want to farm there himself since he is still single."[19]

The letters indicate that women were aware of their family finances and of their own economic contributions to the family, both in producing goods and in buying and preparing goods for consumption. One woman wrote: "[My husband] does not make so much but I do everything myself I bake bread and cake and pie so that does not cost too much."[20] She went on to report the cost of staples such as eggs, flour, and sugar, placing these prices in the context of wages for both men and women. Further, women on farms often detailed family holdings in land and stock, showing extensive knowledge of the financial situation of their holdings.[21] Geertje Ruisch reported both how many bushels of grain they had harvested, and the price at which they sold their crop. In one letter, she apologized for not writing sooner by listing some of her duties, including milking, watering the animals, sewing and darning: ". . . so you can certainly understand that there is not much time left over."[22]

Regardless of women's duties in the fields or other business, they remained responsible for housekeeping and were primarily responsible for child care. They also handled nursing the sick, food storage and preparation, and making clothing. Several writers expressed the opinion that a mother was more indispensable to children and to a household than a father.

> . . . it is lucky for the children, that if the Lord had to take one of us that is was E[nno] and not me. Now at least the housekeeping can remain up to par.[23]

Despite this recognition of a woman's roles in the home and family, the letter writers indicated that wives had limited power in familial decision making, as was the case in the Netherlands. When there was a clash of wills, a wife did not have the ultimate say. Klaaska Noorda exemplified this pattern. Klaaska wrote an apologetic letter to her mother explaining why her new baby was not named Simon, after a maternal family member. Her mother, back in the Netherlands, was quite upset about the matter, so Klaaska replied:

> I already let you know earlier that I am not the master, but that I gladly would have had it so. . . . I called him Simon all the time at first but Onne wanted him to be called Geert and so finally he was baptized Geert.[24]

Both cultural norms and economic conditions contributed to the Dutch immigrants' maintenance of the patriarchal system. But it was not the same system that prevailed in the American middle class; the demarcation of women's and men's spheres among the Dutch was not entrenched in the same way. While certain jobs, particularly within the house, were clearly viewed as women's work, others were more flexible. The same applied in terms of social relations. Dutch immigrant women noted close relationships to both sexes, while native born women tended to relate much more exclusively to other women.

Conclusion

In conclusion, the writings of Dutch immigrant women in the late nineteenth and early twentieth centuries illustrate several themes. Activities surrounding children, church and sickbed were only part of women's roles as arbiters of social reproduction. Maintaining ties to family and friends and carrying on familial and ethnic traditions were crucial to the creation of Dutch-American society. Religion was an important component of this. These Dutch women, unlike their native-born counterparts, used religious terminology often. It served as a unifying cultural force and a core around which to structure meaning in their lives. Along with these aspects of social reproduction, these women recognized their productive work as important to their families' economic success. Their work spaces were not as clearly delineated into separate spheres as among the native-born, white middle class. Such distinctions might come with prosperity, or more likely with the second generation and beyond.

NOTES

[1] Etje Houwerzijl to Mom, Walker, MI, 29 December 1917. Unless otherwise indicated all translations used in this paper are mine. While I am not a skilled linguist, I have tried to convey both meaning and tone as it appears in the original. The letters are found at the Heritage Hall Collection, Calvin College, Grand Rapids, Michigan.

[2] Michel Foucault posits this view. See for example: *The Order of Things* (New York: Pantheon, 1971) and *Archeology of Knowledge*, trans. A.M. Sheridan Smith (New York: Pantheon, 1972). This type of analysis differs from that of Susan Sniader Lanser or Suzanne Bunker, both of whom discuss women's writings in terms of encoding. My position lies between them. While I agree that women can choose how to present their writing through "indirection, contradiction, deviation, and silence," I also argue that the words and the models they choose for this process come out of their specific material and cultural situation, out of a particular historical and philosophical moment, which sets rather distinct parameters on those choices. Lanser, "Feminism (Suppressed/Expressed) and Literary Form," paper presented at the Midwest Modern Language Association Convention, 1980; and Bunker, "Midwestern Diaries and Journals: What Women Were (Not) Saying in the Late 1800's," forthcoming in James Olney, ed., *Studies in Autobiography* (Oxford University Press, 1988), p. 21 (typescript).

[3] For methodological comparison see Frances Ferguson's discussion of how to read public letters: "Interpreting the Self Through Letter," *Centrum,* 1 (1981), pp. 108-110.

[4] Thus far I have not found a sufficient number of letters by Dutch immigrant women of Catholic, Jewish, and non-affiliated religious background to make comparisons between these womens' writing styles. Hence my discussion of Dutch immigrant women refers to Protestants only.

[5] Hendriene Mesink Bos to friends, sister and brothers, nieces and nephews [cousins], St. Anne, IL, September 1909, Heritage Hall Collection.

[6] This contrasts my findings for writings by German immigrant women in the mid-west during the same time period. See Suzanne Sinke, "'Send News Soon': Letters from German Immigrant Women," paper presented at the Missouri Valley History Conference, March 1988, pp. 4-5.

[7] Martje Smit to Mother and Brother, East Orange, SD, 14 May 1881, Heritage Hall Collection.

[8] For example: ". . . you have to open all the trunks when you have so many with you . . . I just said that I could not understand they did not see the cigars. . . my luggage had already been inspected when Miss Neter gave me the tobacco,. . . thus I was able to bring that off quite well." Anne Kuijt to Gerrit and Letha, Chicago, 23 December 1907, Heritage Hall Collection.

[9] Lubbigje Schaapman to Willamientje Beltman, Salida, CA, First day of Easter, 1912, Heritage Hall Collection, Heritage Hall translation.

[10] Robert P. Swierenga, "Dutch Immigrant Demography, 1820-1880," *Journal of Family History,* 5 (Winter 1980), p. 398.

[11] Klaaska Noorda to Mother, Brothers and Sisters, [n.p., probably Oakharbor, IL], [n.d., 1890s], Heritage Hall Collection.

[12] Etje Houwerzijl to family, Byron Center, MI, 3 June 1923, Heritage Hall Collection.

[13] Dina Maria Oggel to sister and other family, Pella, IA, 11 May 1899, Heritage Hall Collection.

[14] Anja Kuijt to Gerrit and Letha, Chicago, IL, August 1908, Heritage Hall Collection.

[15] Lubbigje Schaapman to Willamientje Beltman, Salida, CA, 19 March 1911, Heritage Hall Collection, Heritage Hall translation.

[16] Etje Houwerzijl to family, Byron Center, MI, 3 June 1923, Heritage Hall Collection.

[17] Lubbigje Schaapman to Willamientje Beltman, Salida, CA, January 1913, Heritage Hall Collection, Heritage Hall translation.

[18] For example: ". . . we have to work hard too for hired hands and domestics are not available that is not the same as in the Netherlands. they earn good wages here. you can't get hold of a domestic for less than two or three dollars a week. . . ." Anje Nieveen Mulder to Uncle S. Smit, Stuttgard, KS, end March 1889, Heritage Hall Collection.

[19] Aaltje to uncle, Sibley, IA, 6 June 1907, Heritage Hall Collection.

[20] Anna Kuijt Bates to Gerrit and Letha, Morgan Park, IL, 15 January 1918, Heritage Hall Collection.

[21] An exception helps prove the point. Etje Houwerzijl wrote that her husband had been especially solicitous of her needs, speci-

fically a stomach condition and the duties of caring for six children, because he did not expect her to work in the fields. After his death she took over much of the work, but left management of farming implements and some of the heaviest work to helpful neighbors. Etje Houwerzijl to family, Byron Center, MI, 3 June 1923, Heritage Hall Collection.

[22] Geertje Ruisch to friend, Alton, IA, 19 April 1885, Heritage Hall Collection.

[23] Etje Houwerzijl to family, Byron Center, MI, 3 June 1923.

[24] Klaaska Noorda to Mother, Brothers, Sisters, Nephews, and Nieces, Oakharbor, IL, 19 October 1896, Heritage Hall Collection.

THE FLEMISH MOVEMENT IN SOUTHWESTERN ONTARIO, 1927-1931[*]

Joan Magee
University of Windsor, Windsor

The American scholar Shepard B. Clough, who made a study of the Flemish Movement, wrote in 1930 the following brief statement:

> . . . few [Americans] know there is a Flemish movement. An exception should be made, however, in respect of the Flemish immigrants located in Chicago and Detroit. Those of the latter city have kept alive a certain consciousness of Flemish nationalism. A Flemish newspaper of Detroit, *Gazette van Detroit*, prints lengthy accounts of events concerning the Flemish movement. . . . Flemings are ever on the alert to win the sympathy of Flemish-Americans. Occasionally a Fleming will arrive from Flanders with pamphlets and papers and sometimes lantern slides with which he is expected to reap a golden harvest. Thus far little aid has come from the Flemings of Detroit who are not particularly wealthy and who number only a few thousand. Flamingants can hardly expect any real help from America, at least not in the near future.[1]

With these few words Shepard Clough dismissed the importance of the Flemish Movement in America. Yet material which has recently come to light in Windsor, Ontario shows that the determined efforts made by Flemish workers to gain support for their cause are not without significance. At the least, it was a gallant effort, one led by two men, Adolf Spillemaeckers of Antwerp and Father Ladislas Segers of Zondereigen.

Adolf Spillemaeckers, the leader of the Flemish Movement in the Great Lakes area, arrived in Detroit as a young man of 19, shortly after the end of World War I. He did not enter the United States legally. Now a man of 91, he tells his own story in the following words:

> I was a firebrand and gave speeches in Antwerp for the cause. The Belgian veterans who had gone to America wanted someone to come over to help them collect support and money to help with the Flemish Movement; and I was the one who was chosen. At that time we had to wait a very long time on a list. Friends, soldiers, were so anxious to get me over here that they wrote me and asked me to come over right away. They knew I had been a very young activist. So I came to Chatham, Ontario, with another friend. We had been working (as draftsmen together) in a factory in Antwerp. My friend had three brothers living in Detroit. . . . We arrived in Chatham,

175

by train. There was nothing there, nothing . . . just grass, at that time, . . . prairie grass! Then after waiting a couple of hours a farmer from Wallaceburg who had been written to and knew just about when we would arrive, drove up in a buggy to pick us up. They were very happy to have us. I herded the cows for the farmer. It was mixed farming there. One day that same week a business man from Detroit came in to buy eggs and butter and so forth. The farmer's wife said, "We have two young fellows here so nicely shaven that you just can't see that they are different from real Americans." He said, "Let's see them." When he saw us he said we could go along with him. He gave me a cigar to smoke. "Just say 'Yes, yes, yes' at the Customs." We got pulled across in the ferry, and while they were pulling us over to the other side I got sick. It was my first cigar. And on the other side the veterans were already waiting for us. And at that very minute Flandria-America was born![2]

Five years later, Adolf Spillemaeckers was deported back to Belgium in a round-up of Belgian immigrants who had entered the United States illegally. However, he returned, as did so many others who were deported. The second time he emigrated he entered the United States directly and legally. There he continued his work with Flandria-America, concentrating in particular on founding drama clubs and assisting with Flemish cultural programmes. While he worked in Detroit as a draftsman during the week, each weekend he would visit a Belgian community in Ontario or the Great Lakes region of the United States. He was particularly active in Wallaceburg, Chatham, Leamington, Blenheim, and Windsor.

Dramatic performances in Dutch were important events in the social life of immigrant Belgian communities in America. They continued the traditions of the old country, where even small rural villages had amateur play groups. Just as music was an integral part of Belgian club life and festivity, so were "theatre festivals" enjoyed. The Detroit community had its own successful amateur theatre groups even before World War I, and by 1922 these had increased in number, including *Moedertaal en Volksvermaak* (Mother Tongue and Ethnic Amusement), the Belgian American Dramatic Club *'t Roosje bloeit in 't Wilde* (The Rose Blooms in the Wilds), *Kunst en Vermaak* (Art and Amusement) and *Hooger Op* (Higher Up), among others. A number of members of these groups wrote plays for their group to perform, although the choice was usually made from the many plays suitable for amateur theatre groups which were available from Belgium. Often these were comedies or plays with a theme from World War I, in which many of the young Belgian veterans in the audiences had served not many years earlier.

While Adolf Spillemaeckers used his training as an elocutionist to prepare members of Flandria-America to perform patriotic plays, another Flemish patriot, Father Ladislas, was preparing to leave Flanders for America. On March 21, 1927 a proposal had been made by the General of the Capuchin Order in a letter written to the Belgian province of the Order by Father Fredegand of Rome:

> . . . a great number (several thousand) of Flemish and Dutch immigrants are settling in his diocese, namely in the counties of Kent and Essex, and in the near future their number will increase considerably.
>
> In view of his own obligation to care for their spiritual welfare, the Bishop has asked Father General to accept a settlement in his diocese, with priests who can serve them in their own language. He offers Blenheim, where there is a small church, no rectory as yet, but would seem to offer fair prospects for future development. Father General would like to know if the Belgian Province would have four priests available to serve these people in Flemish in Ontario, which is, as you know, one of the most prosperous provinces in Canada. These four priests would not have to leave as a group; two could start, and two more could be added later.[3]

This proposal was accepted by the Belgian province of the Order and, on August 29, 1927, Father Willibrord of Mortsel and Father Ladislas of Zondereigen left Antwerp by ship.

The Capuchins visited the Belgian and Dutch Catholic communities regularly, preaching missions and visiting in the homes. On one of these occasions, they met Adolf Spillemaeckers from Detroit who was drawn to Wallaceburg by Father Ladislas' celebration there of the anniversary of the Battle of the Golden Spurs on July 11, 1302. In his column in the *Gazette van Detroit* under the pseudonym "P. Fleming," Spillemaeckers wrote:

> Last night I came home dead tired at 10 o'clock at night, and took a glance at the *Gazette van Detroit*, and saw to my great pleasure that the Flemings of Wallaceburg were also going to celebrate the anniversary of the Battle of the Golden Spurs . . . the great Flemish victory of 1302.
>
> Wallaceburg is a rural community that is very industrious. The 7,000 Flemings and Zeelanders who live there get along well together, and earn a good living working in beets, tobacco, sugar, the glass factory, etc.
>
> On Sunday I was awake before six and decided to go to the 8:30 Mass, very anxious to meet the Flemings, hear

them sing their Flemish songs and bring them greetings from Flandria-America. Having arrived at the church I had the inexpressible pleasure of meeting Father Stanislas [sic], from the recently established Capuchin cloister in Blenheim, who to the joy of the Flemish and the Dutch comes every week to say Mass and preach in their own language . . . but a surprise! The leaders of the Flemish Choir were urgently called to work in the sugar factory, and the entire anniversary celebration would have come to naught if the priest hadn't in a suitable manner, within the course of the service, reminded the faithful of the meaning and results of the Battle of the Golden Spurs of 1302.[4]

It was by no means coincidental that both men were celebrating the anniversary of the Battle of the Golden Spurs of 1302 that day, each in his own manner. Their common interest in the Flemish Movement brought them together repeatedly in the next three years until Adolf Spillemaeckers returned to Belgium in 1931.

Both Adolf Spillemaeckers and Father Ladislas were strong and active supporters of the Flemish Movement, a movement which remained little known outside the Low Countries during the 1920s, although it was one of the major issues in Belgium's national life. It was at the height of the effort to achieve political, linguistic, psychological, and material improvement for the Flemish people, that Adolf Spillemaeckers and Father Ladislas endeavoured to help their people both in Belgium and in Canada.

Father Ladislas, like so many of his parishioners, had served in the trenches in World War I. He had been one of the group of soldiers of the Front Movement in the War, a movement which has been explained as follows:

> The rank and file of the Belgian army which, for four years resisted the Germans on the IJzer front, consisted overwhelmingly of Flemings (80%), whereas the officers were almost all French-speaking. The tiny minority of Flemish officers could hardly outweigh the rabid anti-Flemish feelings of the officers' corps. But the army also counted Flemish intellectuals who had joined as volunteers. . . . In the trenches they continued their Flamingant activities: debating sessions, entertainment shows, literary gatherings, etc. Due to the circumstances of the soldiers' everyday life . . . it also had moral and religious aspects. It was supported by a great number of clerics: chaplains or stretcher-bearers. Hence the ever more predominant motto: "*Alles voor Vlaanderen, Vlaanderen voor Kristus*" (All for Flanders, Flanders for Christ).[5]

Father Ladislas (or Ladislaus as it was more correctly spelled), as was mentioned in the *Gazette*, was one of those clerics who had served as a stretcher-bearer on the IJzer Front and who had "served through the entire War at the side of our boys, had suffered with them, together with them had borne the heavy burden of army life, was a witness of their sufferings, sacrifices, their courage and their heroic deeds."

Father Ladislas frequently needed a projector and screen to show the pictures which he used to illustrate his vividly-presented lectures to crowds, many of whom "would recognize the places . . . or hear repeated stories of events in which you yourself took part." On these occasions he would write to Adolf Spillemaeckers, who would bring his equipment to Windsor and leave it at a pre-arranged address so that it could be picked up for Father Ladislas' use.[6] The mutual support of each other's efforts led to a regular correspondence between the two men. One letter, written four months after their first meeting in Wallaceburg at the church service in celebration of the Battle of the Golden Spurs, included the following:

> I would be very happy if you were able to come to Wallaceburg. Please answer soon with the good news that you will be there. The audience which I hope to observe from very close proximity will consist half of Flemings and half of Dutch Zeelanders. Perhaps the Dutch are the most numerous. A wonderful means of furthering brotherhood among those of the same Netherlandic stock!
>
> The Dutch and Flemish get along rather well — though they are somewhat contentious in their respective internal politics. But my humble opinion is that we would be best to come right out with the idea of forming a brotherhood of those of the same stock. It's a marvellous occasion for that. Now, everything you do is well done! . . .
>
> Can you, then, bring the lantern and screen along? If not, I'll expect a line from you.
>
> Good friend, God preserve you idealistic and full of fire, in spite of hard reality.[7]

Soon the friendship between the two men led to a surprising admission. In the fall of 1929 Father Ladislas wrote the following:

> Dear Wolf, hang on to your pen! A friend keeps no secrets from his friend: I am Vossenberg. But you will keep that a secret from even your best friend, won't you![8]

Adolf Spillemaeckers was greatly surprised, because Vossenberg was the pseudonym of one of his fellow columnists in the *Gazette van Detroit*, and an ardent supporter of the Flemish cause.

This knowledge had to be kept a secret, since the higher clergy in Belgium did not approve of the pro-Flemish activities of elements in the clergy. It was claimed that there was a policy of sending these men to small communities where their work would have little effect.[9] In any case, the official attitude towards such activities was made clear in a letter suggesting that it would be more appropriate for priests to spend their time and energy on work for the Kingdom of God and not in labours for the kingdom of an independent Flanders. The pen-name Vossenberg allowed Father Ladislas to reach thousands of Flemish readers through the pages of the *Gazette* in full confidence that his identity would never be guessed. After spending 33 years working in the mission field with the Flemish in Canada, much beloved by all for his unremitting efforts to help them, he died August 19, 1961 with his identity as the inspiring Flamingant Vossenberg still a secret.

With the encouragement, openly of Adolf Spillemaeckers and quietly of Father Ladislas, the Flemish Movement in southwestern Ontario grew more successful year by year from 1927 to 1930.

At this point the Flemish Movement in southwestern Ontario was dealt a series of blows. Jozef Lecluyse, considered by his fellow members of Vlaanderen's Kerels as "the heart of the Movement" was killed in an automobile accident in December 1929. The Great Depression brought unemployment and despair to many of the Belgians, and thousands returned to Belgium. Among those who returned was Adolf Spillemaeckers. Vlaanderen's Kerels remained active for 40 years, disbanding in 1968. Little remains to show the existence of the Flemish Movement in America except newspaper accounts in the *Gazette van Detroit*, a copy of the constitution of Vlaanderen's Kerels, and a number of photographs and letters in private collections.

NOTES

[*] An expanded study of the topic under consideration in this article has appeared in chapters 4 and 5 of my book, *The Belgians in Ontario: A History* (Toronto: Dundurn, 1987).

[1] Shepard B. Clough, *A History of the Flemish Movement in Belgium* (New York: Octagon Books, 1968), pp. 283-284.

[2] Adolf Spillemaeckers, "The Flemish Movement in Canada." Unpublished sound recording, November 12, 1985, Windsor, Ontario.

[3] Multicultural History Society of Ontario, Bel. 2001, Doc. 1.

[4] *Gazette van Detroit*, July 13, 1928.

[5] M. de Vroede, *The Flemish Movement in Belgium* (Antwerp: Flemish Cultural Council and Flemish Information Institute, 1975), pp. 49-50.

[6] Jozef Segers (Father Ladislas) to Adolf Spillemaeckers, December 8, 1928.

[7] Jozef Segers (Father Ladislas) to Adolf Spillemaeckers, undated (December 1928).

[8] Jozef Segers (Father Ladislas) to Adolf Spillemaeckers, undated (November 1929).

[9] Clough, p. 251.

BIBLIOGRAPHY

Capuchins of Central Canada. Orangeville, Ontario: Capuchins of Central Canada, n.d.

Clough, Shepard B. *A History of the Flemish Movement in Belgium. A Study in Nationalism*. New York: Octagon Books, 1968.

De Vroede, M. *The Flemish Movement in Belgium*. Antwerp: Flemish Cultural Council and Flemish Information Institute, 1975.

Easton, B. E. "62 Year Record of Sugar Beet Labour Force in Ontario, and Kent County, 1902-1963." Unpublished report to the Kent Historical Society, Chatham, Ontario, April 20, 1964.

Gazette van Detroit, 1916-

Golden Anniversary, St. Mary's Blenheim, 1927-1977. Blenheim, Ontario: Capuchins of Central Canada, 1977.

Louden, Gertrude. "The History of the Sugar Industry In Wallaceburg, with Reference to the Agricultural Program and the Beet Labour Problem, 1901-1959." Unpublished report to the Wallaceburg Historical Society, October, 1977.

Multicultural History Society of Ontario, Bel. 2001, Doc. 1.

SYSTEM-THREATENING OR SYSTEM-TRANSFORMING?: THE SIGNIFICANCE OF *VERZUILING*

Stanley W. Carlson-Thies
Northwestern College, Orange City

The strongly *verzuilde* character of Dutch society during a large part of this century has raised for political scientists primarily one central question: how was a viable democracy maintained despite the division of society into *zuilen* – into Catholic, socialist, liberal, and orthodox Protestant subcultures? The significant of *verzuiling*, in this view, is the threat it posed to the political system. Taking as given the segmentation of the society into rigid, self-contained blocs, the key question, put lightly, has been: why didn't the Netherlands become Northern Ireland or Lebanon?

The search for an answer has given rise to an entire subfield in comparative politics and to greater sophistication in the analysis of all political systems. To account for the democratic stability of the Dutch and a number of other plural or *verzuilde* societies, "consociational democracy" theorists, chief among them Arend Lijphart, have called attention to deliberate decisions by the leaders of the subcultures to counteract divisive forces, and to the introduction of political practices and structures which facilitate the accommodation of conflicting demands.[1] Although the theory has received much criticism, it remains powerful both as an analytic scheme and as a set of recommendations for political leaders in deeply divided societies who favor democracy over dictatorial rule.[2]

But for the Dutch case, as least, I wish to suggest a different assessment of the significance of *verzuiling* for the political system. Instead of regarding it as system-threatening, consider the alternative conception of *verzuiling* as system-transforming. Rather than a focus on how disintegrative tendencies were counteracted, the key issue in this conception is how diverse fundamental perspectives, religious and ideological, all claiming public as well as private relevance, were integrated into the socio-political order. The *verzuilde* society was the outcome of a successful battle to create rules and institutions permitting the expression of deep differences not just in private practices but also in the public sphere. For just as the subcultures had to be "created" out of the raw material of religious and class distinctions by people who regarded those distinctions as the appropriate bases for forming groups and organizing activities, so also a socio-political framework had to be crafted which incorporated, rather than ignored, such distinctions; indeed, without that framework there could have been no *verzuilde* society.[3]

The Public Dimension of *Zuilen*

For this alternative view, start by considering again the characteristics of *zuilen* and of the *verzuilde* society. It is easy enough to bring to mind oddities like the much-maligned Catholic goat breeders' association or the housewife who will accept the fresh fish on sale only if it is wrapped in a Catholic or Protestant newspaper, depending on her – I mean the housewife's, not the fish's – faith. The more important image, leaving aside nuances, is of a society in which a Protestant worker belongs to a Protestant union, reads Protestant newspapers, and sends his children to Protestant schools; while a socialist worker, employed in the same factory and living in the same town, belongs instead to the socialist union, listens to socialist radio programs, and votes for the socialist party; and their Catholic work colleague goes his own way not only in attending Mass, but also by watching Catholic television, reading Catholic magazines, and insisting on a Catholic hospital when sick. The liberal civil servant who rides to his work on the same tram, on the other hand, abhors all intrusions of religion and ideology into social and political affairs, and thus is devoted only to those newspapers, television programs, clubs, and schools which play down any broader relevance of inner convictions.

Notice two distinctive characteristics of a society organized in this fashion. The first is the wide diversity of options available in the various institutional sectors. There is not just one union for all workers in a particular trade or factory, but several varieties of unions; there is not just one kind of hospital or elementary school or university but several. That is to say, within the single nation several distinct convictions of how the many activities of life ought to be carried out can all be pursued. This is neither a society dominated by one religion nor a society with a homogeneous secular culture. Protestant convictions about labor relations, the schooling of children, and the care of the ill have institutional expression just as do Catholic convictions about the same issues, and those who seek guidance from Reason instead of Revelation have their own institutions exemplifying that perspective on life.

The second defining characteristic is closely connected with the first. The religious and ideological diversity in activities and institutions is not restricted to the private realm, but extends into the public sphere and into the very institutions of the state itself. People choose friends, marriage partners, and Sunday activities on the basis of deep conviction. They can also join unions or political parties which represent and embody one or another fundamental vision of life. But even beyond this, people can choose among different, ideologically-colored, options in the areas of education, broadcasting, and health and social welfare – all of these very public, government-controlled, services. A central, even constitutive, reality of the Dutch *verzuilde* society was this structuring in accordance with deep convictions of not only private activities and institutions, not only intermediary organizations like unions and parties, but also services and institutions clearly belonging to the sphere of government responsibility. The pillars, we might say, extended up into the state itself.

A Protestant worker could easily decide to send his children to a Protestant school rather than to the government-operated, secular public system because schools of all perspectives received equal public funding and had equivalent legal standing. A socialist worker could easily find socialist programs on the radio because the broadcasting system, as structured by government, did not restrict the expression of particular viewpoints on the airwaves nor leave their presence to chance, but rather required each broadcaster to exemplify a particular perspective. Similarly, a Catholic worker could confidently plan on entering a Catholic nursing home in his waning years because the government did not discriminate, in its funding, between religious and secular health and welfare organizations.

Compare the situation in the United States. Here, too, there is a variety of institutions reflecting different fundamental commitments. But such institutions are all regarded as private; they have to raise their own funds and are not universally accessible. Public services take a common approach and government will fund only those non-government initiatives which also ignore particularistic perspectives. Thus, although we have not just secular public schools but also Catholic, Jewish, Christian Reformed, fundamentalist, and other schools and colleges, only the government-operated, secular educational institutions enjoy full public funding. The other schools must raise the bulk of their income from tuition fees, investments, bake sales, bingo games; if they get any government money, it is only for those activities which are demonstrably not tainted by the convictions which these schools were created to exemplify. Similarly, although the various levels of government depend to a surprising degree on religious facilities to care for the health and social needs of the population, funding is provided only to the extent that those facilities are able to provide services not measurably colored by religious distinctives. Americans regard only common activities and institutions as being genuinely in the public interest and thus eligible for government support.[4]

The Liberal Public Order and Its Opponents

A social and political order like this was the goal of the liberals who gave to the Netherlands in 1848 the constitutional foundations for parliamentary democracy and who dominated political life for much of the rest of the nineteenth century. In the existing arrangement, a kind of "enlightened" or generalized Protestantism held sway, despite the formal equality of all faiths. In place of this, liberals wanted all public institutions and initiatives to take a common, secular, approach, with religious conviction restricted to the churches and to private life.

Liberalism, of course, has many dimensions and produced many important advances. What is crucial in the present context, however, is the belief of J.R. Thorbecke and his liberal colleagues that religion is a private affair which must not be permitted to intrude into the public realm. In their view, the essential characteristic of the state and of the public order more generally – institutions and activities of more than narrow scope – was precisely their universality; the state and the public realm were preeminently the places where all citizens met as equals, unburdened of all sectarian distinctives. And it was only when the state disregarded the diverse religious convictions present in the nation that it could fulfill its central responsibility of treating each citizen the same as any other. Religious views and initiatives were permissible, even valuable, but were to be kept strictly private. Church and state were to be separate, but also religion and public life.[5]

These were the convictions the liberals wove into the public order by means of the new constitution and their long years of government leadership. Therefore, those citizens who believed, in opposition to the liberals, that their religious convictions were relevant for every area of life and ought to be embodied even in institutions playing a public role, had to battle to transform the new public order, to force the state to adopt different rules about how religious initiatives and institutions were to be treated. The *verzuilde* society, with its unions and political parties flying distinct ideological banners and its multiple, ideologically-colored, versions of the different public services, thus could only be the outcome of a successful battle by citizens who refused to restrict their beliefs to the private areas of life. Catholics and orthodox Protestants first, and later socialists as well, fought to replace the liberals' model of how the state should deal with *levensbeschouwelijke* diversity – the variety of religious and ideological views – with a new, pluralistic model. For the emancipation all three groups sought was the freedom to be themselves, rather than unrestricted admittance to a society of liberal design.[6]

The liberals' public order ideal was expressed most clearly and controversially in their redesign of elementary education policy.[7] First, all formal religious instruction was banned from the government-run schools; this, according to the liberals, made these schools suitable for children from every religious background, and thus truly public and legitimately entitled to government funding. Second, to protect the religious rights of parents unhappy with secular schooling, religiously-inspired, non-governmental, schools were guaranteed the right to exist. But such special schools, because of their sectarian approaches, were deemed private and denied all direct government assistance.

This two-track policy was increasingly contested by Catholics, who came to favor specifically Catholic education, and by those Protestants who found acceptable only schooling based on the Bible. Although the two groups disagreed on the specific religious content to be given to schooling, they agreed that the elimination of all religion from public education did not make it suitable for their children. Nor was either group satisfied with the mere right to maintain at their own expense special schools outside the public system. In their view, the secular public schools were not really common, but rather just as sectarian as special religious schools; the public schools were just as tailored to the views of only a segment of the nation as were Catholic and Protestant schools. But that meant that the government was discriminating on the basis of religion in exclusively supporting the secular public system.

Catholics and orthodox Protestants thus began demanding for their schools, as a matter of justice, the same government funding the public schools enjoyed. And independently the two groups began calling for a new education policy in which the government would support equally every variety of elementary school - Catholic, Protestant, Jewish, and secular. This was not a fight against neutral education but rather against a "neutral" state which in reality was biased against religious schooling. Nor was it merely a fight to obtain money; as J. Kappeyne van de Coppello, the great liberal leader of the 1870s, acknowledged, the demand for equal treatment of all schools was thoroughly subversive of the very foundation of the state.[8]

As such, the battle for financial equalization was fierce and lengthy, providing much of the political drama for more than fifty years and contributing much to the reshaping of the political landscape. It was the school cause, more than anything else, which made widely attractive to orthodox Protestants and Catholics the notion of building their own, confessional, political movements, and which doomed conservatism to a steady decline. When the liberals in 1878 hardened their position with a school law revision which further privileged public schools at the expense of special religious schools, their confessional opponents were galvanized to increased political activism and to combining in an alliance dedicated to overturning liberal rule and to revising the state's treatment of religious initiatives.

The first step to a pluralistic public education system was taken ten years later, when Catholics and orthodox Protestants jointly won control of the government and changed the school law to give to special religious schools a share of the education funds collected from all citizens. The final step came in 1917, when the constitution was modified to require complete financial equality between public elementary schools and special religious schools. The confessional parties had demanded this reform as the price for permitting consideration of other constitutional changes, and their goal was supported by the socialists, organized since 1894 in an increasingly powerful party, who had early decided for reasons of tactic and principle not to stand in the way of confessional workers desiring for their children religious schooling.[9]

The new constitutional rules effectively broadened the definition of public education, for special religious schools were given full government funding without being required to abandon their distinctive educational philosophies. As a concession to the liberals, it remained the government's obligation to ensure to all children easy access to neutral public schools, whereas the initiative for new special schools had to come from parents.[10] But the elementary education system had been radically reshaped, and with it, the public order. State neutrality in the face of diverse convictions had been reinterpreted, for this area of policy, to require not exclusive support of a secular, supposedly common, approach, but rather equal treatment of all perspectives. In its elementary education policy, the state now took account of, rather than ignored, the diversity of perspectives held by the citizens. Similar rules were later adopted for the other levels of education, giving the Netherlands an education order pluralistic to its core.

The identical issue of how the state ought to deal with a diversity of perspectives was posed in another important policy area in the 1920s with the advent of radio broadcasting. The original radio programming, following liberal preferences, was designed to appeal to the broadest possible audience. But orthodox Protestants, Catholics, and socialists quickly formed their own radio associations, each of these desiring to use the new technology to reach members of its own subculture and to spread its views to the whole society. Despite this, liberals again promoted a "national" broadcasting system which would emphasize common interests and views and allocate only a minor role to programs appealing to specific groups. But Catholics, Protestants, and socialists joined together in opposition, demanding a system giving all groups and perspectives equal access to the public airwaves. There was no neutral or common perspective on the important issues, in their view; an unbiased broadcasting system could only be achieved by allowing each of the subcultures to produce its own programs.

It was this pluralistic model, not the "national" one, which the government followed when it adopted broadcast regulations in

1930. The actual transmission facilities were operated by a public corporation, but the bulk of the programming was supplied by the four subculturally-rooted broadcast associations, to which the government allocated equal shares of the available air time.[11] Instead of assuming that all Dutch people shared the same fundamental perspective, the government had accepted the visible diversity of views and guaranteed access to the public airwaves to all of them. Television broadcasting was later regulated in a similar fashion.

A Pluriform Public Order

Thus, by the 1930s, state policy for dealing with the multiple fundamental convictions of how private and public activities ought to be carried out had been transformed. Equality of treatment no longer was understood to require the state to ignore *levensbeschouwelijke* differences, but rather to embrace them. In such areas of public concern and prime governmental responsibility as education and broadcasting, a new framework for relating state and society, a new public order, had been created. These public services did not have a common approach and were not designed and delivered exclusively by government institutions. There were, instead, multiple options, designed and delivered chiefly by institutions rooted in the subcultures, with the government playing a supervisory and supportive role. The liberal public order had been transformed into what we might call a pluriform public order, with rules and structures designed to incorporate the array of fundamental convictions even into the very services for which the state assumed responsibility.

It was this pluriform model which guided the construction of the welfare state after World War II. The government assumed new health and social service responsibilities and dramatically increased the amount of money it devoted to such policies. But most health and welfare services were actually delivered not by government but by institutions rooted in the subcultures and reflecting their different views.[12]

There was a certain inevitability to this development. The subcultures were well-developed, already extending into the public realm in other policy areas. There is a sense in which *verzuiling*, this particular way of organizing people and institutions, had become, as J.E. Ellemers says, a "self-perpetuating mechanism."[13] But in a deeper sense, the pluralistic development of the welfare state ought to be seen rather as the deliberate extension to a new area of public action of the same state response to *levensbeschouwelijke* diversity which had been crafted for education and broadcasting.

It seems generally accepted that the *verzuilde* society reached its peak of development in the 1950s. Catholics, orthodox

Protestants, socialists, and liberals all had elaborated their own way of doing things, and those different ways were embodied in a whole array of public as well as private activities and institutions. The state's attitude towards religious and ideological diversity, and with it, the pattern of state/society relations, had been transformed. Significantly, that peak of development was reached despite the widespread disruption of the institutional matrix during five years of Nazi occupation, and despite the strong appeal of the *doorbraak* activists, in and out of government, for a reconstruction of society along more conventional lines.

The End of the Pluriform Public Order?

Since the 1960s, numerous cultural and religious developments have combined to weaken the division of the society into subcultures. A short list would include the steep decline in the number of faithful churchgoers; the decreasing tendency of even the remaining faithful to regard a close connection between religion and "profane" activities as natural and necessary; the success of socialists in portraying their party and other activities as suitable for all and open to contributions from every faith perspective; and an increasing individualism and generalized distrust of leaders, both of which cast suspicion on all institutions and make less likely stable commitment to any grouping and comprehensive ideological or religious perspective. Moreover, the massive development of the welfare state, despite its incorporation of subcultural initiatives, appears to have been accompanied by, and to have encouraged, a widespread faith in professionalism, in neutral expertise, weakening the notion that the separate subcultures had distinctive approaches to offer.[14] And governments, even when dominated by the confessional parties, have now and again adopted policies fostering homogeneity in the name of promoting efficiency, democratization, or reductions of the budget deficits.[15]

Without a doubt, the pillars have been tottering for years and their outlines are by now largely eroded. Correspondingly, questioning about the rationale and need for the traditional pluriform arrangements has become widespread. Yet the notions that inner convictions have broad relevance and that public arrangements ought to facilitate their institutional expression have hardly disappeared. On radio and television, TROS and Veronica, with their American-style, non-ideological programming, have become very popular, yet conservative Protestant views have gained enough support to enable the Evangelische Omroep to join the broadcasting system, and the socialist VARA, the Catholic KRO, and the orthodox Protestant NCRV have all renewed their commitments to programming reflecting their respective orientations. If the formation of the Christen Democratisch Appèl out of the three most important confessional parties in one sense proves the declining relevance of older lines of distinction, the merger nevertheless has resulted in a revival of specifically Christian reflection on public policy.

Similarly, it is striking how the enormity of the continuing economic and welfare state crises has prompted from the major political forces not a pragmatic consensus but a revival of their distinctive ideological perspectives.[16] Moreover, several recent issues and policies have compelled renewed reflection on how the state should deal with *levensbeschouwelijke* diversity. Think, for instance, of the revision of the media law and the restructuring of the broadcasting system, the increasing size of the Moslem population, and the rise in the number of parents indifferent to the religious character of their children's schooling.[17] The final chapter in the story of how the Dutch state will accommodate differences of view is far from being written.

Did the advancing "segmented integration" of Dutch society ever have the potential of turning it into another Northern Ireland or Lebanon, where the subcultures are not only distinct but at war with each other?[18] Perhaps the better comparison, if such comparisons are useful, is instead with the Belgium of the past few decades. During these years, public activities, institutions, and even the very structure of the Belgian state have been transformed, so that Dutch-language citizens may have equal opportunities, in public and private life, with the long-dominant Francophones.[19] For in the Netherlands it was the deep desire of Catholics, orthodox Protestants, and socialists to be able to manifest in all sectors of life their distinctive perspectives which drove them to create subcultures and battle to transform the liberal public order.

NOTES

[1] See Lijphart's *The Politics of Accommodation: Pluralism and Democracy in the Netherlands*, 2nd ed. (Berkeley: University of California Press, 1975); *Democracy in Plural Societies: A Comparative Exploration* (New Haven: Yale University Press, 1977); and *Democracies: Patterns of Majoritarian and Consensus Government in Twenty-One Countries* (New Haven: Yale University Press, 1984). See also the reader edited by Kenneth D. McRae, *Consociational Democracy: Political Accommodation in Segmented Societies* (Toronto: McClelland and Stewart, 1974).

[2] See esp. M.P.C.M. van Schendelen, "The Views of Arend Lijphart and Collected Criticisms," *Acta Politica*, XIX (January 1984), pp. 19-55. For Lijphart's response to his critics, see esp. his *Power-Sharing in South Africa*, Policy Papers in International Affairs, no. 24 (Berkeley: Institute of International Studies, 1985), ch. 4.

[3] Consociational theory regards *verzuiling* to be supportive of the political system, not threatening, if the elites of the subcultures have decided to cooperate despite their differences. Moreover, it regards the system-transforming devolution of many services from government to the subcultures as a key feature of viable, democratic, plural societies. What the theory seeks to explain, however, is the assumed incompatibility of stable democracy with the existence within a nation of differences so deep and comprehensive that the society is *verzuild*, i.e., people pursue their affairs in segmented rather than common institutions. The alternative view of the Dutch case suggested here regards such deep and comprehensive differences to have been threatening only to the <u>liberal</u> socio-political order, which required common public institutions and the privatization of religious conviction.

[4] There are exceptions, of course, e.g., the chaplaincy in the armed forces; moreover, although the treatment of the religious/secular and private/public distinctions as identical appears firmly entrenched, this is a relatively recent phenomenon.

[5] On the liberals and religion, see, e.g., I.A. Diepenhorst, *Historisch-critische bijdrage tot de leer van den christelijken staat*, 2nd printing (Amsterdam: Noord-Hollandsche Uitgevers Maatschappij, 1943), ch. 4; and H. G. Leih, *Kaart van politiek Nederland* (Kampen: J.H. Kok, 1962), chapter on liberalism. C.H.E. de Wit, "Thorbecke, staatsman en historicus," in *Thorbecke en de wording van de Nederlandse natie* (Nijmegen: SUN, 1980), pp. 5-176, includes very helpful material on Thorbecke's public order conceptions.

[6] Cf. J.M.G. Thurlings, "The Case of Dutch Catholicism: A Contribution to the Theory of the Pluralistic Society," *Sociologia Neerlandica*, 7, no. 2 (1971), pp. 118-36; Thurlings, *De wankele zuil. Nederlandse katholieken tussen assimilatie en pluralisme*, 2nd ed. (Nijmegen: Van Loghum Slaterus, 1978); and J. Klapwijk, "Christelijke organisaties in verlegenheid," in C. Rijnsdorp, et al., *Christelijke organisaties in discussie. Een bijdrage* (Den Haag: Uitgeverij Boekencentrum, 1979), pp. 21-66.

[7] The actual 1857 law was the work of a non-liberal cabinet, but liberals had set the boundaries for it. For accounts of the school dispute which pay attention to structural issues, see P.A. Diepenhorst, *Onze strijd in de Staten-Generaal*, vol. 1 (Amsterdam: Dagblad en Drukkerij De Standaard, 1927); P.W.C. Akkermans, *Onderwijs als constitutioneel probleem* (Alphen a/d Rijn: Samsom, 1980); and Ph. J. Idenburg, *Schets van het Nederlandse schoolwezen*, 2nd ed. (Groningen: J.B. Wolters, 1964), chs. 3-4.

[8] See his response to the confessional petitions against his 1878 school law, reprinted in J.C. Rullmann, ed., *Gedenkboek bij het vijftig-jarig bestaan van De Unie "Een School met den Bijbel"* (Kampen: J.H. Kok, 1928), pp. 133-42, at p. 142.

[9] Erik Hansen, "Marxism, Socialism, and the Dutch Primary Schools," *History of Education Quarterly*, XIII, no. 4 (Winter 1973), pp. 367-91.

[10] Confessionals also had to accede to the liberal and socialist demand that the state retain a large role in the supply of schooling and that the standards for all state-financed education be drawn from the state-operated schools. Their ideal had been, and is, for all schools to be governed by non-state associations, and some of them feared, rightly, that the adopted scheme hampered the ability of special schools to fully express distinctive approaches. The term *pacificatie* was applied by contemporaries to these compromises on the structure of education, not to any log-rolling or other deal involving universal suffrage, the other major constitutional change made. The full account is Cassianus Hentzen, *De politieke geschiedenis van het lager onderwijs in Nederland. De financieele gelijkstelling, 1913-1920* (Den Haag: R.-K. Centraal Bureau voor Onderwijs en Opvoeding, [1925]).

[11] A small amount of air time went to a liberal Protestant broadcaster, and the regulations imposed on the four major associations the ill-conceived requirement of producing by turns a general program. On the broadcasting system, see esp. Hans van den Heuvel, *Nationaal of verzuild. De strijd om het Nederlandse omroepbestel in de periode 1923-1947* (Baarn: Amboboeken, 1976).

[12] See, e.g., Maria Brenton, "Changing Relationships in Dutch Social Services," *Journal of Social Policy*, 11, pt. 1 (January 1982), pp. 59-80.

[13] Ellemers, "Pillarization as a Process of Modernization," *Acta Politica*, XIX (January 1984), p. 140.

[14] Cf. Brenton, "Changing Relationships," pp. 67-8.

[15] See, e.g., S. Griffioen, "De verhouding van staat en maatschappij," in *Waar staat de staat?* (Den Haag: Boekencentrum, 1984), p. 41.

[16] For the CDA, see, e.g., the discussion documents "Appèl en weerklank" and "Van verzorgingsstaat naar verzorgingsmaatschappij," published together as a special edition of *CD Actueel* in 1983. For the social democratic party (PvdA), see, e.g., *Schuivende panelen. Continuïteit en vernieuwing in de sociaal-democratie,*

4th printing (Amsterdam: PvdA, 1988). For the liberals, see, e.g., *Liberaal bestek '90. "Een kansrijke toekomst - verantwoorde vrijheid"* ([Den Haag:] VVD, n.d.).

[17] See, respectively, L.B.M. Wüst's superb discussion of the value of a pluriform broadcasting system: "Mediabeleid en de waarde van intermenselijke communicatie," *Christen Democratische Verkenningen*, 2/88 (1988), pp. 74-89; C.J. Klop, "De Islam in Nederland. Angst voor een nieuwe zuil?," *Christen Democratische Verkenningen*, 11/82 (1982), pp. 526-33; and Fons van Schoten and Hans Wansink, *De nieuwe schoolstrijd. Knelpunten en conflicten in de hedendaagse onderwijspolitiek* (Amsterdam: Vereniging voor Openbaar Onderwijs, 1984).

[18] Johan Goudsblom, *Dutch Society* (New York: Random House, 1967), p. 31.

[19] See Kenneth D. McRae's excellent study, *Conflict and Compromise in Multilingual Societies, Volume 2: Belgium* (Waterloo, Ontario: Wilfrid Laurier University Press, 1986).

MEDIEVAL NETHERLANDS HISTORY
THE BURGUNDIAN PERSPECTIVE

Arthur L. Loeb
Harvard University, Cambridge

I   Introduction

Although the Unions of Utrecht and Atrecht in 1579 following the Pacification of Ghent the previous year are frequently considered to signify the partition of the Netherlands, it is the fall of Antwerp in 1585 which actually marks the division.[1] Whereas the Union of Utrecht encompassed most of the Dutch-speaking southern provinces, and these regions housed the most orthodox calvinism, the capture of Antwerp by the Spaniards caused an exodus to the north, which in turn spurred the unprecedented flowering of commerce, arts and letters there during the early seventeenth century, which became known as the Golden Age.[2]

As a result, medieval Netherlands history is frequently taught from the perspective of the provinces of Holland which actually constituted a relatively minor portion of the northern Burgundian domain, a region which developed relatively late.[3] Events such as the reign of Jacoba van Beieren and the wars between Hoeks and Kabeljouws are presented as isolated occurrences rather than in the context of the development of the modern European states.

The author has designed and taught an interdisciplinary course at Harvard under the auspices of its Committee on Nondepartmental Courses, entitled "Burgundy, The Rise and Fall of the Middle Realm."[4] The purpose of this course was to bring together the various disciplines known as political and cultural history, art history, musicology, dance history, the history of religion, iconography, architectural history, viticulture and food history in order to demonstrate the interrelations between such topics as the battle of Agincourt, the van Eycks and the miniaturists, Henry V, the poetry of Charles d'Orléans, Jeanne d'Arc, the music of Guillaume Dufay and Jacob Obrecht, the Feast of the Pheasant, the sculptor Sluter of Haarlem, the court of Margaret of Austria, all of which might have been referred to in some courses on Shakespeare, on the poetic forms, on the Cluny ruins, or on the "waning" of the Middle Ages.[5]

When information from different sources in different disciplines was assembled, a pattern emerged in which the Low Countries constitute an important domain in a strongly interconnected group of states, whose *traits d'union* were different branches of the Valois dynasty. This article outlines the history of the Low Countries in this context, represents the relations between Valois, Plantagenets and Wittelsbachs graphically, and concludes with a section describing how this interdisciplinary course was implemented.

II The Fourteenth Century

The various affiliations of Alsace and Lorraine in modern times, and the recent Benelux aggregation are reminders that the failure of the tripartite subdivision of Charlemagne's empire at Verdun of 843 AD engendered forces which have continued to shape history for more than a millennium.[6,7] In particular, the four Valois Dukes of Burgundy, Philippe le Hardi, Jean sans Peur, Philippe le Bon and Charles le Téméraire in the later fourteenth and most of the fifteenth century strove for the recreation of a middle kingdom independent of either France or the Empire.[8,9,10]

Around the beginning of the fourteenth century, the second member of the Avesnes family to be Count of both Holland and Hainaut (Henegouwen), Willem III, found himself dynastically connected to most of the reigning, and usually warring, families of Europe. Upon the unexpected demise of all male members of the senior branch of the French royal family, the Capets, the brother of Willem's wife Jeanne de Valois ascended the French throne as Philippe VI. Willem and Jeanne had two daughters, one of whom, Margaretha, became the second wife of the Emperor, Ludwig of Wittelsbach, while the other, Philippa, married King Edward III of England. Accordingly, Willem and Jeanne counted among their grandchildren not only Albrecht, Count of Holland and Hainaut, but also Edward, the Black Prince and his brother John of Gaunt (=Ghent, his birthplace!), the Duke of Lancaster. This relation of the Counts of Holland to both the Plantagenets in England and the Valois in France put the Counts of Holland in a power-balancing position in the Hundred Years' War between England and France.[11,12] When Albrecht's son Willem VI went to England to attend the wedding of his cousins Richard II of England (son of the Black Prince) and Isabelle de France, he received a warning from his father not to become embroiled in the dangerous English intrigues.

Meanwhile Willem and Jeanne's nephew, King Jean II of France, inherited the Duchy of Burgundy from his mother, and in turn bestowed it upon his youngest son, Philippe le Hardi, whose wife, Margaretha van Male, was heiress to Flanders, Brabant, Artois, and the County of Burgundy (later known as Franche Comté). It is significant that Margaretha's inheritance was situated on both sides of the border between France and the Empire: Flanders and Artois were French fiefs, whereas Brabant and the County of Burgundy were Imperial. Through Philippe's marriage this Valois prince extended his influence eastward and northward into Imperial lands. It should not be forgotten that by that time Flanders with its well-developed textile industry and trade with England was one of the most prosperous regions of Europe, and that during the last quarter of the fourteenth century Brussels, the capital of Brabant at least equaled Dijon as a center of Burgundian power and splendor.[13] The work of Claes Sluter and Claes van de Werve from "Les Pays Là Bas" can still be admired in Dijon, notably their *pleurants* (mourners) on the tomb of Philippe and Margaretha.[14] The traveler should not fail to visit the castle of Germolles between Beaune and Cluny, which Philippe built for his bride. While Philippe's royal brother Charles V of France ruled prudently, their splendor-loving brother the Duc de Berry commissioned his famous Books of Hours from the Netherlandish Limburg brothers.[15]

III Dynastic Politics

King Charles V died in 1380; his son Charles VI was repeatedly incapacitated, probably by the hereditary disease porphyria. As a result, tension developed between some of the appointed guardians, namely the king's brother, Louis Duke of Orléans, and the royal uncle, Philippe of Burgundy. After Philippe's death in 1404, civil war broke out between the Orléans and Burgundy adherents. Burgundy had further extended its influence in the Netherlands through the double marriage of Philippe's daughter Marguerite to Willem VI of Wittelsbach, Count of Holland and Hainaut, and of Philippe's son Jean sans Peur with Willem's sister Margaretha. First Louis d'Orléans (in 1407), and later Jean sans Peur (in 1419) were assassinated by their opponents.

The common "family tree" is of little use in a graphical presentation of the dynastic power flow in the fifteenth century, for the frequent intermarriages between different branches of the same family change the tree structure to one having many closed loops. Attempts to force these family structures into a tree format resort to multiple listings of the same person, or to total disregard for descent in the female line. The author therefore developed a Kinship Graph[c] to represent the relationship between a number of persons relevant to a given argument.[16] Figure 1 is an excerpt of the Kinship Graph relating about four hundred persons relevant to Burgundian history in the late Middle Ages.

After 1419 our cast of characters includes two grandchildren of Philippe le Hardi: Philippe le Bon, son of Jean sans Peur and of Margaretha of Wittelsbach, and his double cousin Jacoba of Wittelsbach, daughter and heiress of Count Willem VI of Holland and Hainaut and of Marguerite of Burgundy, as well as a grandson of Charles V: Charles d'Orléans, son of Louis d'Orléans and of Valentina Visconti.[17,18] The royal branch of the Valois family was racked not only by the intermittent attacks of insanity suffered by the king, Charles VI, but also by the scandals caused by the behaviour of the queen, Elizabeth (Isabeau), a distant Wittelsbach cousin of the Counts of Holland. Their eldest daughter, Isabelle, had been sent to England in the closing years of the fourteenth

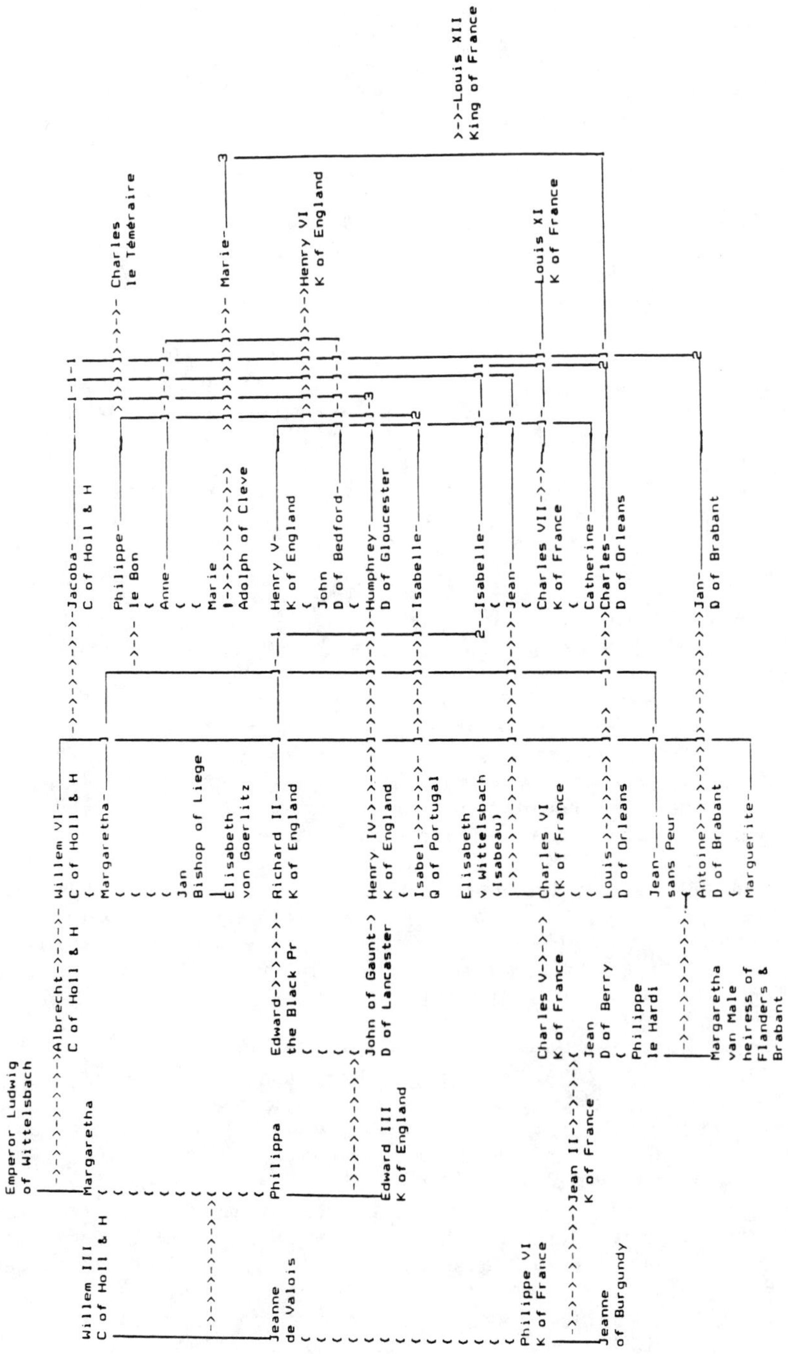
Emperor Ludwig of Wittelsbach
Willem III C of Holl & H
Margaretha
Albrecht C of Holl & H
Willem VI C of Holl & H
Margaretha
Jacoba C of Holl & H
Philippe le Bon
Anne
Jan Bishop of Liege
Elisabeth von Goerlitz
Marie
Adolph of Cleve
Charles le Téméraire
Marie
Louis XII King of France
Jeanne de Valois
Philippa
Edward III K of England
Edward the Black Pr
Richard II K of England
Henry V K of England
Henry VI K of England
John of Gaunt D of Lancaster
Henry IV K of England
John D of Bedford
Humphrey D of Gloucester
Isabel Q of Portugal
Isabelle
Elisabeth v Wittelsbach (Isabeau)
Isabelle
Jean
Philippe VI K of France
Jean II K of France
Charles V K of France
Charles VI (K of France
Charles VII K of France
Louis XI K of France
Catherine
Jeanne of Burgundy
Jean D of Berry
Louis D of Orleans
Charles D of Orleans
Philippe le Hardi
Jean sans Peur
Margaretha van Male heiress of Flanders & Brabant
Antoine D of Brabant
Marguerite
Jan D of Brabant

Figure 1: Kinship Graph for this article.

```
-_____ and ∫ , or _____
                        |
                        |
                        | indicates marriage relationship.
  _____ 1, 2 or 3 indicates that this person is the first,
         second or third spouse.
  ] indicates that two lines cross, but do not intersect.
  >->-> indicates parent-to-child relationship.
  ( indicates sibling relationship.
  E  indicates Emperor.
  K  indicates King.
  Pr indicates Prince.
  D  indicates Duke.
  C  indicates Count(ess).
  Holl & H indicates Holland and Hainaut.
```

****

century as the child bride of the widowed king, Richard II. When Richard was replaced, and probably murdered at the instigation of his cousin Henry IV, the English delayed her return to France, but eventually she did return, and in 1406 became the wife of her young cousin Charles d'Orléans. At that auspicious occasion Jacoba became engaged to Isabelle's younger brother prince Jean. When Jean's elder brother died, the couple became Dauphins of France, and Jacoba would have become Queen of France if her husband had not also died young, to be succeeded as Dauphin by his brother Charles, well known as the protégé and sponsor of Jeanne d'Arc.

We saw previously that Margaretha van Male, Philippe le Hardi's wife, had been heiress not only to Flanders, but also to Brabant. In order not to be too brazen about his designs on the Low Countries, Philippe had designated as heir to Brabant not his elder son Jean sans Peur, but his younger son Antoine. Although Jean sans Peur refused to support the royal, or Orléans partisans in the war against England, his younger brother of Brabant fought on the French side, and was killed in the battle of Agincourt in 1415, being succeeded as Duke of Brabant by his son Jan. Antoine had been a pawn in Philippe le Hardi's grand scheme of expansion in the north: The Luxemburg dynasty had, about a century earlier, developed an Imperial branch, which produced several emperors as well as kings of Bohemia, and a French branch including the well-known St. Pol family. Antoine's first wife, Jeanne de Luxembourg, brought St. Pol into the Burgundian domains; after Jeanne's death Antoine married the Imperial heiress Elisabeth von Goerlitz.

Although Shakespeare in *Henry V* gives the impression that the English victory at Agincourt was immediately followed by the marriage between Henry V and fair Catherine, a daughter of the sick king, Charles VI, this marriage in point of fact did not occur until five years later. At that occasion the king and queen appointed Catherine and Henry V their heirs, disowning the Dauphin Charles.

Catherine's eldest sister, the tragic Isabelle, widow of Richard II and wife of Charles d'Orléans, had died in 1409 giving birth to a daughter, Jeanne, leaving her husband, fourteen-year old Charles, with the responsibility for his daughter, three little brothers and a three-year old sister, as well as the leadership of the royal, anti-Burgundy faction. After Charles's second marriage, to Bonne d'Armagnac, herself a great-granddaughter of Jean II, this faction was called the Armagnacs. Charles was captured at Agincourt, leaving the responsibility for the Orléans family in the hands of his illegitimate half-brother, Jean Dunois, who had been lovingly reared by Charles's mother, Valentina Visconti.[19] It was Dunois who first supported and became a friend to Jeanne d'Arc when she championed the cause of the disavowed dauphin Charles. Charles d'Orléans spent almost thirty years in captivity in England, where he wrote much of the poetry, in both French and English, which made him one of the foremost poets in French literary history.[20,21,22,23]

IV **Jacoba**

In 1417 both Jacoba's father, Count Willem VI, and her husband, the young Dauphin Jean, had died. At a family council at Biervliet, Jacoba was confronted by two of her uncles: her mother's brother, Jean sans Peur, insisted on her marriage to her cousin Jan of Brabant, while her father's brother, Jan of Wittelsbach, Bishop of Liège, decided that she needed his protection in the County of Holland, and installed himself there as leader of the Kabeljouws (Cods), while Jacoba had the support of the Hoeks. The Kabeljouws represented principally the merchants in the prosperous commercial centers, while the Hoeks were the party of the powerful nobility.

A marriage contract between the reluctant Jacoba and her cousin Jan was signed on August 1, 1418, and dispensation from the ban on consanguinous marriages was granted by pope Martin V on December 22, but revoked two weeks later. The papal schism had seriously weakened the position of the popes, and dispensations were granted and revoked according to the prevailing political winds. However, Jacoba and Jan were secretly married in the Hague on March 10, 1418, and a public ceremony was celebrated on April 10. The Emperor now forbade the bans, and formally bestowed Holland, Zeeland, and Hainaut on Jan of Wittelsbach, who promptly renounced his episcopal vows to marry Antoine's widow, Elisabeth von Goerlitz.

Following the assassination of Jean sans Peur at the bridge of Montereau in 1419, a number of treaties put Jacoba in a perilous situation. Jean's son Philippe le Bon, Jan of Brabant, and Jan of Wittelsbach essentially divided up her inheritance, and the Burgundians formally allied themselves with the victorious English against the Orléans/Armagnac faction who supported the disinherited Dauphin. Remarkably for that time, Jacoba refused to let her husband usurp her rights, and when the latter replaced her ladies-in-waiting from Holland with Burgundian ladies of his own choosing, Jacoba made a terrible scene and with her mother, Marguerite of Burgundy, quit the court in Brussels, settling in great style in Quesnoy in Hainaut in the spring of 1420.

Jan of Brabant attempted a reconciliation, but even his own Brabant rebelled against him, with the result that he was temporarily replaced as Duke by his brother, Philippe de St. Pol. In February 1421 Jacoba declared her marriage to Jan illegal, and left Quesnoy very quietly for Calais, where she requested and received a visum for England from Henry V. In England she was warmly welcomed by Henry's brother, Humphrey, the Duke of Gloucester, and comfortably installed at Windsor in the company of her former sister-in-law, Queen Catherine. On December 6, 1421 the future Henry VI was born there, and held at his baptism by his godmother Jacoba. Jacoba and Humphrey became engaged, embarrassing Henry V, who saw in this alliance a threat to his treaty with Philippe le Bon. Philippe consistently opposed any marriage by his independent cousin which would undermine his designs on the strong united middle realm envisioned by his grandfather, Philippe le Hardi. However, Henry V's premature death in August 1422 removed these obstacles, and in February 1423 Jacoba, now Duchess of Gloucester, announced her marriage officially to her estates of Hainaut.

Holland meanwhile was quiet under the rule of Jan of Wittelsbach, and Philippe le Bon sought to strengthen his English alliance through the marriage of his sister Anne to another brother of Henry V, John, the Duke of Bedford. In October 1423, the two cousins and sisters-in-law, Jacoba, Duchess of Gloucester and Anne, Duchess of Bedford became naturalized English citizens. A year later, Humphrey and Jacoba crossed over to Calais, and in the company of Jacoba's mother Marguerite made their triumphal entry into Mons, where Humphrey was recognized as Duke of Hainaut on December 5, 1424. A month later, Jan of Wittelsbach died, possibly poisoned by Jacoba's half-sister and her husband, Beatrix and Jan van Vliet. Jan van Brabant assumed the leadership of the Cod party, and Philippe le Bon attempted to incite Hainaut to a rebellion against Humphrey.

These events mark the pinnacle of Jacoba's remarkable career. Humphrey's position in England was undermined by his uncle, the Bishop of Winchester, and he had to return home, where he fell under the spell of Eleanor Cobham, and ultimately abandoned Jacoba, getting the vacillating pope Martin V to annul their marriage. In 1428 Jacoba was forced to come to an agreement with her cousin Philippe (Zoen van Delft), where she agreed not to marry again without Philippe's approval. Jeanne d'Arc rallied France to the cause of the Dauphin in 1429, but like Jacoba was eventually defeated by the Burgundians. The next year Philippe married Isabelle of Portugal, whose mother had been a daughter of John of Gaunt, and founded the Order of the Golden Fleece, one of those Camelotian institutions so popular in the waning of the Middle Ages. One of the prominent knights of this order, Frank van Borselen from Zeeland, secretly married Jacoba in 1432. When news of the marriage leaked out, Jacoba saved her husband's life by agreeing to abandon all her claims to her Wittelsbach and Burgundian inheritance. Attacked by consumption, she died on October 9, 1436, and was buried in the Hague.

V The End of the Hundred Years' War

The English gradually lost their grip in France. The fickle Humphrey had attempted a landing in Flanders in 1435, and young Henry VI appealed to his beloved aunt for assistance. Anne of Bedford had died in 1431; her widowed husband married another of the Luxembourg princesses, Jacquette, but died shortly afterward. Eleanor Cobham was convicted of treasonable witchcraft in 1441, and condemned to walk barefoot through London with a two-pound taper in her hand, after which she was imprisoned for life. Frank van Borselen had a long and distinguished career in the service of the Dukes of Burgundy until around 1470.

Interesting are the parallel adventures of the two widowed French princesses, Henry V's widow Catherine, and his brother John's widow Jacquette, the dowager Duchess of Bedford.[24] Catherine met a fairly obscure Welsh knight, Owen Tudor, and appears to have married him secretly, at least so claim their descendants, the English royal House of Tudor. After the death of Bedford in France, Jacquette was escorted back to England by Sir Richard Woodville, later to become Lord Rivers, whom she subsequently married. Their daughter Elizabeth married Sir John Grey, who was killed in the Wars of the Roses; one of their descendants was the unfortunate Lady Jane Grey, who ruled England for a day upon the death of Edward VI, but was beheaded by Bloody Mary. Jacquette, however, was not about to allow her daughter to remain a widow for long, and according to legend persuaded Elizabeth to stroll in the woods where King Edward IV was wont to pass. Their romance and marriage, and the "upstart" Woodvilles' influence, considerably upset the older families at court. It should not be forgotten that these upstarts were also scions of the House of Luxembourg, and appear to have shared their mother's French accent at what was a self-consciously English court.

Domestic problems further weakened the English position in France, whereas the Dauphin, now Charles VII, proved to be a crafty ruler, like his grandfather Charles V an administrator in the modern style.[25] Elisabeth von Goerlitz's uncle, the Emperor Sigismund, declared war upon Burgundy; the balance of power in France was restored, and the treaty of Arras in 1435 led to the reconciliation between Charles VII and Philippe le Bon, and the dissolution of the English-Burgundian alliance.

Charles d'Orléans, still in captivity in England, and Philippe le Bon's duchess, Isabelle of Portugal, John of Gaunt's granddaughter, were able to initiate peace negotiations, and in 1440 Charles d'Orléans was finally released, over the objections of Humphrey of Gloucester. His beloved wife Bonne d'Armagnac, subject of so much of his poetry, as well as his daughter Jeanne had died in 1432, and Charles took as his third wife Philippe le Bon's niece, Marie of Clèves. Their son Louis was to be King Louis XII well into the sixteenth century. It is interesting to speculate how much Charles d'Orléans heard from his first wife, Isabelle about the mysterious death of her first husband, Richard II in the late fourteenth century, and how much of this Charles passed on to his son, the first French king in the sixteenth century!

The city of Bruges, long independent in spirit, had rebelled against Philippe in 1436, and the rebellion soon spread into all of Flanders. Philippe is reputed to have sworn that he would never enter the city again unless accompanied by a prince greater than himself. When Charles d'Orléans had been released and married to Marie, Philippe in a magnificent gesture invited his niece and nephew-in-law to accompany him on a mission of forgiveness to Bruges. At Quesnoy they were received by their (great) aunt Marguerite, the dowager Countess of Holland and Hainaut. Altogether, the following decades are marked by magnificent, typically late medieval celebrations of peace and forgiveness: the old leagues are dissolved. Notably, Philippe convened in 1454 the magnificent Feast of the Pheasant, ostensably to call a renewed crusade.

VI **The Habsburgs**

Tensions between the Royal and Burgundian Valois branches resumed when Philippe's son Charles quarreled with his father over the increasing favor enjoyed by the de Croy family, and defected to the royal court, whereas the Dauphin Louis, in rebellion against the King, sought refuge at the Burgundian court. When both had succeeded their fathers by 1470, Louis XI proved to be a modern politician, in opposition to Charles le Téméraire, who saw himself as successor to Alexander the Great and the other worthies, hanging on to the medieval code of chivalry, which died with his defeat at Nancy in 1477.[26,27]

Charles le Téméraire left his daughter Marie under the guardianship of her stepmother, Margaret of York, sister of Edward

IV.[28] The marriage between Charles le Téméraire and Margaret of York in Bruges in 1468 had been in the grand Burgundian style, a style adopted by Margaret's flamboyant brother, Edward IV. Gordon Kipling stresses the influence of the Burgundian court on the Tudor one, culminating in the Elizabethan renaissance.[29] Charles had hoped to persuade the Emperor, Frederic III of Habsburg, to create a Burgundian Kingdom, and to arrange a marriage between Marie and the Emperor's son, Maximilian. Although a Burgundian Kingdom was not to be, the marriage did materialize, and was very happy: unfortunately Marie died very young.[30]

From Marie Maximilian inherited much of the Low Countries, which had gradually developed some degree of unity, marked by the establishment of the States General in 1464. Although Burgundy proper became permanently attached to France, one cannot properly understand the significance of medieval Burgundy without including consideration of the period 1477-1530. Incidentally, Kipling mentions that as late as 1501 the wedding of Margaret, daughter of Marie and Maximilian to Philibert of Savoye took place in Dijon![31]

Margaret, who had been called after her step-grandmother Margaret of York, so beloved by Marie, settled in Mechelen after the death of her husband, where she raised her nieces and nephews, among them the later Emperor Charles V, whose father Philippe le Bel had died, and whose mother, the Spanish princess Juana had become insane.[32,33] Otto von Habsburg in his biography of his ancestor Emperor Charles V stresses the Burgundian character of this grandson of Marie and Maximilian.[34] At her exquisite small palace Margaret became a sponsor of the visual arts and music. Among her protégés at Mechelen were the composers Josquin des Prés and Pierre de la Rue. A beautiful black and gold dance manual in her possession, then already many decades old, and a book of *chansons* from her collection are preserved, and serve us as important sources of music and dance of that time.

Margaret and her erstwhile sister-in-law Louise de Savoie, met in 1530 to arrange a peace between Margaret's nephew, Charles V, and Louise's son, François, the King of France. François, a grandson of Charles d'Orléans's brother, had married Claude, the daughter of Louis XII (hence the prince-poet's granddaughter). With this, sometimes known as the Ladies' Peace Treaty, the Burgundian era, and the strife between Bourguignons and Armagnacs may be considered to come to a close. Burgundy proper returned permanently to France, but Charles V, native of Ghent and heir and direct descendant of Margaretha van Male, retained control of formerly French Flanders, so long the source of power and wealth to the Valois Dukes.

VII Implementation of the Course

About thirty students enrolled in the course, which was given at Harvard as a Dudley House course for credit under the auspices of the Committee on Non-departmental Courses. Several students were able to count the course for credit in their history concentration. One student was a graduate student in law. The class met for an hour three times each week; in addition, the course was subdivided into task forces on food and viticulture, on history and religion, on iconography, on women's biography, on music and on dance, which met separetely. Requirements were a verbal midterm research report and a final project, including a report to the class. The final project could vary in format, but had to include a written component. Some of the final projects were:

Erasmus and the Mystic Tradition,
The Role of Women in Courtly Life and Love,
Medieval Medicine in France and Italy,
Wine in Burgundy,
Mythical Beasts in the Middle Ages,
Manuscript Books in Burgundy from the Middle Ages to the Renaissance,
Behind the Arras: the Tradition of Weaving in Burgundy,
Burgundian Court Dance,
Heraldry as a Graphic Representation of Dynastic Structure,
The Dance of Death
The Impact of the Establishment of the New Middle Kingdom: the Burgundian Possessions in the Low Countries, and
Protocol and Courtly Etiquette.

The course was graced by guest lecturers bringing their special expertise to illustrate the Burgundial civilization. Ann Fehn lectured on the mythological prehistory of the Burgundians as described in the *Nibelungenlied*. Historiography was introduced by comparing Wagner's nineteenth-century approach with the original, and the author accompanied by David Beyer and narration by Ann Fehn performed Ludwig Tieck and Johannes Brahms's *Magellone*, the romance about a Burgundian prince and a Neapolitan princess. Robert Bousquet lectured on the literary significance of Charles d'Orléans, and on the *formes fixes (rondeau, ballade* and *virelay)*. Marianne Teuber brought us her expertise on the van Eycks, van der Weyden, and the miniaturists. Ingrid Brainard conducted a workshop and lectured on Burgundian court dance, and also led the task force on dance. Jean Doten discussed performance practice and style characteristics of Burgundian music, with particular reference to Dufay's *Missa Se La Face Ay Pale*; this mass was performed by the Collegium Iosquinum under direction of the author. The scoring of the mass for this performance was based on the forces shown in van Eyck's *Ghent Altarpiece*.[35] Ian Siggins of the Divinity School related the modern devotion to Erasmus, Kenneth Conant demonstrated his research on Cluny, Konrad Oberhuber reviewed the art at the court of Maximilian, and Franklin Ford rounded off the course with a lecture on the heritage and continuing influence of Burgundy through later centuries.

Near the end of the semester a symposium was held: the lecturers and their topics were as follows:

Ingrid Brainard:	An Exotic Court Dance and Dance Spectacle of the Renaissance: *La Moresca.*
Ian Siggins:	The Preaching of a Disciple: The Sermon Books of Johannes Herolt, O.P.
Arthur L. Loeb:	Kinship Graphs.
Peter Jordan:	Brittany.
Robert Bousquet:	The Sorrows of Marguerite of Austria, as Reflected in the Music of Pierre de la Rue.
Konrad Oberhuber:	Is there a Middle Style of Painting?
Geoffrey Hindley:	Low Countries' Influence on English Composers in the Early Fifteenth Century.
Barbara Wheaton:	The Medieval Banquet: What It is, And How to Eat It.

The symposium concluded with a banquet, for which Dr. Wheaton acted as consultant.[36] The banquet was based on accounts of Philippe le Bon's Feast of the Pheasant; students presented results of their investigations: a meat pie outfitted with a mechanical bird, a gryphon made of marzipan according to a medieval recipe, a sample of an Artesian tapestry.[37] The menu was researched by the leader of the task force on wine and viticulture, Lotje Loeb, and based on various medieval sources.[38]

The music task force performed a *chanson* to a text by Charles d'Orléans composed by one of the students according to the rules given in a fifteenth-century manual, and the dance task force demonstrated dances from Margaret of Savoie's dance book. Barbara Wheaton presented a peacock prepared by her according to a mediaeval recipe.

NOTES

[1] Hugo de Schepper: *Belgium Nostrum, 1500-1650* De Orde van den Prince, Antwerp (1987).

Hugo de Schepper, "Netherlandic Statemaking through Princely Judicature in the 16th Century," pp. 211-226 in this volume.

[2] L.J. Rogier: *Eenheid en Scheiding, Geschiedenis der Nederlanden 1477-1813*, Het Spectrum, Utrecht/Antwerpen (1962).

[3] H.P.H. Jansen: *Middeleeuwse Geschiedenis der Nederlanden*, Het Spectrum, Utrecht/Antwerpen (1965).

[4] Arthur L. Loeb: "Burgundy: The Rise and Fall of the Middle Realm," in *New Developments for Teaching and Learning*, Alvin White, ed. Jossey-Bass, San Francisco (1981).

[5] J. Huizinga: *Herfsttij der Middeleeuwen*, Tjeenk Willink, Groningen (First Printing 1919, Thirteenth Printing 1975).

[6] cf. for instance: Franklin L. Ford: *Strasbourg in Transition 1648–1789*, Harvard University Press, Cambridge (1958).

[7] Ruth Putnam: *Alsace and Lorraine from Caesar to Kaiser*, G.P. Putnam & Sons, New York (1915).

[8] Robert E. Lerner: *The Age of Adversity, the Fourteenth Century*, Cornell University Press, Ithaca (1968).

[9] Jerah Johnson and William Percy: *The Age of Recovery, the Fifteenth Century*, Cornell University Press, Cambridge (1970).

[10] Richard Vaughan: *Philip the Bold*, Harvard University Press, Cambridge (1962).
" *John the Fearless*, Longmans, London (1966).
" *Philip the Good*, Longmans, London (1970).
" *Charles the Bold*, Longmans, London (1973).
" *Valois Burgundy*, Anchor Books, Hamden (1975).

[11] Kenneth Fowler: *The Age of Plantagenet and Valois*, Exeter Books, New York (1967).

[12] Desmond Seward: *The Hundred Years' War*, Constable, London (1978).

[13] Otto Cartellieri: *The Court of Burgundy*, Haskell, New York (reprint of the 1925 edition).

[14] Wm. R. Tyler: *Dijon and the Valois Dukes of Burgundy*, University of Oklahoma, Norman (1971).

[15] *Les très riches heures de Jean, Duc de Berri*.

[16] Copyright registered.

[17] Ruth Putnam: *A Mediaeval Princess, Jacqueline, Countess of Holland*, G.P. Putnam & Sons, New York (1904).

[18] H.P.H. Jansen: *Jacoba van Beieren*, Krusemans, den Haag (1976).

[19] Enid McLeod: *Charles of Orleans*, Viking, New York (1970).

[20] Ed. Sally Purcell: *The Poems of Charles of Orleans*, Carcanet Press, Cheadle, Cheshire (1973).

[21] Norma L. Goodrich: *Charles of Orleans, a Study of Themes in his French and his English Poetry*, Librairie Droz, Geneva (1967).

[22] John Fox: *The Lyric Poetry of Charles d'Orléans*, Clarendon Press, Oxford (1969).

[23] Ed. Pierre Champion: *Poésies*, Librairie Ancienne (1923).

[24] Mortimer Levine: *Tudor Dynastic Problems (1460-1571)*, George Allen and Unwin Ltd. (London) and Barnes and Noble Inc., Harper and Row, Publishers, Inc., New York (1973).

[25] M.G.A. Vale: *Charles VII*, University of California Press, Berkeley (1974).

[26] Pierre Champion: *Louis XI*, Books for Libraries Press, Freeport, New York (1929, 1970).

[27] Philippe de Commynes: *Memoirs*, translated with an Introduction by Michael Jones, Penguin (1971).

[28] Mary Clive: *This Sun of York*, Cardinal, London (1975).

[29] Gordon Kipling: *The Triumph of Honor, Burgundian Origins of the Elizabethan Renaissance*, The Sir Thomas Browne Institute, Leiden University Press, Leiden (1977).

[30] Mart Janssonius: *Maria van Bourgondië, Bruid van Europa*, Thieme, Zutphen.

[31] Gordon Kipling: op. cit., p. 103.

[32] Jane de Iongh: *Margaretha van Oostenrijk*, Querido, Amsterdam (1941).

[33] E. Winker: *Margarete von Oesterreich*, Georg D.W. Callwey, Munich (1966).

[34] Otto von Habsburg: *Charles V*, Praeger Publishers, New York/Washington (1979).

[35] Elisabeth Dhanens: *Van Eyck: The Ghent Altarpiece*, Viking Press, New York (1973).

[36] Barbara Ketcham Wheaton: *Savoring the Past*, The University of Pennsylvania Press, Philadelphia (1983).

cf. also: "Kookboek in de ene, Woordenboek in de andere Hand," De Volkskrant, April 23, 1988.

[37] Johanna Maria van Winter: *Van Soeter Cokene*, Grolsch Spiegel Historiael (1971), reprint Fibula-van Dishoeck, Haarlem (1976).

[38] Adapted by Lorna J. Sass: *To the King's Taste, Richard II's Book of Feasts and Recipes*, The Metropolitan Museum of Art, New York (1975).

Constance B. Hieatt and Sharon Butler: *Pleyn Delit*, University of Toronto Press, Toronto (1976).

NETHERLANDIC STATEMAKING THROUGH PRINCELY JUDICATURE IN THE 16TH CENTURY

Hugo de Schepper
Katholieke Universiteit, Nijmegen

The Emperor Charles V finished the Netherlandic territorial unification process by adding Tournai-Tournaisis (1521), Frisia (1523), Utrecht and Overijssel (1528), Drenthe and Groningen (1536) and finally Guelre-Zutphen (1543) to the Burgundian-Habsburg patrimony.[1] Together with the other regions, Brabant, Limburg-Overmaas, Luxemburg-Chiny, Flanders, Artois, Hainault, Holland, Zeeland, Namur, Malines, Valenciennes, the chatellenies of Walloon Flanders (Lille-Douai-Orchies) and of the Debattenland, they formed the so-called XVII Netherlands or Provinces. Formally the Netherlands or Belgium - synonymous denominations of the period - constituted no more than a confederation of "states." Traditionally Belgian as well as Dutch historiography continues to be based on the formal view of the 16th-century Netherlands - with emphasis on the plural - as a merely personal union of principalities, in which the unity only is supposed to have been expressed by uniting the titles of Duke, Count and Lord of Brabant, Holland, Flanders, etc. in one and the same person, Charles V and after him Philip II, as legal successors to the Dukes of Burgundy. Each of these principalities is supposed to have maintained its own jurisdictional limits and separate legal systems are said to have prevailed over unity. The autonomy of the provinces in the 16th century is heavily emphasized.

Curiously though, historiography, in spite of adhering to the concept of confederation with its so-called provincial juridical systems, still continues to refer to the "Southern" and "Northern" Netherlands as historic entities in the 16th century. The catalogue issued at an exhibition in the Leyden municipal archives in 1985 represents the professors at Leyden University who in 1585 fled from Flanders and Brabant, as being of foreign extraction and in particular from "België." In 1986, seven coordinated exhibitions were staged in different Dutch cities with the general motto: "De eeuw van de Beeldenstorm. De *Noordelijke* Nederlanden in de zestiende eeuw." These are a few of the many examples which once more for the benefit of a wider public confirm the state-nationalistic - or finalistic - historiography which looks upon Dutch c.q. Belgian history as a permanent breach between "België" and "Holland." In spite of some Dutch and Belgian historians such as Geyl, L. van der Essen, H.A. Enno van Gelder, Poelhekke, J.A. van Houtte and Kossmann, the historiography of and within the two Netherlands of today is, indeed, too often based on what Kossmann, on the evaluation day of the new *Algemene Geschiedenis der Nederlanden,* called "the trivial reality of the contemporary state boundaries." W.P. Blockmans, too, points out in a recent article that the identifications of the contemporary state are "more or less consciously purposely adopted by historiographers, especially in school books, but also, more disguised, in research." How often, indeed, are the present state boundaries still used as territorial demarcation lines of historic-scientific research concerning periods for which they have no relevance. In the Ancien Regime this mostly goes for the period up to 1648 and in some provinces even longer. Nevertheless scientific foundations in Holland and in Belgium as a rule only set assignments within those state-national demarcation lines. Apart from a few felicitous exceptions all periods and aspects in the new *General History of the Netherlands* are "neatly" divided into Northern and Southern segments. In this way falsification of history is virtually being supported on a large scale. What started as a pragmatic simplification contributes, by means of repetition, to a brainwashing of historical consciousness. Along those same wrong lines of thought, the centralization which the Netherlandic sovereigns Charles V and mainly Philip II of Spain wanted to effectuate, among other things by imposing the national church as an enforced religious system, would have clashed with particularistic traditions by which, against the background of the economic crisis, the revolt broke out and the Netherlands almost naturally broke up into Northern and Southern parts. Consequently it is customary for present historiography to avoid talking about Netherlandic unity and solidarity.

Arguing against both a state-nationalistic approach and a pure emphasis on autonomy, I mean to arrive at a different conclusion in various fields, without making a premature distinction between the two kingdoms of today, Belgium and Holland, which today divide these historic Netherlands.

1. In his thesis on 16th-century tapestry in Leyden and later on in his book on the late 15th-century, early 16th-century Leyden painter Engebrechtsz, the American art historian Jeremy Bangs rejects the distinction between the italianizing "South-Netherlandic" visual arts and the so-called traditional "North-Netherlandic" arts. The terms "Northern" and "Southern" Netherlands have indeed also established themselves in related historic disciplines as inaccurate concepts. Art historians in the two Low Countries invariably speak even for the 16th century of "North-" and "South-" Netherlandic schools of painting. Painters such as Jan Gossaert (Maubeuge? about 1480-Breda 1532) and Antonio Moro (Utrecht, 1517/19-Antwerp, 1576) do give them a hard time: even more so because of their repeated moves from the "North" to the "South" and vice versa. The first one, for instance, one of the first Renaissance painters in the Netherlands, initially stayed at Bruges and Antwerp and afterwards in Middelburg and Utrecht successively, as court painter of Philip of Burgundy, marquis of Veere. In 1985 paintings by him as a "South-Netherlander" were shown in Brussels at the exhibition "Luister van Spanje en de Belgische [sic!] steden" and a year later at Amsterdam as a

"North-Netherlander" at the exhibition "North-Netherlandic Art in the Age of Iconoclasm." Bangs on the contrary considers such distinctions the result of artificial apriorities and an idealizing and intuitive approach. He tends to view the provinces of Brabant, Holland, Flanders, Utrecht and Zeeland as a cultural unity. With respect to Leyden, Bangs demonstrates that this city, from a cultural and artistic point of view, was in no way different or inferior to Brabant and Flemish towns, and he is of the opinion that his statement holds good for the Holland towns in general. In their splendid volume on the Burgundian Netherlands up to 1530 Professors Prevenier and Blockmans also underline the "very close connections between the existence of a highly developed urban economy, the course of the statemaking process and the exceptional cultural activities in the Netherlands." They speak of unity and of "a common way of life." In this respect they distinguish in the Burgundian Low Countries a number of zones within concentric semi-circles, the center of which is situated along the shore and the density of which diminishes as one gets further removed from the sea. Brabant and particularly Flanders at that time set the tone, and Holland, which had had a somewhat later start, joined them in this before the end of the Burgundian era. How much more rightly can the presentation put forward by Prevenier and Blockmans be applied to the subsequent decades.

As I hope to show, both the state-nationalistic approach and an over-emphasis on particularism are equally irrelevant in other aspects. Estates and cities did get hold of a powerful expedient for defending medieval provincial and local particularism by means of the taxation system, and as to control and inspection of expenditures on subsidy income, the Estates largely acquired financial autonomy in the 40s and 50s of the 16th century – also with the intent of to rationalize monetary transactions in the country.[2] Still I would like to argue that this form of autonomy was only partially able to rescue the formal autonomy of the provinces in matters of "justice" and "policy," and in some respects it did not check state formation. They could not refuse the ordinary princely petitions for money and even they provided extra financial support to defend the common Netherlands against foreign enemies.

Prior to definitive recognition of their sovereign authority the respective dynastic hereditary successors were expected at the moment of succession to take an oath and state that they would respect the fundamental privileges of the province concerned. Only then the prince was recognized in the execution of his high-ranking public rights by the constitutional representatives of the subjects of the province in question. Princely sovereignty, consequently, was formally conditioned in all provinces by a variety of mostly oral and local customary laws, which had spontaneously established themselves over the centuries. Although the sovereign's decrees took precedence over local customary law, the prince's lawmaking power mainly covered administrative law, procedural law, monetary regulations, maintenance regulations for dykes, dunes, bridges and roads, and the *jura circa sacra*; in short it mainly imposed rules with regard to public life. Princely edicts hardly ventured into the field of civil law, unless the matter under consideration had to do with public life, such as matrimonial affairs or possession cases. The percentage of edicts devoted to private law during the reigns of Charles V and Philip II is assessed at only 1.5 and 4, respectively. Consequently, the relations between the subjects as private individuals continued to be mainly determined by unpredictable and poorly organized local customary law; customary laws even within all juridical systems were different to a larger or lesser extent. Most local courts of oldermen (*schepenbanken*), feudal courts and other traditional courts of customary law were competent to pronounce sentences in civil conflicts and criminal cases and ruled according to their own local and unwritten legal customs. The greater the distance between those local government bodies, the greater the difference in law. But town and village councils hardly even functioned as "makers" of new civil law. Instead they adapted themselves in these matters mostly to the central pattern of government; only the prince was authorized to set these rules, although in the 16th-century he used this competence to a limited degree. In carrying out princely law, or in areas that did not conflict with it, town magistracies issued rules in a lot of matters such as closing hours of inns and taverns, Sunday rest, quality of products and organization of the local market, weights and measures, maintenance of roads and squares, mendicity, heresy, and other matters of local public order.

From 1531 on, the sovereign for his part entered the world of civil law mainly by officially codifying and ratifying unwritten legal customs, in an attempt to realize greater legal uniformity and judicial security. In 1531, Charles V gave orders to work on this in a systematic way. From now on the interpretation of customary law would be reserved for princely councils. The repeated orders for its ratification were only reluctantly and partially obeyed, however, because — and with some justification — the local authorities dreaded losing some of their local independence and power. As a result of this opposition only about twenty customary laws acquired, between 1531 and 1579, the character of princely written law.

With regard to civil law, the normative impact of the central authority on the local level remained limited. The Netherlands did not yet have a long tradition of general regulation; this was only gradually coming into existence. In this sense we may in fact speak of local autonomy with regard to the preservation of old legal customs. We should not refer to provincial autonomy in this respect, however, since numerous circles of customary laws existed within each province and beyond the provincial boundaries. Prior to 1531 there were indeed over 600 different sets of customary law, so that the separate legal systems did not coincide with the provincial boundaries. The traditional view of the Netherlands as a personal union of independent principalities should therefore, in my opinion, be regarded as an over-idealization of provincial autonomy.

In addition to this, the sovereignty of the Netherlandic prince was legally more or less restricted by written rights and liberties acquired or exacted from medieval emperors, princes, dukes and counts by the respective principalities in the course of earlier centuries, as well as by cities, guilds, crafts and classes. Nevertheless the actual value of those parchment sheets should not be exaggerated, for they are only the reflection of the real balance of power between prince and subjects at a given time.[3] Although for instance the "Great Privileges" of 1477 had granted the Provincial Estates *de jure* the right to convene at their own initiative, this right soon appeared non-existent *de facto*. Apart from a few exceptions the sovereigns tightly held on to the right of convening the Estates. Within the framework of the 16th-century Netherlands distance as well as the relatively small economic and demographic significance of provinces like the Groningen area, Overijssel, Frisia, Guelre-Zutphen and Luxemburg worked to their advantage in terms of individuality and autonomy. Although the Provincial Estates and the local authorities kept on referring to their privileges and liberties, the application of these did not depend much on *legal* positions but rather on fluctuations in positions of *power*.

However important the involvement of lower administrative levels was in establishing written laws of the Netherlands, the task of the provincial courts of justice, princely in any case, was restricted to supplying advice at the request of the government. Later these courts tested placards and decrees against legal customs, privileges and actual circumstances in the province involved, in as far as the variety and even contradictory elements in legal customs and privileges within the province made this feasible. The Provincial Courts were, to be sure, the direct or indirect continuation of the medieval *Curiae* which preceded the integration of the separate principalities into the Burgundian-Habsburg Netherland, but after their integration they became instruments used by the prince and the central authorities. In contrast to the local institutions in general the Provincial Courts of Justice were composed of lawyers in the service of the prince; they wanted to make a career in his service. Obviously, effective realization of the national-sovereign principle had to clear away a number of medieval relics and limitations. This required an obedient and professionalized body of modern judges and civil servants who restricted themselves to carrying out technical tasks for which their mostly academic and juridical training had prepared them.[4] Important matters of foreign policy and defense, however, escaped consultation with the lower levels, especially under Philip II.[5] Moreover, participative decision-making is not to be identified with autonomy.

II. Alongside – and in spite of – important particularistic and autonomistic indicators, also in the fields of "Justice" and its sequel "Policy," I cannot but record an ever greater princely capacity to govern as well as an integration of the Netherlands into the Netherland in the singular. There was a clear interaction between the economic networks that came into being and state formation. Both social-economic and demographic factors on the one hand, and politico-judicial factors on the other, cooperated or coincided in transforming society and in increasing the governing capacity of the state.[6] The creation and expansion of supra-provincial state institutions at the expense of provincial autonomy and the permanent reciprocal relations with lower level authorities induced uniformity of administrative and judicial methods and regulations; the old ones were replaced by more rational and effective modern ones. Bureaucratization up to and including the provincial level was closely connected with the formation of the monarchic state. Although at the local level the penetration of more rational and uniform administrative methods has possibly led only partially to greater administrative efficiency, we should recognize that in the 16th century lawyers, for instance, got access to the magistracies of large cities and that in pronouncing sentences the magistrates of smaller towns more and more often appealed to the legally trained City Pensionary for the passing of sentences.[7] Very probably they felt the princely professional lawyers breathing down their necks; indeed, they were summoned to a higher court for passing "evil sentences" and in cases of well-founded appeals they were fined.[8] Also, written judicial procedures penetrated urban magistracies and gradually replaced the oral ones.

The movement of administrative and judicial uniformity to lower levels was not as important, however, in peripheral regions as in central provinces. On the periphery, indeed, statemaking progressed at a lower speed than in what should be regarded as the focal area of the Netherland: namely the Northwestern provinces around the Scheldt-, Maas- and Rhine-estuaries, in particular Brabant, Holland, Flanders and Zeeland. Since 1433, these had, anyway, already been part of the then still Burgundian confederation of states and had in various fields a level of development different from that of the other parts of the country, including the so-called non-patrimonial provinces in the Northeast which were only added much later by means of acquisition or warfare. Recently, Professor Woltjer rightly stated that the highly urbanized Flemish-Brabant-Holland economy and culture throughout the 16th century should be regarded as a unity. Within the community of interest of the central area, the center had moved inwards, around 1500, from Flanders to Brabant namely, although the latter province had developed at a later date than Flanders. Until

1583/85 Holland, Flanders and Zeeland were indisputably oriented to political, judicial, economic, intellectual-cultural – and from 1559 onwards also ecclesiastic – epicenters in Brabant and this much more intensively so than the other provinces. Some 70% of the students at the university of Louvain originated from those parts of the country; Brabant supplied half of these students. In the Northern and Eastern outlying districts, however, students preferred German universities. Contemporaries looked upon Brabant as the *Hooftprovintie der Nederlanden* (Main Province of the Netherlands) and upon Brussels as the *Princelycke Hoofdstadt van 't Nederlant* (Princely Capital of the Netherland). In Netherlandic economic-maritime expansion in the periods of 1495-1525 and 1540-1565 as well as in intercontinental trade, the focal area with Amsterdam and especially Antwerp as chief centers of growth was most important. In the Amstel city, with its some 500 ships, the main emphasis was on shipping, as, by the way, was the case all through the province of Holland. In the Scheldt city with its hinterland commercial capitalism was accentuated. But both influenced and complemented each other. Flanders and Brabant strongly availed themselves of Holland and Zeeland shipping; the Holland and Zeeland shippers largely took care of the Netherlandic shipping trade on the river Scheldt. Flushing, Arnemuiden, and other Zeeland towns were outports of Antwerp, just like the Flemish Sluice. Holland ports, too, acted as entrepots for Antwerp. Brabant, Holland and Flanders had the largest concentration of Netherlandic industrial production, in which the countryside also took part, representing two thirds of Netherlandic capital. While the economy of the surrounding areas was mainly founded on agriculture, in the three focal provinces commercial capitalism, domestic industrialization, and even early-capitalist small companies were coming on. The market mechanisms that ruled economic life, wagework in towns and countryside and the means of production in the hands of urban bourgeoisie were other common characteristics in the core area. As a matter of fact, around 1550, nearly two thirds of the about three million Netherlanders lived within this expansive economic region, into which the small Zeeland islands were dragged along, and it featured a high degree of urbanization, namely some 45 percent. Of the 15 largest Netherlandic towns 13 were situated in Brabant, Holland and Flanders.

As the towns determined production relations and economic order in the surrounding countryside, at the same time the political influence of the town patriciate in the central area increased, not only in the gatherings of the respective Provincial Estates, but likewise with regard to policies for the country. This growing influence came at the expense of the other politically vocal orders, the clergy, the nobility and the yeomen, which at the time were flourishing in the periphery. The Burgundian-Habsburg sovereigns relied on and supported the new socio-economic, intellectual-cultural and politically dominant town elite. As far as state finance was concerned, they depended on the capital of the well-to-do urban bourgeoisie in the focal region; as to justice and policy, the princes appreciated their professional expertise and their new patterns of political and juridical thought. Of the 47 Netherlandic members and civil servants of upper middle class origins that could be traced geographically and who were appointed to the three government councils between 1531 and 1579, almost two thirds came from the central area, including Zeeland. For those (32 in all) who were appointed according to tradition way because of their noble prestige and feudal origins, the ratio was exactly the reverse: almost two thirds, 20 that is, originated from the Walloon provinces, from Luxemburg, and from Guelre; only four came from Brabant, three from Holland, four from Flanders, and one from Zeeland. In contrast to the Northwestern region, where clergy and landed gentry probably hardly owned 10 percent of the agricultural land, the clergy and the nobility in Luxemburg and in the Walloon provinces, with their predominantly agricultural economy apart from the respective metal industries, could easily maintain their socio-economic and political status. In the Tournaisis area, for instance, the church owned three quarters of the countryside. In Utrecht the Chapters occupied a prominent economic and socio-political position, and in Guelre, Limburg-upon-Vesder and Overmaas the old noble families and the monasteries employed many leasehold farmers. Although the old Hanseatic towns in the Estates of Overijssel had just as many votes as the knights, they became less important in the 16th century because of the rise of the Holland trade centers, whereas the nobility rose in importance; in Salland and in Twente (both in the province of Overijssel-Drenthe) 30 percent of the land was in the hands of the nobility. The other areas in the East and up North also had an agricultural structure. In Frisia and the surrounding area of Groningen ecclesiastic institutions possessed a fifth or as much as a quarter of the land. But in contrast to Guelre, Overijssel, Limburg-Overmaas, Luxemburg and the Walloon provinces, Frisia, Groningen and Drenthe had hardly known feudalism. However, according to Woltjer, Frisia had from an economic and intellectual-cultural viewpoint, closer links with Westphalia than with the Habsburg Netherlands. For that matter, the whole peripheral area from Groningen down to Luxemburg was more oriented towards its neighbours in the East; even the more centrally situated province of Utrecht was rather directed towards Guelre than towards Holland. In all these boundary areas the degree of urbanization was conspicuously lower than in Brabant, Holland and Flanders. Except for a few middle-sized towns, their towns were small; they were few and far between and in the various Estates they were hardly of any political significance.

The different integration rates which relate to the socio-economic discrepancies in structure, are also apparent from the rate of unification and centralization of "justice," more specifically through laws imposed by or on behalf of the prince, through recording of legal customs and especially through princely forensic practice at the prince's courts. Preference for the more rational codified laws with a general validity, rather than the over six hundred different and unpredictable local customary laws, had to do with the humanist mentality of the educated groups of the population and also with the needs of the economy. Of the decrees of general tenor issued by Charles V and Philip II, 80 percent came about not only at the request of towns, crafts, and other legal bodies, but also at the request of private individuals. At the same time, regarding imposed law, the role played by town councils, who possibly had the best reasons for relying on their former autonomy, was reduced; as was mentioned earlier, their powers became more and more restricted to supplementary work in local affairs and matters of local administration. Likewise, provincial legislation did not add up to much, probably not even to 10 percent of central legislation. By directing a great many petitions to the sovereign and his government on the most divergent and sometimes futile affairs, both private persons and local authorities gave impulses to monarchic expansion and centralization and accepted princely centralization. They obviously looked beyond local and provincial horizons, more so than has so far been assumed. Either consciously or unconsciously they must have sensed that all other "residual" power rested with the sovereign and his government: not only to issue general legal instructions, but also to provide licenses, pardons and other personal favors, to sanction marriage settlements, last wills, debt-settlements and other agreements, to pass sentences in civil cases and to have these executed; in short, the power to decide in all new situations for which no provisions had been made yet.

By far the largest number of requests originated from the commercial-maritime provinces of Brabant, Holland, Flanders and Zeeland, and vice versa most decrees of general tenor were intended for these centrally-oriented provinces. With the exception of Frisia, which was among the first to have its customary rights converted - by the prince - to a single customary rule for the whole province, the majority of the 330 customary laws that were officially codified before 1580, came from Flanders, followed by Brabant and Holland, despite resistance from local authorities.

Besides rules imposed by the sovereign and reduction of customary law, forensic practice by the prince's courts is the third and possibly the main criterion for defining the extent of centralization and formation of the Netherlandic State. Historians are, from the point of view of contemporary state organization, with its division of powers, inclined to look at legislative work in particular. Whether this holds good for the 16th century is subject to serious debate. For issuing legal rules was no more than a sequel to or derivation of *Justitia*, hence frequently occasional and corrective legislation. The monarch, in his function of Supreme Judge and Protector of law and order, has rightly been awarded a key position by legal historians, because in line with

16th-century political ideology, he probably had the greatest impact on social phenomena from this position of power.

Princely judicature was virtually exclusively the task of university-trained lawyers, familiar with Roman law as well as with Canon law and with the comments by learned annotators and post-annotators. Attorneys and barristers pleading before the princely courts referred to that collection of erudite and written laws in dealing with the juridical questions of their clients in order to defend them. Although it may hardly be seen as a matter of systematic adoption of scientific law into the national legal system, nor of jurisprudence-forensic practice, central and provincial princely courts of justice responded to the need for legal security, objectivity and wider legal validity that continued to grow as commercial relations exceeded village, town and provincial boundaries. The customary law courts could not offer similar provisions. In comparison with sentences passed by lower customary law courts monarchic sentences could in fact already be executed within a wider territory.

The number of final verdicts of the central courts, Great Council of Malines and Privy Council, seems to prove the breakthrough and extension of centralization.[9] The Great Council was the main Court of Justice for the 15th and 16th centuries, but from 1517 onwards and possibly even earlier the Privy Council, next to the sovereign or his regent, was also requested to judge cases in first and last instance. Since roughly 80 percent of the cases considered here relate to civil lawsuits, which were brought before the princely courts by the parties themselves, and thus not initiated by princely courts, one can speak, in my opinion, of acceptance of legal centralization and "statification." Legal bodies as well as private individuals tried to get justice as close as possible to the source of all justice, "the sovereign judge," in all kinds of conflicts, not excluding neighbourhood quarrels. This was not only the case with appeals to a higher court because people were dissatisfied with the so-called "evil" sentences by local courts and other customary courts, but also directly and increasingly from the very start in first instance because people got more and more confidence in princely judicial practice. In seeking justice the parties at law did not want to have anything to do with privileges *de non appellando* and *de non evocando*, nor with the opposition of local authorities to princely courts. No sooner had the Estates exacted the Great Privileges in 1477, by which, among other things, the Great Council was reduced to a court of judicature for exceptional cases, than parties at law went once again calmly ahead seeking justice from the Great Council, as if there were nothing wrong with this. Even the Estates, the defenders of privileges and advocates of financial autonomy, were seeking justice at princely courts against those who were deficient in making payments to them. In the beginning of the 16th century, the Great Council pronounced an average of about 40 judgments a year. Not even half a century later this number had more than tripled, that is 135 annually. The Great Council and the Privy Council together, in the period of 1546-1550, pronounced on the average some 170 judgments a year. Because we do not yet exactly know the averages of final sentences in the princely judicature at the provincial level, 170 probably is only the tip of the iceberg. A poll conducted in the verdict registers of the Princely Council of Brabant seems to confirm this: there were about 250 sentences overall during those years, including voluntary and interlocutory ones.

It is true that these statistics can give no more than a general impression, but they do illustrate the degree of the sovereign's extension of power concerning actual or litigious judicature, as well as the related *verrechtelijking* and statemaking process, mainly in those provinces that in other respects also constituted the Netherlandic central area.[10] Around 1500 it was still Flanders that played a leading role by being responsible for 32 percent of the Great Council verdicts, whereas Holland took care of 10 percent less. Almost 50 years later Holland had not only caught up with Flanders, but even slightly outstripped it (28 and 26 percent, respectively). The small province of Zeeland, which initially followed in the wake of Holland with 13 percent, did drop back to 7 percent, but with some 10 ten verdicts a year it occupied the next level, meanwhile joined by Artois. In the entire central judicial practice, including the Privy Council, Flanders with 41 verdicts a year and Holland with 40 were very close. Brabant, including Malines, followed with "only" 22 sentences. This had to do with the fact that since about 1500 the Council of Brabant acted as provincial and central princely Court of Justice at the same time. Princely forensic practice had probably pervaded that province most intensively. Artois and Zeeland boasted 14 and 12 sentences a year, respectively. Walloon-Flanders, Namur, Luxemburg-Chiny, Hainault-Valenciennes, Tournai-Tournaisis and Utrecht ranged from 8 to 2 sentences a year, in this order, whereas Guelre, Frisia, Groningen and surroundings, Limburg-Overmaas and Overijssel-Drenthe closed the ranks with 1 or not even a single sentence. Excepting Artois, obviously in the agricultural provinces the old customary judicature structures persisted. Through feudal courts, *laathoven*, census courts and other traditional courts, such as *Etstoel*, Great Clearing, Headmenchamber, knights courts and other parishes, judicature remained, in the case of conflicts, fully or partially in the hands of noblemen, yeomen, customary-law judges, chapters and abbeys; it was only with great difficulty that princely central and provincial judicature gained some ground in the peripheral area and in some of these provinces it was hardly the case. Even the prince took this into account when composing his courts of justice in the periphery. Deviating from the normal pattern in the focal area with lawyers of roman-canon formation, in Guelre half the princely court were costumary practicians. The judicial process in the provincial court of

Guelre knew indeed more feudal and customary legal elements, while the princely central and provincial tribunals in the nuclear area applied the burgundo-roman-canon procedural law.[11] In Groningen and surroundings the prince did not even have a provincial council of justice; Hainault and Luxemburg had strong provincial feudal courts beside the princely courts. It is also striking that in the Eastern areas the number of enclaves directly depending on the German Emperor or other Eastern neighbours, was particularly high. They were able to withdraw from Netherlandic statemaking and have their own, often outside the Burgundian patrimony. Besides the numerous "pebbles" Liège, Bouillon and Ravenstein may well illustrate this.

III. The question of whether this statemaking corresponded to a sense of solidarity is generally no longer being asked, the more so as in general any queries as to Netherlandic state formation meet with negative responses. In my view, however, all forms of solidarity, whether ideological, social, provincial, and even local, need not necessarily be inconsistent with growing national unity and joint interests. In the narrow sense Erasmus meant by *patria* his native province of Holland, and in a wider sense the conglomerate of the Netherlands which for him comprised the focal provinces of Brabant, Holland, Flanders and Zeeland; from 1524 onwards he also frequently used *Brabantia* as a part for that whole. At the time of the Netherlandic Rebellion, when regionalism had once again gained ground, "beggars" from Brabant, Holland, Flanders, and Zeeland were loudly singing not about the Netherlands in the plural, but about: "Nederlant let op uw saeck" (Netherland, have your interests at heart), or about: "Nederlant, ons aerts prieel" (Netherland, our paradise on earth), and so on, in the singular. In the *Wilhelmus*, the alleged composer, the Brabander Marnix van Sint-Aldegonde, attributed the verse "O edel Nederlant soet" (O noble, sweet Netherland) to that other Brabant man Orange. From the middle of the 16th century onwards the names *Nederlanden* in the plural and *'t Nederlan(d)t* in the singular were definitely interchangeable, but more and more with a distinct preference for the singular. Even in French this seems to have been the case, also with a preference for *le Païs bas, au Païs bas,* and *du Païs Bas*. Other expressions in French for indicating the *XVII Provincies* were: *Flandre(s), Provinces Belgiques* and *nostre païs Belgique*. In map-making the singular forms, in Dutch as well as in French, are preferred to the plural ones. It could hardly be a coincidence that from about 1540 onwards the terms *Lingua Belgica, Belgicus, Belgis* and *Nederduytsch,* or *Onse Nederlantscher sprake* and *Onse Nederlantsche taele* as synonyms came to replace the terms *Lingua Teutonica, Teutonicus, Vlaemsche, Duytsche,* or *Dietsche tonghe*. The cultivation of the mother tongue by Renaissance poets and of the history of the *patria* by humanist historians also points to a growing sense of belonging to the Netherlandic state, Belgica or Belgium; in short a growing identification with the state alongside the existing identifications at other levels. Although at court French was used as the medium of communication, the Brabant dialect was, under the influence of centralization, state formation and economic interaction, well on its way of becoming the basic written language, whether or not mixed with Flemish or Holland dialects, the two most common combinations with the Brabant dialect.[12] The fact, for instance, that Rembertus Dondonius (Malines 1517-Leyden 1585) in his famous *Cruijde Boek* (his Book on Herbs and Spices) added a list of plants in "Brabantsche ende Nederlantsche" points to identification of the Brabant language with the state language. Also, the Flemish upper classes, which commonly used the French language in the Burgundian time, made use more and more of the Netherlandic language in their lawsuits at the Central Courts of Justice. Even in Frisia, where the Frisian language is used by the people, the Netherlandic language became the *Lingua vernacula*. Even the cosmopolitan Erasmus had raised the Netherlandic language to a sister language, superior to what he referred to as "bastard languages." Jan Cauweel, publisher of *rederijker* literature, insisted on the duty of "we, Netherlanders" to enrich and embellish "onslieder tale" (our own native tongue).

To what extent examples of this kind represent a smaller or rather a larger part of the Netherlandic population, remains a question that needs further research. Recently Professor Craeybeckx put forward that the witnesses were too numerous and until the end of the 17th century too emotional to be doubted.[13] It goes without saying that a sense of solidarity was more prominent with scholars and writers in the nuclear regions, with merchants trading beyond their town boundaries, with the large number of civil servants employed by the prince, and with their clients and social relations, the network of which was strongly expanding, by the way. As a matter of fact, I was struck in this respect, by the great mobility of civil servants and magistrates, who started their careers in local councils and afterwards were in the princely service in different provinces in spite of prevailing regional privileges.

CONCLUSION AND EPILOGUE. The provincial or autonomist way of thinking by Belgian and Dutch historiography is possibly related to the final result of the Revolt, the Republic in particular, when government largely reverted to the old provincialism and an intensified particularism. For the aversion to Philip II's extension of powers, felt to be rather bold, and to the lack of liberty that went with it, had once more stimulated former particularisms. In my opinion however, this was rather felt to be a weapon against absolutism than an issue or cause in connection with the Revolt, except perhaps regarding finance. On the other hand I have tried to point out here the relation between region and center and the various gradations in state formation and integration of the Burgundian-Habsburg "Netherland." From an intellectual-cultural, socio-economic, demographic and politico-institutional point of view Brabant, Holland, and Flanders set the tone. This central area was not monolithic, though, and each had its specific sub-centers, but the provinces concerned showed a lot of interaction. Zeeland joined in for the most part in this central area of North-western provinces. In the surrounding peripheral districts centri-petal forces abated to various degrees. In certain respects even Frisia (law), Utrecht (art), and Artois (judicature) patterned themselves in the end on the central area. The focal area knew a *modus vivendi*, a compromise between centralism and autonomism or regionalism, between the powers of the sovereign and those of the Estates. In fact, I submit that this paradoxical pair – autonomism and centralism – was not so paradoxical.

The statemaking process in the Netherlands, which actually had reached its federal phase as early as 1531, remained, however, confined to the largely integrated community of interests around the Rhine-, Maas- and Scheldt-estuaries, whereas the other provinces remained stuck in the phase of the personal union of states and continued their relations with the center only on a confederal basis. The autonomy of the region was certainly greater in the peripheral areas than in the four main, urbanized provinces of the country. In the field of finance they undoubtedly showed a high degree of provincial and local self-government. It is true that this way they were able, to a great extent, to participate in central decision-making, but regarding the issue of rules and regulations provincial autonomy was out of the question. Mutual relations between private people continued to be ruled by local customary laws and this could be referred to as local autonomy, but the addition of new laws lay within the competence of the central authorities. The acceptance of the center is most conspicuous, though, in the field of judicature. But, again, it was mainly the provinces of the core area that participated in it. In the peripheral agricultural areas the customary legal structures per-sisted more easily and there was a greater degree of independence. Owing to the Revolt the center did not have sufficient time to establish its influence in those borderline area.

In the last quarter of the 16th century the integration and state formation of the Netherland and of the central area in par-ticular came to an abrupt halt as a result of the Revolt against the Spanish king who thought he could treat the country as a kind of conquered land, and against what was felt to be lack of freedom and intolerance. The brusk encroachment on the provincial and local autonomy in financial matters by the Duke of Alva and even the artificial fuss created around this, played a significant role in this respect. This conflict, unintentionally, led to the disso-lution and disintegration of the country. Twelve years after the Netherlandic Revolt had broken out in 1568, it looked as if the country would fall apart along more or less the same dividing lines between focal and peripheral areas. Differing socio-economic structures, religious-cultural discrepancies and possibly the roles played by clercs and/or noblemen or yeomen in the border areas, even though they had for the most part come to belong to the Netherlands no earlier than under the reign of Charles V, were the decisive factors in this, as it is well known. But after some 50 to 60 years of conflict the military-technical and financial contest between Spain and the rebels left the country torn into a Northern and a Southern part, along an incidental and arbitrary frontline running straight across the central area. In this way two Netherlandic states came into being: the Roman-Catholic, Spanish, or Royal Netherland and the United Netherland or Republic of the United Provinces of Calvinist signature. The North-South split traversed the existing center-periphery relations.

NOTES

[1] This paper is mostly based on the first chapter in the extended version of my inaugural lecture at the Katholieke Universiteit Nijmegen: *Belgium Nostrum 1500-1650. Over Integratie en Desintegratie van het Nederland* (Antwerp, 1987), pp. 1-17; and on my article "La organización de las 'Finanzas' públicas en los Países Bajos Reales 1480-1700. Una reseña," in: *Cuadernos de Investigación Histórica* 8 (Madrid, 1984), pp.7-34. Except as noted I only refer to them.

[2] See also J.P. Peeters, *De financiën van de kleine en secundaire steden in Brabant van de 12de tot het midden der 16de eeuw* (Antwerp, 1980), pp. 327-345 and 485-518; J.D. Tracy, "The taxation system of the county of Holland during the reigns of Charles V and Philip II 1519-1566," in: *Economisch- en Sociaal-Historisch Jaarboek* 48 (1985), pp. 71-118; id., *A Financial Revolution in the Habsburg Netherlands. "Renten" and "Renteniers" in the county of Holland, 1515-1565* (Berkeley/Los Angeles/London, 1985).

[3] See R. van Uytven en W.P. Blockmans, "Constitutions and their applications in the Netherlands during the Middle Ages," in: *Belgisch Tijdschrift voor Filologie en Geschiedenis* 47 (1969), pp. 399-424; J.J. Woltjer, "Dutch Privileges, Real and Imaginary," in: J.S. Bromley and E.H. Kossmann eds., *Britain and the Netherlands* 5 (The Hague, 1975), pp. 19-35.

[4] See H. de Schepper, "Vorstelijke ambtenarij en bureaukratisering in regering en gewesten van 's Konings Nederlanden, 16de-17de eeuw," in: *Tijdschrift voor Geschiedenis* 90 (1977), pp. 362-363.

[5] See H. de Schepper, "Ensayo sobre el modelo del proceso de decisión política en los Países Bajos de Felipe II, 1559-1598," in: P.J.A.N. Rietbergen, F.M.A. Robben and H. de Schepper eds., *Nijmeegse Publicatiën over de Nieuwe Geschiedenis*, 2 (1988), pp. 151-172.

[6] See H. de Schepper, "Vorstelijke ambtenarij en bureaukratisering," pp. 358-377. See also K. Koch, "Staatsvorming en conjunctuurontwikkeling," in: *Acta Politica* 13 (1977), p. 333; R. Rose, "Disaggregating the Concept of Government," in: Ch.L. Taylor ed., *Why Governments Grow? Measuring Public Sector Size* (Beverly Hills, 1987), p. 161; Ch.Tilly, "Western State-Making and the Theory of Political Transformations," in: Ch.Tilly ed., *The Formation of National States in Western Europe* (Princeton, 1975), pp. 602 and 635.

[7] See L. van Buyten, "Bureaucratie en bureaucratisering in de lokale besturen der Zuidelijke Nederlanden, 16de tot 18de eeuw," in: *Tijdschrift voor Geschiedenis* 90 (1977) pp. 503-523; H.de Ridder-Symoens, "De universitaire vorming van de Brabantse stadsmagistraten en stadsfunctionarissen. Leuven en Antwerpen 1430-1580," in: *De Brabantse Stad. Vijfde Colloquium* ('s-Hertogenbosch, 1978), pp. 21-126.

[8] See W. Wedekind, "Quelques remarques sur les voies de recours auprès du Grand Conseil de Malines au 16e siècle," in: *Consilium Magnum 1473-1973* (Brussels, 1977), pp. 449-456.

[9] Interlocutory sentences or "administrative" decisions and appointments of voluntary judicature are not taken into account.

[10] I hope it will be possible to relate the final results of this research to results of local and regional historic-demographic research.

[11] See A. Zijp, *De strijd tussen de Staten van Gelderland en het Hof 1543-1566* (Arnhem, 1919), pp. 22-24 and 205-227. See also note 4.

[12] See also the article by G. Hanson, B. Holtman, and R. Howell, "Evaluating the Influence of *Zuidnederlands* on the Language of Holland in the 16th and 17th Centuries," pp. 61-75 in this volume.

[13] See J. Craeybeckx, "De Val van Antwerpen en de scheuring der Nederlanden, gezien door de grote Noordnederlandse geschiedschrijvers van de eerste generatie," in: J. Craeybeckx, F. Daelemans, and F.G. Scheelings eds., *1585: On separate Paths. . . . Acta Colloquii Bruxellensis* 22-23 XI 1985 (Colloquia Europalia VI, Brussels, 1988), pp. 124-125.

REPUBLICAN CULTURE IN EARLY MODERN EUROPE:
THE DUTCH REPUBLIC AND THE SEARCH FOR DIPLOMATIC RECOGNITION

Matthew T. Holland
University of North Carolina, Chapel Hill

In the history of the Dutch Republic the Treaty of Antwerp (1609) is an important event. Besides marking the beginning of the Twelve Years Truce, the Treaty created a new sovereign state, recognized on paper by adversary and friends alike. An important and perhaps crucial stage of the so-called Eighty Years War had ended bringing to the new nation full diplomatic recognition. Looking back upon this important year, one might think that it constituted a break with the preceding history of the rebellious provinces. In at least one important way, however, there was more continuity than hiatus between the collection of provinces that preceded the Treaty and the Dutch Republic that followed it. The Dutch conduct of foreign affairs continued as before, with the same fundamental expectation that their allies would remain actively involved with the defense of the Low Countries. Indeed this belief survived the turbulence of the coup of 1618 and even the expiration of the Twelve Years Truce. Spoiled by the various alliances and assistance which the French and English had arranged in the previous years, the Dutch were unprepared to accept the fact that their allies had begun to treat them like competitors, or at least a state that should live from its own means. The feeling that the Dutch could rightfully expect help ran deep and remained consistently one of the facets of republican culture in the United Provinces.

The collision between expectation and reality came with three Dutch embassies between the summer of 1620 and the end of 1622, when their ambassadors negotiated at Venice and London for agreements leading to the formation of an enormous anti-Habsburg league. The idea of such a league was not new in 1620. John of Oldenbarnevelt had worked to build one earlier, but it had never materialized.[1] The Dutch envisioned their league not as a monolithic organization, but as a series of bilateral defensive alliances between the United Provinces and England, France, Venice, the Protestant Union, the Hanseatic league, Denmark, Sweden, the Swiss Cantons, and perhaps Savoy.[2] The Dutch wanted to be a hub at the center of many spokes, and believed that such an arrangement would save them from renewed Spanish aggression. The embassies of 1620-1622 went to Venice and London but failed to obtain any agreement. Now that the Dutch were a sovereign state, they did not figure so prominently in the foreign policies of their allies. The Dutch were no longer the center of attention, as they had been in the reigns of Elizabeth I and Henry IV.[3] But even though the objectives of all three embassies were rebuffed the Dutch did not change their overall belief that the allies would soon come to their senses and form an alliance. The Dutch persisted so diligently throughout the period of the Twelve Years Truce that we may more easily understand their effort if we think of it as a second search for diplomatic recognition.

The famous coup of 1618, like the Treaty nine years before, also lends the false impression of a break with the past. True, the Orangists toppled Oldenbarnevelt from power, removed many of his supporters from municipal offices, and drastically reduced the power of the office of Grand Pensionary. The source of greatest influence shifted to Prince Maurice of Nassau, and families that served him came to enjoy more opportunity and prestige. On the other hand some of the most important veterans remained in power. The most prestigious of them, Francis van Aerssens, had sworn himself the enemy of Oldenbarnevelt in 1614, yet Aerssens completely adopted Oldenbarnevelt's project for an international league. Aerssens personally led the embassy of 1620 to Venice and the embassy of 1622 to London, to secure the league that Oldenbarnevelt had envisioned. Yet Aerssens was thoroughly Orangist. He became the diplomatic mentor of Constantine Huygens, who came from one of the families most closely bound to the dynasty of Orange-Nassau. The smooth transition of power and the continuity of foreign policy shows the distinctive resiliency of the Dutch political system in the early seventeenth century.

Along with foreign policy, the Dutch attitude about their centrality in European politics remained unchanged from the Treaty of Antwerp past the end of the Twelve Years Truce. In part the foreign policy derived from their attitude, which in turn grew more persistent from the increasing aloofness, and even condescension, with which older more established neighbors treated the Dutch. The fact that the Dutch had no king created problems for them, and the Princes of Orange-Nassau were no substitute. The undefined Dutch constitution pinpointed no clear source of sovereignty, which provided considerable frustration for those wishing to conduct diplomatic relations with the United Provinces. Moreover, the Dutch nation was born of rebellion against sovereignty, so that it constituted in the eyes of other Europeans a kind of anti-state. One historian recently observed that the Dutch fought to become a nation so they could avoid becoming a state.[4] The Dutch in turn wove their own national myth from the threads of the rebellion. They insisted they had a special covenant with God because they had survived oppression, and ordeal, and then freed themselves. They were the ancient Israelites reborn.[5] The speech that Francis van Aerssens delivered to the Doge and Senate during his embassy of 1620 displays the centrality of the Revolt in Dutch self-definition.

The Dutch, therefore, had to contend with the threefold stigma which Europeans attached to the little Republic. The circumstances of their nation's creation made them suspect. They were rebels. The fact of their nation's novelty made them unworthy. They had no ancient lineage. And the nature of their nation's undefined constitution made them tedious in negotiations. Their nation had no single source of sovereignty. What happened when the Dutch bumped against the condescension which older, more established states pressed upon them? The correspondence of Constantine Huygens casts light on this side of the problem. Huygens between 1620 and 1622 was just beginning his diplomatic career. On the Venetian embassy of 1620 he held a commission as secretary, as he also did on two embassies to England, in 1621 and 1622. The letters which he wrote on the two latter journeys tell us something of the frustration of being Dutch and of being republican in the early seventeenth century.

This essay shall examine briefly the attitude of the Dutch, and the attitudes of Venice and England toward them, in the years around 1621. The evidence comes from Aerssens' report to the Estates-General describing his Venetian embassy, from Huygens' letters, and from the Venetian diplomatic correspondence which not only mentions the league frequently, but also contains descriptions of the English attitude towards the Dutch. Together the three sources paint a portrait of the energy with which the Dutch pushed for their league, the indifference with which the Venetians approached it, and the hostility which it received from the English. In spite of their frustration over the league, however, the Dutch only momentarily revised their belief that their allies would actively help them.

The embassy of 1620 left for Venice in April, but before then Aerssens had discussed the possibility of an "understanding" between the two republics. In December of 1619 the Dutch had successfully negotiated with Venice a league for free trade in the Mediterranean, and later on England joined it.[6] Commercial leagues, however, were not the same as defensive leagues in the minds of the Dutch.[7] Aerssens publicized his embassy as a trip to confirm the commercial league, but he probably intended more.[8] His instructions, sanctioned by the Estates-General, stated that he should "deduce how far it was from the wish of Their High Mightinesses that the already established alliance might give way to a closer bond for mutual preservation and assistance." They added that Aerssens should try to persuade Venice to advance the interests of Frederick V of the Palatinate to regain the Crown of Bohemia. At least Venice should assist the general situation of the Protestants in Europe, since Spain was a common enemy. He was to suggest that the Dutch Republic maintain a permanent ambassador in the Most Serene Republic, to speed negotiations for any help.[9]

Once in Venice, Aerssens emphasized the common interests of the two peoples. In his introductory speech to the Doge and the Senate he mentioned that friendship could produce a fruit that would strengthen the "deux republiques comme fondée sur des interestz commun." He made the struggle against Spain an important theme. Later in the same speech he justified his embassy, referring at length to the past war in the Low Countries, which he described as a fight for the conservation of liberty, rights, and privileges. More importantly, Aerssens hinted that if the "greatest king in Europe" had judged the Dutch worthy of his assistance, then so should Venice. Here he meant Henry IV of France.[10]

The Venetians listened but the Dutch message did not persuade them to do much more than before. Aerssens had hoped to gain at least some assistance for Frederick V until the English provided more help, but the Venetians limited their interest mainly to Italian affairs. They told the Dutch that they could offer some support only after the Turk was tamed. The embassy left on July 5, 1620.[11]

The Savoyard ambassador at Venice had told Aerssens that help for the Protestant cause would naturally have to come from King James I. The Dutch had wanted help from him, and doubled their effort after the diplomatic defeat in Italy. Six ambassadors with their entourage left the United Provinces on January 23, 1621. Their orders were to accomplish in England what had failed in Venice: secure a non-commercial defensive alliance, obtaining the promise of military support for Frederick V. By this time Frederick had suffered his calamitous defeat at the Battle of the White Mountain (November 8, 1620), and earlier Spinola had invaded the Palatinate. If the Dutch could persuade James to lend substantial support to the effort against the Habsburgs, then other Protestant states, and perhaps even recalcitrant Venice, might lend a hand. The gamble was not unrealistic in this particular case. Frederick happened to be the son-in-law of the English monarch. Surely the Dutch could persuade the English to observe the interests of dynasty, or at least the interests of the Evangelical Faith. Perhaps they might even forget temporarily their obsession with the East Indies and the Fisheries questions.[12]

Unfortunately for nearly everyone except the Spanish, James styled himself something of a seventeenth-century Woodrow Wilson. Ever since his accession he had wanted Europe to view him as its peacemaker. In contemporary terms this meant balancing friendly relations with Protestant states against equally friendly relations with the Habsburg dominions. Likewise it meant moving beyond cordial relations, to dynastic alliances. James gave away his daughter Elizabeth to a match with Frederick, so the Prince of Wales deserved a Spanish bride. This line of thought obsessed James, while the fearsome prospects of war in Bohemia, the Palatinate, and the Low Countries turned into three horrible realities.[13]

The Dutch embassy met with failure almost at once. Everyone had known that condescension cradled James' attitude toward the

230

Dutch Republic, because it was a brand new state created in the spirit of rebellion. He did not like novelty and he certainly did not favor rebellion. The Venetian ambassador in London noted that James listened intently when the Spanish ambassador Gondomar told him it was worrisome that ". . . people nowadays took to revolution so easily and seemed so inclined to throw off their duty to their sovereign, with the idea of living like Republics." Gondomar had added that, "it would be necessary for the monarchical powers to devote themselves to bridle such pernicious temerity."[14] The Dutch might insist, as they had at Venice, that a bitterly fought struggle to preserve ancient liberties gave birth to their state and thus they deserved respect. James continued, nevertheless, to pay no attention. In fact, when he discovered that the envoys had with them no instructions allowing them to discuss commercial issues, he refused to grant them a personal audience. He referred their negotiations to the Privy Council, where they could expect to receive nothing but hostility. Later the Venetian ambassador observed that the Dutch had not seen the King since their first audience with him, adding with surprise that James had offered the Dutch nothing but the worst of treatment.[15]

The Dutch were not so astonished. The English had raised their commercial grievances before this visit. That the English did so now should not have amazed anyone. The secretary to the embassy made note several times of the lack of progress during the stay.[16] Finally in April the envoys returned to their homeland, promising the English that they would return empowered to discuss commercial grievances.[17]

A new embassy arrived in London in December. Francis van Aerssens himself led the party of envoys, so that anyone who bothered to notice would realize how much importance the Dutch placed upon concluding an agreement with James I. Aerssens possessed an excellent reputation everywhere in Europe. He had earned it during his rise to power, after the death of Oldenbarnevelt.[18] Three East India Company commissioners also formed part of the embassy, so that the Dutch arrived fully prepared to discuss commerce, even though they considered it to be of secondary importance to the critical political situation in Christendom. The Dutch believed James had a duty to help the Protestant cause, and that honor demanded his active participation. They did not think he could possibly refuse. They needed only to give him a little more time before the clouds would lift from before his eyes. That they held this view Constantine Huygens made clear in his letters to his parents. He enjoyed a commission as secretary to the embassy, and recorded the discouragements of the Aerssens mission in great detail.

When the Dutch tried to limit discussion in their first meetings, James diverted their negotiations into the Privy Council again. The conferences in the Council brought no progress, but much frustration. In February, 1622, Dutch and English relations had come dangerously close to a complete rupture. The Council's negotiations broke down, as James ordered that the Spanish must be allowed to recruit English mercenaries for their campaigns on the Continent.[19]

The two disappointments together really angered the Dutch. For the first time they clearly saw that their expectations had been foolish and that the United Provinces might have to survive on their own. Huygens described the events with a great deal of ire. To a report about James' order concerning the mercenaries, Constantine added cynically that James had qualified the command by adding that the mercenaries could not be used in the Palatinate. "So they shall be used against us," Huygens wrote, "the King knows that naturally. It does not bode well for the Republic, with Jülich occupied [by Spanish troops], Germany [also] in their hands, which we must fear, France divided by faction, England rocked into slumber, the Grisons smashed, Switzerland threatened!"[20] The course of events seemed even more incredible when the Dutch remembered that late in the previous year James had dissolved a Parliament which enthusiastically voted money for military aid in the Palatinate. At the time, the dissolution of Parliament had appeared farcical and full of comedy, but that was before the Dutch ran into their recent troubles.[21] Months later, in August of 1622, Huygens observed that James slept while Christendom suffered.[22] Clearly, relations had fallen apart.[23]

The King decided to end the deadlock in the same month that Huygens accused him of sleeping. James scheduled a special session of the Privy Council over which he would preside. The commercial problems began to receive fruitful treatment, and the way seemed open to a discussion of the defensive alliance. The appearance of progress, however, was only a mirage, even though the Dutch refused to believe it. The two sides concluded no hard and fast agreement about defense, and early in 1623 the Prince of Wales left for Spain on his famous escapade to win the hand of the Infanta. The Dutch returned to their formerly unrealistic expectations. They thought, once again, that time would eventually bring James to see the light of day. Eventually he would see through the Spanish chirade that had fooled him for so long. Eventually he would stop the indignities which the Dutch suffered at Court. In any case such indignities were not James' fault, but that of a group of "rascals raised from the mud to great dignities," according to Huygens.[24] Since James had found the wisdom to intervene personally in the negotiations over commerce, then surely he had the best interests of the Dutch at heart.

Some have said that commercial rivalry had destroyed the good relations between the two Maritime Powers.[25] Such a conclusion offers only an English point of view and ignores the Dutch. In truth commerce cannot be blamed; James and his ministers used commercial grievances as pretext for putting off discussion of the problem that really bothered the Dutch. The strategy succeeded brilliantly. The ambassadors went home empty-handed.

Thus the second search for diplomatic recognition failed in 1622. Past experience with numerous alliances had lulled the Dutch into the confident belief that a league against the Habsburgs could be assembled. But their newly recognized sovereignty brought no more influence in international diplomacy. Instead sovereignty earned cold responses from the old allies. The league did not materialize. Former friends, England above all, largely abandoned the United Provinces to their own devices at the outset of the Thirty Years War. At the end of 1622 their fortified city, Bergen op Zoom, withstood a great siege conducted by the famous Spanish general Spinola. Other Spanish plans were enacted and the Dutch survived those too. Denmark entered the war later on, and then so did France. Eventually the Dutch discovered that they could survive without their league, and later in the century they even considered adopting a policy of neutrality. The embassies of 1620, 1621, and 1622 advanced the Dutch only a little way along the road of political maturity, a road which had to be traversed in order to become a self-reliant nation in the community of European states. Thus, Dutch republicanism in these years meant among other things the naive belief that the United Provinces could always count on loyal allies, friends committed to assisting the little lowlands country as long as Spain threatened the stability of Europe. Oldenbarnevelt's dream of a great alliance was also the dream of other Dutchmen. The vision was so persuasive that even the dismal diplomatic failures in Venice and London shook it only a little.

NOTES

[1] Jan den Tex, *Oldenbarnevelt*, translated by R.B. Powell (Cambridge: Cambridge University Press, 1973), volume 2, pp. 493-494.

[2] In the following volumes of the *Calendar of State Papers Venetian*, at least, occur a number of specific references to this super-league: volume 12 (1610-1613), pp. 17, 278, 559, 112, 115, 281, 175, 217, 281, 283, 292, 491, 503, 520; volume 13 (1613-1615), pp. 11, 25, 226, 232, 88, 238, 307, 337, 383; volume 14 (1615-1617), pp. 169, 171-173, 180, 211, 185, 280, 281, 258, 399, 536, 561, 563, 576; volume 15 (1617-1619), pp. 16, 18, 19, 37, 187, 42, 54, 69, 444, 463, 491, 522, 458, 464, 482-488, 516, 511.

[3] Wallace MacCaffrey explained why Elizabeth was unable to help the Dutch earlier than she did. His point is that she wanted very much to help them. See: Wallace MacCaffrey, *Queen*

Elizabeth and the Making of Policy, 1572-1588 (Princeton: Princeton University Press, 1981).

[4] Simon Schama, *The Embarrassment of Riches* (New York: Alfred Knopf, 1987), p. 62.

[5] Schama, *Embarrassment*, pp. 67-68. See also: G. Groenhuis, "Calvinism as National Consciousness: The Dutch Republic as the New Israel," *Britain and the Netherlands*, volume 7, edited by A.C. Duke and C.A. Tamse (The Hague: Martinus Nijhoff, 1981).

[6] *Calendar of State Papers Venetian*, volume 15 (1617-1619), p. 45; volume 16 (1619-1621), pp. 31, 32, 42, 98.

[7] Simon Schama points out that the Dutch thought of war and commercial enterprise as two separate things which could not be mixed, mainly because their commerce operated comfortably without military assistance, and war seemed only to be a hindrance to commerce. See: *Embarrassment*, p. 253.

[8] *Calendar of State Papers Venetian*, volume 16 (1619-1621), p. 332.

[9] "Rapport" of Francis van Aerssens to the Estates-General, edited by C.A. van Rathaan Macare, *Berigten van het Historisch Genootschap te Utrecht*, part 5, volume 1 (Utrecht, 1853), pp. 46-50.

[10] "Rapport," pp. 93-94; the speech took place June 17, 1620.

[11] Constantine Huygens to his father, no date, *Briefwisseling van Constantijn Huygens*, volume 1 (The Hague: Martinus Nijhoff, 1911), letter #87, p. 54 (hereafter cited as *Briefwisseling*; all citations to this source come from volume 1 only). Huygens was the official secretary for the embassy. See also "Report of the Savoyard ambassador Hieronino Trevisano to the Doge and Senate," June 23, 1620, *Calendar of State Papers Venetian*, volume 16 (1619-1621), pp. 288-289. The Savoyard ambassador was reporting a conversation he had held with Aerssens.

[12] George Edmundson, *Anglo-Dutch Rivalry During the First Half of the Seventeenth Century* (Oxford: The Clarendon Press, 1911), pp. 1-60, and especially pp. 58-60.

[13] G.P.V. Akrigg, *Jacobean Pageant* (Cambridge: Harvard University Press, 1963), p. 323; A.G.H. Bachrach, *Sir Constantine Huygens and Britain* (London: Oxford University Press, 1963), pp. 164-165.

[14] Girolamo Lando, Venetian ambassador in London, to the Doge and Senate, June 25, 1620, *Calendar of State Papers Venetian*, volume 16 (1619-1621), p. 293.

[15] Girolamo Lando to the Doge and Senate, March 26, 1621, *Calendar of State Papers Venetian*, volume 16 (1619-1621), p. 617.

[16] For an example, see: Constantine Huygens to his parents, February 23, 1621, *Briefwisseling*, p. 62.

[17] Despite the discouraging tide of events, the Dutch still considered a league between the United Provinces, the Protestant Union, the King of Denmark, the Hanseatic League, and the King of England to be a reasonable goal. Girolamo Lando to the Doge and Senate, April 2, 1621, *Calendar of State Papers Venetian*, volume 17 (1621-1623), p. 3.

[18] See: *Calendar of State Papers Venetian*, volume 15 (1617-1619), p. 346, where the Venetians predicted that Aerssens would become "the new Oldenbarnevelt."

[19] For details on the deadlock and later progress in the Privy Council deliberations, see *Acts of the Privy Council*, volume 38 (London: His Majesty's Stationary Office, 1932): letter of February 9, 1622, pp. 147-151; letter of August 1, 1622, pp. 304-305; letter of November 19, 1622, pp. 354-355.

[20] Constantine Huygens to his parents, February 4, 1622, *Briefwisseling*, p. 79.

[21] Constantine Huygens to his parents, December 18, 1621, *Briefwisseling*, p. 72. On the fortunes of that Parliament see: Robert Zaller, *The Parliament of 1621* (Berkeley: University of California Press, 1971).

[22] Constantine Huygens to his parents, August 14, 1622, *Briefwisseling*, p. 112.

[23] Huygens used the word "rupture." Constantine Huygens to his father, no date, *Briefwisseling*, p. 112.

[24] Constantine Huygens to his father, September 19, 1622, *Briefwisseling*, pp. 121-123.

[25] George Edmundson's *Anglo-Dutch Rivalry* has this for its thesis.

THE DUTCH REVOLT AND ITS IMPACT ON ENGLAND DURING THE FIRST HALF OF THE SEVENTEENTH CENTURY

Hugh Dunthorne
University College, Swansea

The last twenty years have seen a growing and welcome tendency among historians interested in the Revolt of the Netherlands to consider the rebellion as an international problem. It has been studied in the context both of Spain's international empire and of the international relations of the North Sea; its close links with the French Wars of Religion have been explored; and there have been several works tracing the course of England's involvement in the Low Countries wars. Studies of the English connexion have tended to focus on royal policy towards the Netherlands, and there are good reasons for this. The motives for Queen Elizabeth I's reluctant decision in 1585 to come to the assistance of the Dutch, the effect (or lack of effect) of English intervention on the course of events, the dilemmas created by James I's determination to make peace with Spain - all these were matters of widespread public concern in late sixteenth- and early seventeenth-century England, and they remain the subject of debate and disagreement among modern historians. Yet it is also possible to approach the subject of Anglo-Dutch relations from a different, and less familiar, standpoint. For the other face of England's involvement in the Dutch struggle with Spain - an involvement, incidentally, which by no means ceased with the Anglo-Spanish peace of 1604 - was the impact which the Dutch Revolt and the rise of the Dutch state had upon England and English affairs, particularly during the turbulent first half of the seventeenth century. This impact was equally a subject of concern to contemporaries. Writing shortly after the end of the English Civil War, which led to the overthrow of the monarchy and to the establishment in its place of an English Republic, Thomas Hobbes remarked how 'oftentimes the example of different government in a neighbouring nation disposeth men to alteration of the form [of their own] . . . And I doubt not, but many men have been contented to see the late troubles in England out of an imitation of the Low Countries; supposing there needed no more to grow rich, than to change, as [the Dutch] had done, the forme of their Government.'[1] Such an interpretation of the origins of the English Civil War, it must be said, has not received much support from modern historical scholarship. Indeed, it has hardly been considered. Yet it has implications which are surely worth considering.[2] There is in fact a good deal of evidence, if not always to support, at least to cast light upon the point of view which Hobbes had in mind; and I should like in the course of this article to offer an outline of some of this evidence.

A word must be said first about communications between England and the Dutch Republic in the late sixteenth and early seventeenth century. By the end of Elizabeth's reign the exchange of diplomatic representatives had become established as a regular and permanent link between the two countries. But what is more remarkable - at least so far as the theme of this article is concerned - is the amount of unofficial, even popular contact that there was, much of it the consequence of migration. Since the Middle Ages the commercial interdependence of the two regions had encouraged the movement of merchants and artisans across the North Sea. And the Reformation added to this human traffic streams of religious refugees, first from the Netherlands to England with the onset of the Duke of Alva's regime in 1567, and later in the other direction, as dissenters of various kinds left England for the more congenial religious atmosphere of the Low Countries. From the earliest years of the Dutch Revolt, English, Scots and Welsh soldiers had gone to fight in the Low Countries - mainly, but not exclusively, on the rebel side - their numbers increasing markedly after the Anglo-Dutch Treaty of Nonsuch in 1585. And at the same time a growing stream of English and Scots were seeking an education there, whether as commercial apprentices in the great trading towns, as students at the newly-founded Dutch universities, or simply as gentlemen travellers. By the 1630s around 30 English and Scots churches had been established in the Dutch Republic; and although the total size of the Anglo-Scots community is difficult to calculate, because it was in part a shifting rather than a static population, there seems no reason to doubt Keith Sprunger's recent estimate placing it 'in the tens of thousands.'[3] Dutch settlement in Britain never reached these proportions, but it was spread over a wider geographical area - from Scotland to East Anglia, London, and the South East.

One of the results of so much migration was to make the Dutch language more widely-known among English speaking people than it is today. It has been suggested, indeed, that during the seventeenth century Dutch became for a while an international language for the countries bordering the Baltic and North Seas.[4] Yet even without a knowledge of Dutch or an opportunity to visit the Low Countries, it was still possible for English people to keep abreast of what was happening there thanks to the growth of the Anglo-Dutch printing industry. The Dutch Revolt was the first major rebellion to take full advantage of the printing press; and, in addition to what was published in Holland for the domestic market, a mass of printed material was also addressed to readers in neighbouring countries, especially England - material which ranged in style from sobre reporting to sometimes blatant propaganda (Catholic as well as Protestant) and in format from large-scale histories down to pamphlets and newspapers. The interest which this material aroused in England can be observed at several different levels: in the parliamentary tracts of the 1640s, littered with references to Dutch authorities like Van Meteren and Grotius; in the allusions (not always favourable) to things Dutch in English poetry from Spenser to Milton and Marvell; and, not least, in the theatre.[5] Events like the Sack of Antwerp, the Siege of Ostend and the trial and death of Oldenbarneveldt were all seen during these years re-enacted on the London stage.[6]

With so many strands of communication, it is not surprising that the seventeenth-century English were said to know more about the Netherlands, 'either by sight or relation,' than about any other foreign country.[7] But how did this knowledge effect English life and thought? What, in other words, was the impact of the Dutch Revolt and of the emerging Dutch Republic on England? Let me point to three related areas in which I believe a significant impact was felt: military affairs, religious beliefs, and political and social thought. It makes sense to begin with the military, since it was as a military struggle that events in the Netherlands were most immediately perceived by contemporaries: they spoke of *The Wofull Warres in Flanders* or *The Actions of the Lowe Countries*, hardly ever of 'the Dutch Revolt' as we usually say today.[8] In the early years of the conflict, the armed forces sustaining the Dutch cause were not impressive. To the experienced eye of a professional soldier like Sir Roger Williams, the Welshman who contrived at various times in the 1570s and '80s to serve in both the Dutch and Spanish armies, the technical military superiority of the Spaniards was unquestionable.[9] But in 1588, with the appointment of Maurice of Nassau, second son of William the Silent, as Captain- and Admiral-General of the Dutch forces, the situation began to change. The military reforms which he set in motion over the next two decades - reforms of tactics and military science, of training and discipline - not only made the Dutch army a match for the Spaniards but also won it an international reputation, transforming it into what one military writer called 'the Schoole of War, whither the most martiall Spirits of Europe resort to lay down the Apprentiship of their Service in Armes.'[10] Among those martial spirits were many of the English and Scots officers who were later to serve in the victorious parliamentary armies of the English Civil War - and it is hardly an exaggeration to say that Oliver Cromwell's New Model Army could not have been the force it was without his soldiers' prior experience in the Low Countries.[11] The standard English military handbooks of the time were written by veterans of the Dutch service.[12] Cromwell adopted Dutch tactical methods, particularly in the use of artillery.[13] His disciplinary code was modelled on the one published by the States General in 1590, which had been printed in English in 1637. And, like Maurice of Nassau, he selected and promoted officers on grounds of ability, not social rank.[14] Above all, the activities of the Puritan army chaplains attached to English military units in the Netherlands anticipated the role which such chaplains were to play in the English parliamentary armies of the 1640s. Almost without exception, the army chaplains in the United Provinces were convinced Calvinists, exiled from England because their views were disapproved by the Anglican hierarchy and attracted to the Dutch cause which they saw as a holy war. Like their successors in the New Model Army, they tried through their preaching to create what Thomas Scott, chaplain to the garrisons at Gorinchem and Utrecht, called 'the glorious splendour of the Christian camp'; and they were also ready on occasion to champion the grievances of the rank-and-file soldiers against their officers.[15]

Garrison churches were not the only English religious institutions in the Netherlands. There were also the official churches for the English and Scots civilian population – official in the sense that they were sanctioned and maintained by the Dutch local authorities as English-language branches of what became in 1618 the state Calvinist church. And, thirdly, there were the more radical Separatist congregations, lacking official status but for the most part tolerated. Thanks to the work of numerous church historians, we know a great deal about these groups, about their often faction-ridden history, and about the influences exerted over them by Dutch Calvinism and by more radical groups like the Mennonites. In terms of church government they ranged from Presbyterian to Congregationalist, and in doctrine from orthodox Calvinist to Anabaptist. But what they had in common – or, at any rate, what their ministers had in common – was a dissatisfaction with the current state of the Church of England and a determination to take advantage of the 'Sacred Sanctuary' provided by the Dutch Republic in order to search for a better kind of church.[16] Writing to Archbishop Laud in 1628, the English ambassador at The Hague put the same point another way when he referred disapprovingly to the Republic as a 'nursery to non-conformists.'[17] Consequently, when Laud was impeached by the English parliament in 1640 and the episcopal hierarchy of the Church of England effectively overthrown, many of these exiled nonconformists eagerly returned to England to embark on the reformation of the English church for which they believed their period of Dutch exile had been a spiritual preparation.[18] Within a few years parliament had issued ordinances replacing the traditional Anglican structure with a Calvinist system of church government. And during the period of religious anarchy that followed, many of the sects that sprang up and many of their doctrines and practices – including, for example, the active participation of women in church affairs – can be traced to origins among the English congregations of the Netherlands.[19] This was particularly true of what for its time was perhaps the most radical doctrine of all, religious toleration. The first English plea for religious freedom was made in 1612 by the exiled Separatist John Smyth, influenced partly by Mennonite doctrine but also by the tolerant policy of the *vroedschap* of Amsterdam where he had been allowed to establish his congregation.[20] Taking up the argument in 1641, Lord Brooke pointed to 'the United Provinces (in the Low Countries) who let every Church please her selfe. And how Religion doth flourish There, is known to most men.'[21] Brooke himself certainly knew, from his experience as a student at Leiden in the 1620s. And so did the former minister of the English church at

Rotterdam, Hugh Peter, who strengthened the argument further by remarking on the connexion between toleration and Holland's flourishing economy.[22] But advocates of toleration had to contend also with the widely held view that religious freedom undermined national unity and created 'division and disturbance' in the state. The Leveller Richard Overton, another radical who knew the Republic from personal experience, argued that in practice the opposite was true and that it was the attempt to enforce religious uniformity, rather than toleration, that caused dissension. 'What [had] occasioned the revolt . . . of the Neitherlanders from the King of Spaine,' he asked, if not 'this divelish spirit of binding the conscience?' And as another Leveller pointed out, the unity of the Dutch in successfully defending 'their common liberty' was convincing proof that diversity of religious belief was not incompatible with patriotism.[23]

Toleration, in other words, was as much a political issue as a religious one, and it points to the last area of my subject to be considered: the impact of the Dutch Revolt on English political and social thought. It was an impact felt particularly during the 1640s as deepening political divisions produced among the English - or at least among parliamentarians - a growing sense of the affinity between their situation and that of the Dutch, whose Eighty Years' War was of course still continuing. In thinking about foreign policy, for example, the Puritans had traditionally viewed the Dutch as members of the international Calvinist brotherhood and as a bulwark against the threat of Spanish tyranny, a bulwark which it was England's duty and interest to support. But in the 1640s this view was given an added dimension as England became engulfed in her own civil war - in the eyes of the parliamentarians, a war against much the same threat of tyranny at home as the Dutch had been fighting in their long struggle with Spain. Consequently, when the war began and parliament started to pursue its own independent foreign policy in 1642, its first act was to appeal for support to the States General of the United Provinces and to propose what was really an ideological union based on their common commitment to constitutional government and the reformed religion.[24] The proposal was turned down by the Dutch, precisely because they were still at war with Spain and felt that fighting one war was enough. But this did not prevent the English parliament repeating its proposal to the States General several times down to 1650, always with the same result. Moreover, although English frustration with the States General's unwillingness to cooperate combined with irritation over various minor maritime disputes to produce in due course the Navigation Act of 1651 and the outbreak of the first Anglo-Dutch war, not even this conflict could entirely dispel the view that the English and Dutch Republics were really natural allies.

When it came to justifying the act of civil war and the eventual overthrow of the monarchy, the arguments adopted by parliamentary pamphleteers were equally revealing of their sense of affinity with the Dutch Revolt. For they were largely the arguments that had been employed by William the Silent and his circle in the sixteenth century, based on notions of popular sovereignty, natural law and the right of resistance. Princes existed for the sake of their people, from whom they held their offices in trust; and if they abused that trust, their subjects could lawfully resist – even, said John Goodwin, to the point of 'turn[ing] these servants of their out of their doors, as . . . the Hollanders of late have done.' In more than one parliamentary tract of the 1640s the States General's Act of Abjuration of 1581 and other Dutch documents were cited or quoted at length.[25] It is true that this theory of resistance did not originate with the Dutch, and that the English could have imported it as easily from the political writers of the French Wars of Religion.[26] But it is worth noticing that it was a doctrine that also dominated the teaching of politics and law at several of the Dutch universities at this time, particularly as it had been formulated by Johannes Althusius in his *Politica* of 1603; and the frequent citing of Althusius by English writers on resistance during the 1640s may suggest one way in which those universities were making their mark on English thought.[27]

Finally, the sense of affinity with the Dutch Revolt, and indeed with the Dutch Republic that had emerged during its course, can be seen in the wide-ranging debate which the Civil War set in motion in mid-seventeenth-century England – a debate about constitutional structures, about legal reform, about social and economic improvement. Here, too, it seems likely that the Dutch universities were exercising an influence by directing attention towards the study of republican institutions.[28] Some English readers may also have got to know Hugo Grotius's book *On the Antiquity of the Batavian Republic*, which was essentially a defence of the Dutch republican constitution as it had evolved by 1610 – and, so Grotius argued, as it had always existed. This was his first work to be published in English, appropriately in 1649.[29] Perhaps even more influential were the generally favourable impressions brought back – and in some cases published – by Englishmen who visited the Dutch Republic of the earlier seventeenth century and saw the practical effects of its institutions at first hand.[30] At any rate, when the Rump Parliament in 1649 officially announced the abolition of the monarchy and the establishment of the English Republic, it seemed natural that it should pay tribute to the 'encouragement' it had received from observing 'Our neighbours in the United Provinces' who 'since their change of Government have wonderfully increased in Wealth, Freedom, Trade and Strength, both by Sea and Land.'[31] The causal connexion implied here between the more 'democratical' style of government characteristic of a 'free state,' on the one hand, and the growth of the national economy, on the other, was a point which had been made by earlier observers of the Republic.[32] But now the members of England's new Council of Trade were urging that the country adopt specific economic policies and techniques that had proved successful in Holland – lower customs and interest rates, free ports, active encouragement of immigration, negotiable bills of exchange, insurance.[33] Dutch systems of social welfare and poor relief, with their emphasis on productive labour, were recommended.[34] So, perhaps more surprisingly, were various features of the Dutch legal system, such as civil marriage, partible inheritance, merchant courts and the registration of land. There were fewer lawyers in the Republic than in England, it was said, yet because of its localized court system 'you may get justice as often and as naturally as their cows give milk.'[35] Several plans were put forward for the reform and extension of university education in England, partly along Dutch lines.[36] And Hugh Peter, who believed that with God's help anything was possible, wanted large parts of London knocked down and rebuilt in the style of his adopted city of Rotterdam.[37] How far these and other schemes were actually put into practice is, of course, another matter – but it is a matter which ought to be investigated.

The themes that I have chosen to discuss – the role of the Netherlands as England's school of war, as its nursery of nonconformity and as its model of revolution – do not in themselves provide a complete picture of Anglo-Dutch relations during these years. And I do not want to suggest that the impression made by the Dutch on England, even on Puritan England, was always positive or favourable. This was, after all, also the period of the massacre of Amboyna and of growing Anglo-Dutch commercial rivalry. Nor do I want to suggest, despite the opinion of some of Thomas Hobbes' contemporaries, that the Dutch Revolt can be regarded as a direct cause of the English Revolution. But I would argue that the English of the first half of the seventeenth century were well-informed both about the progress of the Eighty Years' War and about the new state and society that emerged during the course of it. Consequently, when the English found themselves involved in their own civil war in the 1640s and apparently on the threshold of creating their own new state and society, it was natural that some of them at least should have tried to apply the lessons that they felt could be learned from the experience and achievements of their ancient and familiar neighbours across the North Sea.

NOTES

[1] *Leviathan* (1651) in Hobbes' *English Works* ed. W. Molesworth (11v., 1839-45), iii, pp. 313-14.

[2] See the brief but suggestive discussions of G.N. Clark, 'Dutch Influences in British History,' *De Nieuwe Gids* 38 (1923), pp. 505-15, and C. Hill, *Intellectual Origins of the English Revolution* (1965), pp. 280-84.

[3] K.L. Sprunger, *Dutch Puritanism: A History of the English and Scottish Churches of the Netherlands* (1982), p. 5.

[4] [J.J. Orlers], *The Triumphs of Nassau* tr. W. Shute (1613), p. 5; J. Huizinga, *Dutch Civilisation in the Seventeenth Century and Other Essays* (1968), p. 150.

[5] E.g., W. Prynne, *The Soveraigne Power of Parliaments and Kingdomes* (1643), pt. iii, esp. pp. 143-44.

[6] J. Huizinga, 'Engelschen en Nederlanders in Shakespeare's tijd,' *Verzamelde werken* (9v., 1948-53), ii, pp. 350-81. The plays referred to are *A Larum for London or the Siedge of Antwerp* (1602); C. Tourneur, *The Atheist's Tragedy* (1611), II, i, describing the overthrow of the Spanish at Ostend; and J. Fletcher and P. Massinger, *The Tragedy of Sir John van Olden Barneveldt* (1619).

[7] *The Memoirs and Travels of Sir John Reresby* (1813), p. 144.

[8] The titles, respectively, of works by Thomas Churchyard (1578) and Sir Roger Williams (1618).

[9] *A Briefe Discourse of Warre* (1590), urging reform of the English army along Spanish lines.

[10] J. Bingham, *The Tacticks of Aelian* (1616), sig. A2v.

[11] Sir J.W. Fortescue, *A History of the British Army* (13v., 1899-1930), i, pp. 168-69; M. Ashley, *Cromwell's Generals* (1954), pp. 14-15, 28-29, 157-58. James I's peace with Spain did not lessen the numbers of English and Scots troops in the Dutch army, who were by this time in the pay of the States General. During the 1630s they numbered around 12,000.

[12] Besides Bingham, cited above n. 10, these included E. Davies, *The Art of War* (1616), J. Waymouth, *Low-Country Trayning* (1617), H. Hexham, *Principles of the Art Militarie* (1637-40), and R. Ward, *Animadversions of Warre* (1639).

[13] C.H. Firth, *Cromwell's Army* (3rd ed., 1921), pp. 151-52.

[14] Discussing the structure of infantry companies in the Dutch army, John Hexham suggests that 'gentlemen of quality' were expected to serve initially as private soldiers, with the opportunity for preferment 'when the Generall or coronell shall find them worthy and deserving': *Principles*, i, pp. 6-7; cf. Firth, *Cromwell's Army*, pp. 40-53. In an appendix to pt. i of his book, Hexham printed the Dutch army's *Laws, Articles and Ordinances* which may be compared with the English parliamentary army's *Laws and Ordinances* of 1642.

[15] T. Scott, 'The Campe's a Schole' in S. Bachelor, *Miles Christianus* (1625), quoted by Sprunger, *Dutch Puritanism*, p. 264; see also pp. 198-99.

[16] J. Quick, 'Icones Sacrae Anglicanae' (Ms.), quoted by Sprunger, *Dutch Puritanism*, p. 285.

[17] Quoted by Sprunger, *Dutch Puritanism*, p. 11.

[18] See, for example, the favourable account of their Dutch experience given in the *Apologeticall Narration* (1644) of W. Bridge and his fellow-Congregationalists: *Tracts on Liberty in the Puritan Revolution 1638-1647* ed. W. Haller (3v., 1934), ii, pp. 305-39.

[19] Sprunger, *Dutch Puritanism*, ch. xii; K.V. Thomas, 'Women and the Civil War Sects' in *Crisis in Europe 1560-1660* ed. T. Aston (1965), pp. 321-24.

[20] M.R. Watts, *The Dissenters* i (1977), pp. 42-49.

[21] *A Discourse upon the Nature of Episcopacy* (1641) in *Tracts on Liberty*, ii, p. 135.

[22] *Puritanism and Liberty* ed. A.S.P. Woodhouse (2nd ed., 1974), p. 138.

[23] R. Overton, *The Araignement of Mr. Persecution* (1645) and W. Walwyn, *The Compassionate Samaritane* (1644) in *Tracts on Liberty*, iii, pp. 222-23, 241, 286-88.

[24] S. Groenveld, *Verlopend Getij: de Nederlandse Republiek en de Engelse Burgeroorlog 1640-1646* (1986), pp. 39-42, 103-04.

[25] P. Hunton, *A Treatise of Monarchy* (1643), p. 10; W. Prynne, *The Soveraigne Power of Parliaments and Kingdomes* (1643), pt. iii; J. Goodwin, *The Obstructours of Justice* (1649), pp. 11-12 (quotation); J. Milton, *The Tenure of Kings and Magistrates* in *Complete Prose Works* (Yale ed.) iii, pp. 226-27.

[26] J.H.M. Salmon, *The French Religious Wars in English Political Thought* (1959), pp. 3-4.

[27] *The Politics of Althusius* tr. F.S. Carney (1964), pp. 10-11, 95-96, 101, 186-87; E.H. Kossmann, 'The Development of Dutch Political Theory in the Seventeenth Century' in *Britain and the Netherlands* eds. J.S. Bromley and E.H. Kossmann (1960), pp. 97-98; G.P. Gooch, *English Democratic Ideas in the Seventeenth Century* ed. H.J. Laski (1927), pp. 47-48.

[28] Kossmann, 'Dutch Political Theory,' p. 94.

[29] A second edition followed in 1654. Other works of Grotius appeared in English in the course of the 1650s, including *Of the Law of War and Peace*, which in its original Latin had been cited frequently as an authority on the right of resistance.

[30] E.g. Sir T. Overbury, *His Observations in his Travailes upon the State of the XVII Provinces* (1626). Cf. T. Violet, *Humble Proposal against Transporting Gold and Silver* (1661) quoted by J.P. Cooper, 'Social and Economic Policies under the Commonwealth' in *The Interregnum* ed. G.E. Aylmer (1972), p. 122.

[31] *A Declaration of the Parliament of England* (1649), p. 16. Cf. H. Robinson, *A Short Discourse between Monarchical and Aristocratical Government* (1649), p. 15; W. Cole, *A Rod for the Lawyers* (1659) in *The Harleian Miscellany* (10v., 1808-13), iv, p. 310.

[32] Most acutely by Sir Francis Bacon, 'Of the Greatness of the Kingdom of Great Britain' in *Works* ed. J. Spedding (14v. 1862-74), vii, pp. 59-61.

[33] *Early English Tracts on Commerce* ed., J.R. McCulloch (1954), pp. 79-93; J.P. Cooper, 'Social and Economic Policies,' pp. 125, 129-30, 136.

[34] W. Goffe, *How to Advance the Trade of the Nation and Employ the Poor* (1641) in *Harleian Miscellany* iv, pp. 385-89; R. Bush, *The Poor Man's Friend* (1649).

[35] D. Veall, *The Popular Movement for Law Reform 1640-1660* (1970), pp. 206 (quoting H. Peter, *A Word For the Army*, 1647), 217-18, 219-22; N.L. Matthews, *William Sheppard, Cromwell's Law Reformer* (1984), p. 173; *Early English Tracts on Commerce*, p. 81.

[36] *The Advice of W[illiam] P[etty] to Mr. Samuel Hartlib for the Advancement of Some Particular Parts of Learning* (1648) in *Harleian Miscellany* vi, pp. 1-14; Hill, *Intellectual Origins*, pp. 108-09, 123-24. Several of Petty's ideas clearly derive from his two years of study at Leiden, Utrecht and Amsterdam in the earlier 1640s.

[37] *Good Work for a Good Magistrate* (1651), pp. 101-08.

POPULAR SONG-BOOKS IN THE SIXTEENTH-CENTURY LOWLANDS

Hermina Joldersma
University of Calgary, Calgary

Of interest to almost everyone concerned with the Lowlands of the sixteenth century are, or ought to be, its songs and its song-books. From the earliest extant collection, *Het Antwerps liedboek* of 1544, to the last of its genre, *Het Haerlems Oudt Liedt-Boeck* of 1640 (27th edition in 1716), these song-books provide glimpses into the time and its people not to be had from any other source. In a refracted way, the songs in these collections deal with almost every topic of current interest, from history to politics to piety to relationships between the sexes to prostitution to male impotence – the entire gamut. At the same time these songs are part of collections, and the interrelationship between text and context, between song and song-book, adds significantly to our understanding of them both and the society in which they played such an important role. This short paper can give only a brief introduction to what is becoming a very large field, but as introduction it hopes to arouse the interest of scholars in a variety of fields – literature, musicology, sociology, history, women's studies, early publishing, religious studies, linguistics, to name but a few of the more obvious ones – in what I consider to be one of the most fascinating bodies of texts from the sixteenth century.

Though a knowledge of song scholarship is not necessary for working with these texts, it may be helpful to understand the questions and concerns which have informed work already done. Song scholarship in general can be divided into roughly three areas. On area, clearly, is that of commercially produced and disseminated song. So, for example, it would be interesting to examine the social context and textual content of the widely promoted Dutch song-book *Kun je nog zingen, zing dan mee!*, an early twentieth-century collection intended to raise the moral fibre of the common folk by giving them "decent" songs to sing. Another area of scholarship is that of orally transmitted song, songs handed down from one generation to the next by the act of singing. This kind of song transmission is dying out, for a variety of reasons which will not be dealt with here, and song scholarship is concerned with capturing what is still left by interviewing the elderly people who still know both the texts and contexts of these songs, and recording their singing for posterity. In the Netherlands since 1957 the tremendously successful radio programme *Onder de groene linde*, under the auspices of Ate Doornbosch, has been devoted to collecting and broadcasting this orally preserved song. In conjunction with *Het Nederlands Volksliedarchief* he has recently published the first of what is planned as seven volumes of songs drawn from this work (Doornbosch). The third area, that of older song scholarship, falls between these two. It necessarily deals with printed texts, but at the same time many of these texts had lived only in oral form up to that first printing. Walking the tightrope between orality and literacy, between real "folk" song and songs produced with other considerations, say moral or financial, is a challenging task. In this regard those books which I will refer to as belonging to the "family" of *Het Antwerps liedboek* offer a unique perspective, for in their forewords, in their song repertoires, and in their relationships to each other, they provide important clues to song life, and life, in the sixteenth century.

Het Antwerps liedboek occupies a particularly important position in the history of European as well as Netherlandic song because it is the largest, oldest, printed, secular song collection in Germanic literature. It is by far the **largest** of its time: it has 221 texts, with an average of about five stanzas per text and about six lines per stanza, so many songs that even its printer lost an overview and included four of the songs twice. It is the **oldest**, largest song collection: song-books were printed before 1544, of course, but these were less ambitious, containing only sixty songs or less. It is the largest, oldest, **printed** song collection: many sixteenth-century people collected their favorite songs in manuscripts, but *Het Antwerps liedboek* is one of the first instances in which a printer took a gamble and collected songs for commercial purposes. It is also the largest, oldest, printed, **secular** song collection: Symon Cock's *Deuoot ende Profitelyck Boecxken* of 1539 was an ambitious project, as was his *Souterliedekens* of 1540, but both books contain strictly religious songs. *Het Antwerps liedboek*, in contrast, has only four (or five, depending on one's interpretation) religious songs among the 217 different texts.

These texts offer a staggering variety of material. About 25 of the songs are ballads, some of them among the best textual versions of famous international ballads such as the *Tannhäuser* or the *Jüngeres Hildebrandslied*. Another 30 of the songs are historical-political and deal with important events or political figures of the time, such as the political trouble between the emperor Charles V and the dukes of Cleve, Julich, and Gelder around 1543. In some of these songs the Cleve troop leader, Maarten van Rossum, plays a major role; he may be known to modern smokers as the man in stocks on the tobacco package of "Van Rossems Troost." Some of the songs are farces, funny tales in which sexual humor is the salient ingredient. The most famous of these is the well known sixteenth-century song of the peasant who gives his horse and wagon for the privilege of sleeping with the lady of the castle. After the fact, however, the peasant decides that one woman is essentially the same as the next and, through a clever trick, regains not only horse and wagon, but even the lady's favour. The first version of this song is a German one from the late 1440s; the first Dutch version is found in *Het Antwerps liedboek*, and the song lived on in the Low Countries till well into the twentieth century. It functioned as the dramatic kernel for Samuel Coster's *Boere-Klucht van Teeuwis de Boer*, first performed in 1612 (*Wercken* 1-70), and it is possible that Jan Debusschere, a street musician from Roeselaar who lived from 1750 until 1827, was apprehended by the authorities for singing precisely this song (de Bruyne; Joldersma II, 71). By far the majority of songs, about 60, are love complaints, songs in which a disappointed lover mourns an untrue or lost love and hopes that he may yet win her favour. Though all the songs these texts least capture the modern imagination, even they are potentially interesting, for example in the study of literary history, as their amalgamation of medieval and renaissance motifs and traditions may have had some effect on the reception of Petrarchism in the Low Countries in the seventeenth century.

As a book *Het Antwerps liedboek* is no less fascinating. First of all, it has no music, and virtually no indications as to how a particular song is to be sung. Fortunately, many contemporary religious song-books had both musical notation and melody reference, e.g., the book would introduce a song by indicating that it should be sung "na de wise Ick had een ghestadich minneken / gheen schoon" (*Souterliedekens* Psalm 28), and provide the notes as well. Many of these melody references point to the first lines of text from *Het Antwerps liedboek* (here song #98). As a result scholars have been able to trace about ninety of the melodies (Vellekoop), although the last word about the musical notation and certainly about the melody references has not yet been said. One illustration, taken from many, of the complexity of melody references can be found in a religious song manuscript of 1525; it does not provide music but gives the singer a great deal of choice about melodies:

Dese vier nauolgende lyedekens mach men synghen op dese wijsen Die eerste wijse Ic sach mijnheer van valkesteyn Die ander van die hartoch van sassen Die dorde Ic sie die morgen sterre Die vierde wijs Het viel op eenen morghenstont Ende alle ander lyedekijns die men op vier regulen sijnghen mach (Ms II 2631, fol. 11a).

The absence of melodies has also figured in the discussion concerning the intended market for the book as a whole, another subject still open to debate. Certainly some of the songs were what modern scholarship, following the romantic tradition, has called "folksongs," songs so well known among *het volk* that knowledge of the melodies could be taken for granted. Other texts, however, bear clear evidence that they were composed by *Rederijkers*, the professional poets of the day, for educated people like themselves (Joldersma "Volksdichters"). For some of these *Rederijker* texts one may legitimately question whether such poems were ever intended to be set to music, or whether the printer added them in order to increase the volume of his collection and flatter would-be buyers by including their work. Furthermore, did the absence of melodies mean that the book was intended to be cheap, and hence within the price range of more individuals? This, too, is difficult to answer. What constitutes a "cheap" book in the first half of the sixteenth century? An analysis of book prices and wages suggests that a book like *Het Antwerps liedboek* possibly cost as much as a craftsman earned in one day, which, in the words of one scholar, "brought books into the purview of the merely comfortably off rather than of the wealthy only" (Davies 133; Joldersma I, XXXIII). Nor does size provide any clear clues as to cost. By modern standards *Het Antwerps liedboek*, which measures 10 cm in height and 13 1/2 cm in width, is relatively small. But by sixteenth-century standards it is a medium sized song-book, larger than the tiny *Kamper liedboek* (which does have music), smaller than a number of others, such as the aforementioned *Souterliedekens*.

Additional evidence that *Het Antwerps liedboek* was intended for the less literate of the time might be cited from the book's discussion of the way in which the song material is organized. Only the headings "Een oudt liedeken," Een nieu liedeken," "Een amoreus liedeken," or occasionally a title such as "Van't Vriesken," delineate the end of one song and the beginning of the next. In addition to this, the songs are placed in a very loose alphabetical order. In 1544 this alphabetical ordering was quite an innovation, for in his foreword the printer explains proudly:

> Ende op dat ghi lichtelic vinden soudt tgene dat ghi begeert te singen so zijn dese liedekens gestelt, na dordinancie van den. ABC.

Not assuming that his readers understood the alphabet as an ordering principle, however, he continues:

> So dat alle die liedekens dye met een A beginnen, staen voren, die met een B beginnen daer na, die met een C beginnen daer naer. Ende also voort veruolgende. Vaert wel.

Despite this innovative use of the alphabet the book is not entirely problem-free in its song organization, for it seems to have gone through a number of editions, and hence there are three series of alphabets. Interestingly enough, the already more sophisticated *Amstelredams Amoreus lietboeck* of 1589 reprints this part of the foreword verbatim. And it would seem that even today an understanding of the alphabet as ordering principle cannot be taken entirely for granted; in a recent "Funky Winkerbean" comic the highschool principal instructs the graduating students to proceed across the stage in alphabetical order, and explains: "This means that students whose names start with A go first, students whose names start with B go next. . . ."

Het Antwerps liedboek has a fascinating publishing history. Two years after it was printed, in 1546, it was put on the index of books forbidden by the Catholic church as represented by the theological faculty at Leuven. No one has yet been able to conclusively determine why (Joldersma I, XLVI-LII); perhaps, in the words of the Index of 1546, it was simply one of those books

> die beter zijn niet ghelesen dan ghelesen in desen periculuesen tijd ende beeter uut den handen van den ghemeenen peupel ende der jongheren, dan daer in te zyne (Reusch 30).

In any case, the printer of *Het Antwerps liedboek*, Jan Roulans, is known to have produced several other books which were placed on a later Index. He died in an Antwerp prison in 1570, where he had been incarcerated on the charge of printing and selling forbidden books. His wife Lisbeth was banned from the city for religious heresy a few months later, and their entire property, of which the most valuable item seems to have been the printing press, was confiscated.

I have dealt with *Het Antwerps liedboek* in such length because it, as the largest, earliest, printed, secular song collection, stands between the established tradition of the individually compiled song manuscript and the advent of the commercially prepared song-book. Though song manuscripts, the copying of songs into a collection by and for one person, remained a favoured way of capturing a pleasing song for future reference, the enterprising printer saw a market for the printed form of such collections. The printed song-book had a definite advantage over the song manuscript in that it contained many more texts than any individual would ever be able to collect over a lifetime. Yet the printer was at a disadvantage because he did not precisely know the taste of his potential buyers. In trusting his own perceptions of that taste in preparing a song collection, he took a calculated financial risk. *Het Antwerps liedboek* reflects efforts to minimize this risk in the wide variety of songs that it contains. By including almost every song at his disposal, the printer obviously hoped to market a book which would appeal to the largest possible number of buyers.

Het Antwerps liedboek clearly influenced the composition and physical appearance of a number of song-books; five of these, some in fragmentary state (Thiele; van Selm), are known to us. Because such later song-books were selective and transmitted only certain elements, they provide clues to the actual, rather than the perceived tastes of buyers and to the buyers themselves. So the *Amstelredams Amoreus lietboeck* of 1589, for example, reprints forty of the songs besides the foreword. As an added innovation the printer included an alphabetized index of first lines, although in this book, too, alphabetical precision leaves something to be desired. Interestingly enough, the *Amstelredams Amoreus lietboeck* and other later song-books transmit mainly the love complaints and only a few of the older, most famous ballads, leaving out most of the historical-political songs and all those texts whose *raison d'être* is erotic wordplay. This choice makes some sense generally in that historical events and linguistic puns become incomprehensible with the passing of time. Furthermore, it may also be possible that the "immigration" of these song-books from Flanders to the Northern Provinces, part of the larger immigration from the south to the north between 1560 and 1630, may have played a role. Nevertheless, it is telling that very few contemporary or local texts were included as replacements. Further research may indicate that this development corresponds to Burke's thesis of "the withdrawal of the upper classes" from popular culture, beginning already in the sixteenth century (270). Actually, the trend established in the group of song-books under discussion is already clear from *Het Antwerps liedboek* itself; in the first alphabet series about half of the songs were "nieu" or "amoreus," the rest "oudt" or ballads with titles. In the second and third series, in contrast, the songs are virtually all "nieu" or "amoreus." Later song-books, such as the socalled *Amoreuse Liedekens* of about 1615, deal with this difference in that they divide the book into two parts which echo the sections in *Het Antwerps liedboek*. In all of the later books proportionately more space is gradually devoted to the modern songs which change with each generation, i.e., "the hits," until in 1716 the printer of the *Haerlems Oudt Liedt-Boeck*, in its 27th edition, felt called upon to defend the fact that he had included any of the old songs at all:

> Men siet de Jeugt doorgaens begeerig na spickspelder nieuwe Deuntjes, daer door de oude . . . uyt de Liedt. Boecken in het her-drucken gelaten worden, tot ongenoegen dergener die . . . met diergelijcke opgewassen zijn. Derhalven hebbe ick hier in willen voorsien, met het herdrucken van eenige oude begeerde Liedekens . . . op dat elck in't singen verkiesen magh die hem behagen. . . .

In this foreword the printer clearly identifies the buyers of the song-books: "de jeugt." In the rising prosperity of the newly established Netherlands, "de jeugt" were the literate young people with leisure time to fill and money to spend, most likely the sons and daughters of well-to-do merchants. And he also describes their tastes: they were out to purchase the latest in 16th-, 17th-, or 18th-century entertainment — namely new songs in a new song-book. In the Golden Age of the seventeenth-century Netherlands there was no shortage of these; a different family of song-books, with titles such as *Triumphus Cupidinis* (by Ioan Yserman in 1628), or *den Druyuen-tros der Amoureusheyt* (1602), or the *Dubbelde Nieuwe Haerlemse Duyne Vreugd Inhoudende veele Mey*,

Herders en Vreugde Gezangen (1718), flooded the market and, in time, replaced the older books entirely.

The development in Netherlandic song-books from the multidimensional *Het Antwerps liedboek* to the uni-dimensional books of the seventeenth and eighteenth centuries has been decried by scholars as "the decline of the Netherlandic folksong" (Wirth). It cannot be denied, of course, that the books had an effect on the song repertoire of the general population: certain songs not included in the books were forgotten, others were introduced in their place. At the same time, however, such a thesis does not take into account the peculiar relationship between oral and written traditions, as it is precisely through print that we are able to obtain any glimpse at all of popular song in the early modern period. As the historian of popular culture, Peter Burke, puts its: "[i]n the long run, print undermined traditional oral culture; in the process, it also recorded much of it. . . ." (xii). Furthermore, it would be a mistake to conclude either that the orally transmitted song repertoire changed dramatically overnight or that the song-books were primarily responsible for the changes that did occur. Particularly for these questions the series *Onder de groene linde* (Doornbosch) will be of great importance. These volumes record what *het volk* was singing at the turn of the century, thus permitting research concerning orally transmitted song backwards into time, one of the "oblique approaches to popular culture" Burke has called "the regressive method" (83). *Onder de groene linde* also documents, as far as possible, the relationship between the songs and the contexts in which they were sung. This will permit greater understanding into the disappearance of songs due to the kinds of social and political changes inevitable in our ever more rapidly changing society. At the heart of **historically** oriented song scholarship in this direction stand the song-books related to *Het Antwerps liedboek*. Their reaction to this first one provides us with a first-hand look at how popular song fared in the commercially motivated printing production which was essentially upper class. Nevertheless, only *Het Antwerps liedboek*'s relatively unselfconscious collection of all that was remotely singable and sung in the sixteenth century affords us the basis of comparison and gives us a unique glimpse into the entire song life of that society. Because of this, it is also a window, however small, on some of the truly important concerns of that society.

WORKS CITED

Amoreuse Liedekens. Facsimile ed. J. Klatter, ed. Amsterdam: Buijten & Schipperhein, 1984.

Amstelredams Amoreus lietboeck nu nieus wtgegaen waer in begrepen zijn alderhande Liedekens, die in geen ander Lietboecken en staen, meest al met zijn voys oft wijse daer bi gestellt om alle droefheyt, melancolie te verdrijven. Amsterdam: H. Jz.

Muller, 1589. Facsimile. Maastricht: Burgont & Tebbenart, 1966.

Het Antwerps liedboek: Een schoon liedekens. Boeck in den welcken ghy in vinden sult. Veelderhande liedekens. Oude ende nyeuwe Om droefheyt ende melancolie te verdrijven. Item hier sijn noch toe ghedaen Meer dan Veertichderhande nyeuwe, liedekens die in gheen ander liedekens boecken en staen. Antwerp: Ian Roulans, 1544.

Bruyne, Michael de. "De Roeselaarse liedjeszanger Jan Debusschere 1750-1827." *Ons Heem* 27 (1973): 47-51.

Burke, Peter. *Popular Culture in Early Modern Europe*. New York: Harper & Row, 1978.

Coster, Samuel. *Samuel Coster's Wercken*. R.A. Kollewijn, ed. Haarlem: De erven F. Bohn, 1883.

Davies, C.S.L. *Peace, Print and Protestantism*. The Paladin History of England. Great Britain: Hart-Davis, MacGibbon Ltd., 1966.

Deuoot ende Profitelyck Boecxken, in houdende veel ghestelijcke Liedekens ende Leysenen, diemen tot deser tijt toe heeft connen ghevinden in prente oft in gescrifte. Antwerp: [Symon Cock], 1539.

Doornbosch, Ate, Marie van Dijk, Henk Kuijer, Hermine Sterringa, eds. "Onder de groene linde." *Verhalende liederen uit de mondelinge overlevering*. Vol. I. Liederen met magische, religieuze en stichtelijke thematiek. Amsterdam: Uniepers, 1987.

Druyuen-tros: Een nieu Liedt-boeck / genaemt den Druyuen-tros der Amoureusheyt. Pieter Lenaerts vander Goes, 1602.

Dubbelde Nieuwe Haerlemse Duyne Vreugd Inhoudende veele Mey, Herders en Vreugde Gezangen: Als mede verscheyde Oude en Nieuwe Liedekens. Amsterdam: J. Konynenberg, 1718.

Haerlems Oudt Liedt-Boeck, Inhoudende veele Historiale ende Amoreuse Liedekens: Oock Taefel, Bruyloft ende Scheydt-Liedekens. Haerlem: Vincent Casteleyn, (n.d., c. 1640). Facsimile. Maastricht: Burgont & Tebbenart, 1966. 27th edition: title as above. Amsterdam: Wed. van Gysbert de Groot, 1716.

Joldersma, Hermina. "Het Antwerps Liedboek: A Critical Edition." 2 vols. Diss. Princeton University, 1983.

---. "*Volksdichters of Rederijkers*: Modern Problems with Late-Medieval Anonymity in the *Antwerps Liedboek*." *Papers from the First Interdisciplinary Conference on Netherlandic Studies*. William H. Fletcher, ed. American Association for Netherlandic Studies Papers in Netherlandic Studies 1. Lanham: University Press of America, 1985. pp. 3-9.

Kamper liedboek (fragment). [Kampen: Jan Petreius, c. 1540?] Facsimile. Maastricht: Burgont & Tebbenart, 1966.

Kun je nog zingen, zing dan mee! P. Jonker, J. Veldkamp, K. de Boer, eds. 32nd ed. Groningen: P. Noordhoff, 1941.

Ms II 2631. Signature: Koninklijke Bibliotheek, Brussels: Ms II 2631.

Reusch, Fr. H. *Die Indices Librorum prohibitorum des sechzehnten Jahrhunderts*. Bibliothek des literarischen Vereins Stuttgart 176. Tübingen: H. Laupp, 1886.

Selm, Bert van. "In memoriam 't Dubbelt verbetert Amsterdamse Liedboeck (het z.g. Oud Amsterdamse Liedboek)." *Dokumentaal* 3 (1974): 4-5.

Souterliedekens, Ghemaect ter eeren Gods, op alle die Psalmen van David. Antwerpen: Symon Cock, 1540. Facsimile ed. Jan van Biezen and Marie Veldhuyzen, eds. *Souterliedekens 1540*. The Netherlands: Fritz Knuf, 1984.

T[hiele], P.A. "Fragmenten van een Liedeboek en van een' Reisbundel uit de XVIde eeuw." *De Navorscher* 7 (1857): 1-2.

Vellekoop, K., H. Wagenaar-Nolthenius, W.P. Gerritsen, and A.C. Hemmes-Hoogstad, eds. *Het Antwerps Liedboek. 87 melodieën op teksten uit "Een Schoon Liedekens-Boeck" van 1544*. 2 vols. Amsterdam: Vereniging voor Nederlandse Muziekgeschiedenis, 1972.

Wirth, H.F. *Der Untergang des niederländischen Volksliedes*. The Hague: Nijhoff, 1911.

Ysermans, Ioan. *Triumphus Cupidinis*. Antwerp: Weduwe Iacob Mesens, 1628.